To my dear mother-in-law,

With all my love,

Martin.

4th July, 1931.

A HISTORY OF
KING ALFRED'S COLLEGE,
WINCHESTER

A History of
KING ALFRED'S COLLEGE, WINCHESTER
1840-1980

Martial Rose

Phillimore

1981

Published by
PHILLIMORE & CO. LTD.
London and Chichester

Head Office: Shopwyke Hall,
Chichester, Sussex, England

ISBN 0 85033 393 8

Printed and bound in Great Britain at
The Camelot Press Ltd, Southampton

CONTENTS

LIST OF ILLUSTRATIONS

(between pages 56 and 57)

ACKNOWLEDGEMENTS

In 1960 when Barry Shipley was head of the College's History department he invited half a dozen students to study different periods in the College's history and write up their findings. This present work owes a great deal to those students' research. I am also indebted to the Rev. Michael Benton, who, soon after his appointment in 1969, was interested enough to gather together what seemed a few unpromising remnants of the College's past and form an archival collection, to which he invited Wintonians to contribute. In 1978 when the new library was opened a special room was set aside for the College archives. Bob Perkins and his staff transferred what was now a mass of material, and Margaret Kettle, with infinite care, patience and skill, arranged and catalogued the existing material and also the substantial additional contributions which continued to arrive. Without the dedicated work of these colleagues this book would have taken much longer to complete.

Of the very many others who helped this book on its way I should like in particular to thank: Iris Blake, Bob Breach, Paula Godfrey, Thomas Graty, Ken and Alice Heyes, David Humby, Peter Jacobs, A.I.I.P. (for Plates 1-32, 34-38), Kenneth Kettle, Linden Lawson, Tony Lee (for Plate 33), Alison Leigh, Victor Osborne, Eleanor Phillips, Roger Richardson, Peggy Taylor, Donald Venning and Fred Wheeler.

To the Governors of the College, who granted me study leave in 1978-79, to lay the foundation for this history, I am deeply grateful. My only hope is that they, Wintonians, and others will share a little of the pride and pleasure I experienced in writing it.

To Fred Wheeler

Qualis Vita Finis Ita

CHAPTER ONE

INTRODUCTION

THE HISTORY OF EDUCATION in England shows how at certain times religious interests have brought about giant strides in the advancement of learning, but how at other times, particularly when there has been a clash on denominational issues, religious interests have stifled progress. Church and State were close partners in the founding of the grammar schools in the 16th century, whereas the Church at the turn of the 18th and 19th centuries appeared callously indifferent to the barbaric conditions prevalent in schools of its own foundation. The growing and successful involvement of Nonconformists in educational matters at this time stirred the Established Church into action. The anomaly of the years following the First Reform Act, 1832, was that despite the growing concern by most religious bodies for fundamental education reform, it was religious faction itself that stemmed progress, and this resulted in a dual system of schools and colleges, State and voluntary; a precarious, uneasy, and divisive arrangement. The government's scheme for a unitary national system was set aside in the face of the bitter antagonism between the Nonconformists and the Established Church.

The pressure for electoral reform had come from the rapidly expanding population, especially in urban areas, and the consequent growth of slum living, the enslavement of the poor and their children to cotton, coal, steel, or steam, and the gross inequality of the distribution of wealth. It is not too simplistic to identify the Whigs, who were pressing for electoral reform, with the Nonconformists and free-thinking Radicals; and the High Tories, resistant to change, as adherents of the Church of England. In 1831, for instance, the bishops in the House of Lords voted by 21 to 2 against the Reform Bill. Only the previous November the whole of the country had been shaken by the march of the starving labourers of the southern counties demanding a living wage. The country, too, had been stunned by the severity of the penalties: a few had been sentenced to death, a great many had been deported to Australia. When the Bill was thrown out by the Lords at its second reading, the country was once more, literally, ablaze. In the winter of 1831–32 cholera was added to the wretchedness of unemployment and starvation. Political and economic reasons, quite apart from religious scruples, were to bring the spiritual and temporal Peers to a change of mind. The High Tory Party was at last on the move, and the bishops moved too.

1

During the 1830s a reforming spirit spread within the Established Church, and an earnest attempt was made to throw off the image of an effete, corrupt, over-fed materialism. There was a resurgence of Evangelicalism (a Low Church development) on the one hand, and the first stirrings of the Oxford Movement (High Church) on the other. This reforming spirit was wholly supportive of the government's intention to establish a national system for schools for the children and training institutions for the teachers. However, as the Churchmen viewed education essentially as the process of inculcating Christianity according to the principles of the Church of England, the State religion, then in their eyes all State education was the prerogative of the Church to control. The Nonconformists saw the position very differently. They objected vehemently to the proposed national system of schools under the control of the Church of England, and their protest delayed the establishment of a national system for nearly thirty years. They objected, too, to the government grants to schools which began in 1833 with the sum of £20,000, but rapidly increased to £500,000 a year in the 1840s. Their concern was that a disproportionate amount was being allotted to Church of England schools, although there was no dispute that Church schools were more numerous. The founding of University College, London, in 1828, had come about through the reaction of Dissenters and educational reformers against the privileged position of the Established Church in higher education. Now the position of the Church was being challenged at lower levels.

The Nonconformists had indeed taken the initiative in teacher training. By 1805 Joseph Lancaster, a Quaker, was developing the first training school for teachers, based on the monitorial system, at Borough Road, London. This establishment was taken over by the British and Foreign School Society, a Nonconformist foundation, in 1814. The Established Church responded more slowly. The National Society for the education of the Poor in the Principles of the Church of England opened the College of St. Mark's, Chelsea, in 1841. A government plan in 1835 to establish normal schools in London and the provinces on a national basis resulted in the unfortunate compromise of £10,000 being divided between the two antagonistic Societies, which were required to raise additional sums to promote the founding of their own teacher training schools.

In 1839 Lord John Russell, who introduced to parliament the First Reform Bill in 1832, created by Orders in Council a Select Committee of Privy Council 'to superintend the application of any sums voted by Parliament for the purpose of promoting Public Education'. The Church, especially the High Church section represented by the Oxford Movement, interpreted this move as channelling State funds into educational enterprises unblessed by the State religion. For Nonconformists attending Church of England Schools the hard line taken was that the children should be made to learn the Catechism and attend church services or stay away altogether. 'The vote of protest against the establishment of the new committee was defeated by a majority of only five, and the education grant of £30,000 was carried by the narrow margin of two votes.'[1]

The attempt to set up a training school for teachers at Kneller Hall without denominational bias was also met by a storm of protest and failed. The first training schools were therefore denominational foundations with their oversight and partial funding undertaken by the Committee of Council, whose first Secretary was Dr. James Kay, later known as Sir James Kay-Shuttleworth.

Dr. Kay's appointment was an extraordinary stroke of good fortune for the teacher-training cause. As a civil servant his concern for administration was not blinkered. He was a qualified doctor with experience in Manchester of the great 1832 cholera epidemic. He had been made acutely aware of the deleterious effect on children of poverty, slum-dwellings, bad sanitation, sickness and neglect. He had written strongly and persuasively about such conditions, indicating that the country should make itself acquainted with the dehumanising manner in which the urban poor lived, suggesting that in order to assess such problems accurately, and subsequently to seek solutions scientifically, precise statistical data were required. His work resulted in the founding of a number of Statistical Societies in different parts of the country. The work of these Societies examined closely, among other things, the state of the local schools. The horrific findings, which show neither Jane Eyre's Lowood nor Nicholas Nickleby's Dotheboys Hall to be wildly exaggerated, gave an additional impetus to the reform of education, and in particular to teacher training.

Dr. Kay, when he took up his duties as Secretary of the Committee of Council, was at the same time planning the opening of a training school in Battersea, which admitted its first students in 1840. This was a piece of private enterprise on Kay's part. He resorted to such a measure when it became clear that there was no overwhelming parliamentary will to support a national scheme for the training of teachers. It is of considerable significance that Dr. Kay could bring to bear in his office of Secretary not only a physician's understanding of the physical and mental conditions which contribute to the health of children, but also his extensive experience of educational systems in Scotland, France, Germany, Holland and Switzerland. In addition, he had the personal experience of working out many of the pioneering principles he had gleaned—Pestalozzi's, for instance—within his own residential training school.

Dr. Kay shared with Anglicans and Nonconformists the belief that elementary school teachers should be first and foremost Christian missionaries. His students at Battersea were therefore grounded in religion. But both Anglican and Nonconformist Churches throughout the 1830s had aspired to develop their own plans for teacher training, not through a national scheme such as was defeated in parliament in 1835, nor through private enterprise such as Dr. Kay's, but through the initiative of their own institutions and, as far as possible, with such government funding as might be made available. It was with such an end in view that the Archbishop of Canterbury, acting as President of the National Society, exhorted the diocesan bishops to examine ways in which training schools might be set up, under the direction of the Church, within a variety of dioceses, for the training of teachers who might subsequently be appointed to Church schools within the diocese to teach the children of the poor.

It was following this exhortation that the Winchester Diocesan Board of Education was inaugurated in the Chapter Room on 4 December 1838. One of its first functions was to elect a committee to investigate and report on the conditions of the schools in the diocese.

Members of the committee worked according to their remit throughout 1839, and it was not until February 1840 that they were ready to report to the Board. The bishop called a special meeting of the Board on 6 February 1840 at Farnham Castle, which was then in use as the Bishop's Palace. The bishop began the meeting with a detailed description of the existing provision for education within the diocese, revealing the dire lack of educational facilities in the parishes throughout Hampshire and Surrey. His report merely endorsed for the diocese of Winchester what the Parliamentary Report of 1835 had revealed for the country as a whole. The *Hampshire Chronicle*, reporting the meeting in full, commented: 'There was but one feeling as to the desirableness and necessity of extending and improving education'.[2]

Two resolutions were passed. One was that knowledge of the work of the Board should be given to the rural clergy, so that co-operation between the Board and the clergy, who were responsible for the parish schools, might be facilitated, and subscriptions might become more frequent and more substantial. The other resolution was that one of the most important aims of the Board should be the improvement of masters and mistresses through the facilities afforded by the training schools.

This last generalisation finds more particular expression in the following words of the *Hampshire Chronicle* reporter, who must have been informed of the Board's intention in more detail: 'It is hoped that in the course of the summer a Training School will be opened in Winchester for the purpose of preparing masters to become teachers in Commercial and National Schools'.[3]

That hope, against all odds of time, funding, establishing a constitution for the school, finding the premises, appointing staff and recruiting students, was realized when, on 15 August 1840, the Winchester Diocesan Training School opened its doors.

CHAPTER TWO

ST. SWITHUN'S STREET (1840–1847)

The Formation of the Winchester Diocesan Board of Education

CHARLES RICHARD SUMNER, Bishop of Winchester from 1827 to 1869, was the central figure in establishing the Winchester Diocesan Board of Education in 1838. He was a man with abounding drive and energy, and a keen sense of leadership, taking diocesan initiatives at a time when the bench of bishops had not yet shaken off a century's torpor. His Churchmanship was Evangelical, although he showed no narrowness in the appointment of clergy to the churches of his diocese which, at the beginning of his episcopate, stretched from the New Forest to Clapham, and included the present dioceses of Southwark, Guildford, and Portsmouth. The manner in which Bishop Sumner got to know his clergy, through personal visits and organised meetings, was a model which Samuel Wilberforce was proud to follow, first as the incumbent of Brighstone, Isle of Wight, then as Rector of Alverstoke (Gosport) and Archdeacon of Surrey, later as Bishop of Oxford, and finally, in 1869, on Sumner's retirement, as Bishop of Winchester.

Sumner and Wilberforce were second cousins, and, through marriage, they were both related to Henry Edward Manning and to George Dudley Ryder, who had both been close associates of Samuel Wilberforce at Oxford. They were subsequently to become his brothers-in-law. Sumner appointed Ryder to the living at Easton, a parish on the north-eastern fringe of Winchester. Manning was Rector of Lavington in Sussex, before becoming Archdeacon of Chichester. Ryder and Manning were avowed High Churchmen. Indeed, at a later stage they both defected to Rome, Manning becoming the Cardinal Archbishop of Westminster. But in the late 1830s the cause of education in these parts was strongly promoted by kinsmen, friends, and scholars, mostly of Oxford vintage, and in the Winchester diocese they came under the able leadership of Bishop Sumner. Samuel Wilberforce, son of the great emancipator, stemmed from one of the strongest Evangelical families. At the beginning of his ministry, at least, he was able to share many of the Evangelical sympathies of his bishop.

The Evangelicals and the High Churchmen made common cause in promoting the work of the National Society by spreading an educational system, at both school and teacher-training levels, which adhered to the formularies of the Church of England, which deplored undenominational teaching as advocated by the British and Foreign School Society, and shrank from, as even more abhorrent, any notion of a national system of schooling or teacher-training which precluded religious instruction. Fear of the implementation of such a national system was the more acute in the late 1830s, since not only had government funding been voted for schools and training colleges, but also, now that Catholics, Dissenters, heretics, and even atheists might find their way into parliament, the State Established Church (in its age-old right of inculcating through educational means its liturgy and doctrine), might now, in these prerogatives, be challenged by the State itself.

In a sermon preached in Chichester Cathedral on 31 May 1838, Henry Manning revealed his vision of the Church's role in education. He saw the early successes of the National Society as but the first step towards the fulfilment of a national educational system which would transform the spiritual life of the nation. It was for the Church to shoulder the responsibility of providing education for the parochial schools at the foot of the ladder, and for universitites at the top. Manning looked to the existing framework to establish new intermediate schools, to revive and expand the teaching function of the cathedrals and cathedral institutions for the training both of ordinands and teachers, and to be responsible for the whole gamut of religious education up to university level.[1]

This was a vision perceived less vividly but pursued more doggedly by the Bishop of Winchester, ably supported by Archdeacon Wilberforce, who later, as Bishop of Oxford, not only founded one of the first theological colleges in the country, at Cuddesdon in 1854, but was also the prime mover in establishing the Oxford Training School at Culham in 1853.

Manning was invited to join the Committee of Inquiry and Correspondence, set up to advise the Committee of the National Society, regarding the formation of the diocesan boards. S. F. Wood, another member of the committee, reported to Manning in February 1839:

> There have been great meetings at Lichfield and Warrington, to form boards for Lichfield and Chester Dioceses; at the former, Peel, at the latter, Stanley, spoke; the last with brilliant eloquence. Chichester meets to form a board tomorrow. We have issued our appeal for funds for the central establishment, and in a few days have got about £300 in donations, and £200 annual: the nobility have not as yet been applied to, and I am sanguine of our getting enough to begin. The Archbishop of Canterbury has given a donation of £200 and £100 annual to his own diocesan board.[2]

The setting up of diocesan boards of education was not invariably followed by the establishment of a training school for teachers. Sometimes training schools were formed, but were short-lived, such was the case at Highbury and Chichester. But where plans were well laid, where diocesan control was strong, or inspired by individual initiative, as was the case of Robert Wilberforce's groundwork for the creation of the York and Ripon teacher-training colleges, school and college enterprises flourished.

During the 1830s and 1840s, when the stock of the clergy within the Established Church stood low, the quality, in spiritual and intellectual vigour, of so many of them had never been higher. In the 1820s Oxford had nurtured so many distinguished clerics, many of whom subsequently defected to Rome, but who, at this stage of ferment over the country's educational problems, were concerned to establish a national system under the aegis of the Established Church. They drew support from each other in family groups, in deep and tight-knit friendships, and through tireless correspondence and mutual exhortation. Kinship, friendship, and kindly and wise patronage are all characteristics of the educational progress made within the Winchester diocese. It is of significance that Wood's report to Manning concerning the setting up of the diocesan educational boards refers to Chester, where John Bird Sumner, brother of the Bishop of Winchester, was the diocesan (in 1848 he became Archbishop of Canterbury); and to Lichfield, whose Bishop was the father of George Dudley Ryder, Vicar of Easton. Familial ties, shared educational experience, class affinities, but above all, common religious Anglican convictions, fuelled the drive for the reform and regeneration of the Church's involvement in education.

Who were the clergy whom the Bishop of Winchester called on to support him in this drive? The Dean and Chapter, in service, in cash, and in grants of land, were seen constantly in accord with the diocesan initiative. The Archdeacons of Winchester and Surrey, Hoare and Wilberforce, were powerful and persuasive men, the latter being a tireless and superbly able administrator. The Warden and Fellows of Winchester College, from the very outset, identified themselves with this development, as indeed did the Warden of New College, Oxford. In particular Dr. Moberly, the headmaster of Winchester College, contributed continuously, from his considerable scholarship and his expertise in educational management, to the founding of the Training School in 1840 and to its subsequent management until his retirement from Winchester College in 1866.

Of the very many other diocesan clergy supporting their bishop, Dealtry and Keble were outstanding. The Rev. William Dealtry was Vicar of Holy Trinity, Clapham Common. He numbered among his congregation some of the surviving members of the Clapham Sect. He was a distinguished mathematician, having been Professor of Mathematics at the East India College at Haileybury. He was made a prebend of Winchester Cathedral in 1830, and, later, Chancellor of the diocese. It was under his tutelage, and from his parish, that William Whiting, the author of the hymn, 'Eternal Father, strong to save', joined the Winchester Training School in 1841. Dealtry, as Keble, was to become one of the School's regular examiners.

John Keble had accepted from Sir William Heathcote, his friend and former Oxford student, the living of Hursley, a parish four miles to the south-east of Winchester, in 1835, when he moved from his curacy at Southrop in Gloucestershire. In 1823 he had relinquished his residence in Oriel College,

Oxford, where he had been a Fellow. By nature retiring, reflective, and reserved. he had been surprised, even embarrassed, by the stunning popularity of his volume of poems, *The Christian Year* (1827). It ran into more than ninety editions in half as many years. 'It brought its author a fortune which he expended on the Victorian hobby of church renovation and building Hursley and its (then) subsidiary church at Ampfield.'[3]

Never lacking courage to speak or write what was in his heart, Keble was guided by a deep spirituality, which gave him little zest for the public debate and polemic battle his own work had generated nationally, through writings and sermons, culminating in the Tractarian Movement. The Bishop of Winchester had warmly approved the early numbers of the Oxford Tracts. Keble's High Churchmanship he happily accepted within the broad conspectus of diocesan Anglicanism, and Keble himself, who at the time of the formation of the Winchester Diocesan Board of Education was still Professor of Poetry at Oxford, was looked to as an essential ally in the founding of the Diocesan Training School. Keble retained an active interest in the Training School until he died in 1866. Dr. Moberly's active interest spanned the same period. The bishop did not retire until 1869. The long and continuous service given to the earliest years of the Training School by these three distinguished gentlemen did much to settle the sound and proper foundations for the institution to flourish in the future.

The bishop knew well that, in campaigning for funds for a Diocesan Training School for teachers, for the building of new middle schools for children of tradesmen and the yeomanry, and improving and building new schools for the poor, he had to rely not only on the support of his clergy, but also on a generous reponse from all parishes within the diocese. The clergy worked hard and well. Contributions came from church collections, from humble parishioners,village squires, members of parliament, and a great variety of the landed gentry. The first subscription list which was published with the First Report of the Winchester Diocesan Board of Education, presented to the special meeting on 16 December 1840, records the names and amounts of the subscriptions (annual payments) and donations. There are about five hundred and fifty contributions, including six from M.P.s. The clergy not only proved themselves able canvassers, but also generous donors at a time when both their status and affluence were very much greater than today. Among the gentry who gave generously were Lord Arden (£100); Sir Thomas Baring (£100); the Earl of Carnarvon (£100); H. C. Compton, Esq., M.P., Minstead (£105); J. Fleming, Esq., M.P., Stoneham (£100); Wm Garnier, Esq., Rooksbury (£100); Sir W. Heathcote, M.P., Hursley (£105); Right Hon. C. S. Lefevre, M.P., Heckfield (£50); Mrs. Long, Marwell (£100); Earl of Malmesbury (£21); Hon. Capt. Perceval, M.P.(£100); the Lord Bishop of Winchester (£100); the Dean and Chapter of Winchester (£200); Warden and Fellows of Winchester College (£150). Generous gifts, too, were received from George Eyre of Bramshaw, and from Sir C. Hulse of Breamore. These two families were linked by marriage. The Eyre family was to play a continuing role in the early development of the Training School. Before the new building on West Hill took shape in 1862, two of the most generous donors were George Eyre and William Spottiswoode. (It is of passing interest to note among the contributors two of Jane Austen's brothers: Rear Admiral Sir Francis Austen, and, in the second subscription list, Edward Knight, Esq., of Chawton. Edward Austen had been adopted by the Knight family, and eventually took up residence on their Chawton estate. His son, Rev. W. Knight, also appears as a contributor, as the incumbent of Steventon, Jane Austen's birthplace.)

The bishop's task was to harness the support of the whole diocese, clergy and laity, to promote the advance of education according to the 'suggestions' submitted to the National Society by the Committee of Inquiry and Correspondence set up in 1838, 'for the purpose of collecting information and making plans, which, with the sanction of the Society, should be recommended for general adoption'. These 'suggestions', approved by the Archbishop of Canterbury, and recommended by the bishops, were communicated, in the first instance, to the Dean and Chapter of each diocese.

> Our own Dean and Chapter, on receiving the communication from the National Society, according to the instructions with which it was accompanied by the Lord Bishop of the Diocese, proceeded to invite several of the clergy and laity in the neighbourhood of Winchester to co-operate with them in carrying the recommendations of the National Society into effect. The constitution of the Diocesan Board was adopted as suggested, by which certain official persons, ecclesiastical and civil, became permanent members, and certain others, four clergymen and eight laymen, were invited to accept the office of elected members.[4]

The first meeting of the Winchester Diocesan Board of Education took place on 4 December 1838. Its membership is set out in Appendix I.

One of the Board's first actions was to appoint a committee to gather information, and to report to the Board, 'with respect to the description of existing Schools for the middle classes, the expediency of attempting to establish new schools, and other matters connected with this object'.[5] Membership of this committee was: Sir Wm. Heathcote, Bart., Archdeacon Wilberforce, Rev. Canon James, Rev. J. Keble, Rev. F. Dyson, Rev. F. Beadon, Rev. J. Haygarth, Rev. C. Wordsworth, Rev. J. E. Shadwell, Rev. W. N. Hooper, Rev. R. Payne, W. C. Yonge, Esq., the Diocesan Secretary.

A second committee of the Board was set up 'for conducting the Affairs of the Training School'. Its membership was: Archdeacon Hoare, The Warden of New College, The Warden of Winchester College, Rev. Canon Vaux, Rev. J. Keble, Rev. Edward M'All, Rev. Wm. Nicholson, Rev. Dr. Moberly, Secretary.

The clergy serving on the committees, apart from those associated with Winchester College, were all incumbents of Hampshire parishes in, or not too distant from, Winchester. Archdeacon Hoare and Archdeacon Wilberforce both enjoyed residence in the Close, but the anomaly was that Hoare, the

Archdeacon of Winchester, was Vicar of Godstone, Surrey, and Wilberforce, Archdeacon of Surrey, was Vicar of Alverstoke, Hampshire. The Archdeacons were key members of these two committees.

John Keble was the only member to serve on both committees as well as the Board, a signal mark of the bishop's esteem of Keble's ability and wisdom in the field of educational planning, and also an indication of Keble's own willingness to give his services to such a cause. The representation from New College, Oxford, and from Winchester College, was strong on the committee concerned to see improvements in the educational system allay the social and scholar and outstanding athlete, represented Winchester College on the Schools Committee.

Sir William Heathcote of Hursley, and W. C. Yonge, Charlotte Yonge's father, of Otterbourne, were both conveniently situated for committee meetings in Winchester. More important, they were both passionately concerned to see improvements in the educational system allay the social and political unrest that had simmered in Hampshire and had then flared up in the early 1830s, when Sir William had been prominent in raising a troop of Hampshire Yeomanry to quell the Machine Riots.

The extension of the franchise, consequent upon the 1832 Reform Act, was cause for concern in so far as members of parliament from the middle classes might be returned who were either unschooled in the formularies of the Established Church, or, worse, Dissenters, Roman Catholics, or even atheists. It is clear that all permanent members of the Diocesan Board of Education, apart from the the M.P.s, by virtue of their station in life or their office, were assumed to be members of the Church of England. Of M.P.s that could no longer be assumed, and there is therefore the addition of the clause 'the same being members of the Church of England and Subscribers to the Board'.

The Schools Committee had discovered that there was wretched provision of Church of England schools within the diocese for the middle classes:

> . . . that the education of the sons of our yeomen, tradesmen, and superior mechanics in the diocese, has been hitherto conducted, to a great extent, by Dissenters; and it does not necessarily follow that education has been based on dissenting principles, or conducted in hostility to the Established Church; yet it were a contradiction in terms, as well as an inconsistency, to suppose the least proselyting Dissenter, were he even to instil the doctrines of the Church, to be capable of imparting a Church spirit. The former, indeed, is not probable, the latter is impossible. And yet but for the effort now making on the part of the Church, through her Incorporated National Society, and the Diocesan Boards in connexion with it, the youth of the Church, among the middle classes, would have been suffered to remain almost entirely consigned to teaching foreign to her polity. The Board have endeavoured to call attention to this great want on the part of the middle classes, in the hope of being enabled to relieve it. The cause is worthy of the Church's best exertions. The classes to be benefited are those to whom recent legislation, and other circumstances, have given more than ordinary influence in the state.[6]

The 'recent legislation' referred to above had given half the middle classes in England enfranchisement following the 1832 Reform Act. The State Church needed a strong State voice in parliament to safeguard its tradition and secure its future. It was thought preposterous, indeed dangerous, for the middle classes to be taught predominantly by Dissenters. The Church's parochial schools were for the children of the poor. 'The children of the nobility, clergy, and middle classes . . . are not likely to be found in any of the schools included in our present calculation',[7] reported the Rev. R. C. Fell, Secretary of the Godstone Decanal Board. It was therefore a primary concern of the Winchester Diocesan Board of Education to establish new schools for the middle classes, and to bring the existing middle and commercial schools into union with the National Society. Establishing such a union, whether for parochial, middle school, or for training school for teachers, ensured agreement on terms of union: a full commitment to the Church of England formularies, such as observation of the Liturgy and Catechism of the Established Church; regular church attendance; superintendence of the parochial or diocesan clergy, and the requirement that staff appointed should be members of the Church of England. Union also attracted funds, channelled through the National Society by the Committee of Council on Education of the Privy Council.

It is apparent that the National Society, founded in 1811, for Promoting the Education of the Poor in the Principles of the Established Church through England and Wales, had to rearrange its priorities in the late 1830s, and promote the education of the middle classes. The Winchester Diocesan Board of Education set themselves this aim, but realised that the first need was the provision of teachers, themselves committed to the Church of England, for such schools. Consequently the 'Objects of the Board' are defined as follows:

1. Improvement of Masters and Mistresses through the facilities afforded by Training Schools.
2. Promotion of Middle Schools.
3. Assistance in the primary establishment of Schools.
4. Inspection of Schools (without interfering with the ordinary authorities), connected with Rewards to Masters and Mistresses, and deserving Scholars.[8]

The Board was anxious to found new commercial schools for the middle classes and to appoint schoolmasters 'of high-toned feeling and ardent devotion to their duties. The schools so superintended are likely to set the standard to Commercial Schools in general, exercising an influence similar to that which our Public Schools now exert over the Grammar Schools of the country'.[9]

The reference to the public schools is made 12 years after Thomas Arnold had taken over the headship of Rugby, and led the reform of the English public school system. The Board looked to the improvement of the commercial schools extending to the parochial schools. The training school was expected to provide schoolmasters for both types of school:

... while the standard is set for teachers in Commercial Schools, it is plain all cannot become Commercial Schoolmasters. The age at which most will leave the Training

> School will hardly allow of their taking an independent charge, while they will be
> well fitted to engage as Parochial Schoolmasters, under the superintendence of the
> clergy.[10]

Indeed, many of the early students left the training school at the age of 17
to take charge of parochial schools with two hundred or more children. But the
cardinal sin of a young schoolmaster, whether he aspired to teach in a commercial school or a parochial school, was lack of humility.

> The object to be dreaded in the matter of education is not the amount of know-
> ledge, but the deficiency of Christian principle. The Board desire to instil in the
> training pupil such sound principles that, however highly qualified, he shall not think
> any station beneath him to which he shall be called, if only he may promote the glory
> of God and the edification of the Church.[11]

That the Board's primary target for the newly-trained teachers was the commercial school is underlined by their original intention of annexing to the
training school 'a Commercial School in which the training pupils may learn
the practice of teaching'. This plan was abandoned when the choristers of
Winchester Cathedral and the choristers of Winchester College came together
to form the junior department of the training school.[12] The first indication
that the choristers were to form the junior department of the new training
school appeared in the *Hampshire Chronicle,* 17 February 1840, in an account
of a meeting of the Board held at Farnham Castle on 6 February 1840. The
objects of the Board were set out, followed by the tentative plans for the
establishment of the training school:

> It is hoped that in the course of the summer a Training School will be opened,
> for the purpose of preparing masters to become teachers in Commercial and National
> Schools. Through the liberality of the Dean and Chapter and the College, not only
> has the Board obtained the use of the premises in the Close, at present occupied as
> the College Choristers' School (which will be fitted up for the purpose), but the
> Choristers of both establishments are about to become the junior department of
> the Training School, under their own masters, in connection with a senior department,
> the whole being placed under the superintendence of a principal, in holy orders, of
> superior qualifications and attainments, who has been selected from a list of 13
> candidates. It is confidently hoped that, with divine blessing, the greatest good will
> arise from these new efforts to promote the cause of scriptural education in connec-
> tion with the doctrines and practices of the Church of England.

The Principal, it appears, had already been chosen by February 1840, but
his name is not given at this stage. The premises were secured with a junior
department on hand, but as that junior department was not a commercial
school for the middle classes, there could well be repercussions on the
staffing, curriculum, and organisation of the training school.

When members of the Winchester and Somborne Rural Deaneries met in
St. John's House, Winchester, on 26 April 1840, the Rural Dean of Winchester,
Dr. Williams, who was elected chairman, in his introductory remarks gave a
brief account of the work of the National Society and looked to an improved
system of education as a panacea for the national ills: 'The increase of crimes,
and the existence of civil disorders, and other evils, have made the impression

more general and so strong that the cure for these ills must be looked for in an improved system of national education'.[13] Dr. Moberly was then invited to speak about the plans for the training school. He began by pointing out that the education of the middle classes was in the hands of the Dissenters, the only mitigation being that the pupils were not actually taken to a 'dissenting place of worship'. He went on to indicate that the estimated cost for each pupil at the training school would be from £22–£23 per annum, and that £100 was to be devoted annually to exhibitions for the pupils. Admission would be restricted to those who were prepared to pledge, that when certificated, they would teach in a diocesan school.

In this same edition of the *Hampshire Chronicle* appears notice of the installation, on 25 April 1840, of the new Dean of Winchester, the Very Rev. Dr. Thomas Garnier. It may possibly be the advent of the new Dean that changed the arrangements for the site of the training school, because when the Committee for conducting the Affairs of the Training School reported to the Board in June they 'had engaged the premises, lately occupied by Mr. Blake, for the purpose of commencing the Training School'.[14] Mr. Blake had formerly lived in 27/28 St. Swithun's Street. The Board gave authority to the committee to furnish the house, and at the same time they approved the rules and regulations governing the training school. (See Appendix II.) At this meeting it was announced that 10 exhibitions, to a total value of £100, had been recommended, and, most important, that a young man, the Rev. D. I. Waugh, M.A., who had excelled himself at Dublin University, had been appointed as Principal.

When the Winchester Diocesan Board of Education first met in December 1838, it had seen as its first task the gathering of information relating to the educational provision within the diocese for the middle and lower classes. The committee which was formed to glean this information did not report until February 1840, but the information it then presented was in great detail, giving a systematic account of all day school and Sunday school attendance in each parish in Hampshire and Surrey. The committee, which had been elected to initiate the training school plans, did not wait for the Schools Committee report before taking action, but, by February 1840, had made arrangements for the premises, accepted the choristers, and appointed the first Principal. But the main work of the training school, which was to provide teachers for the diocesan schools, was to rest to a large extent on the findings of the Schools Committee.

Winchester Schools and the beginning of Teacher Training in the City

Soon after the National Society was founded in 1811, at a meeting, with the bishop as chairman, at St. John's House, Winchester, on 19 November of that year, it was resolved to form

> . . . a Society for the nurturing and education of the Infant poor within the County of Hampshire for the purpose of instructing them upon the admirable plan of the

Rev. Dr. Bell in the knowledge of the Bible and of our excellent Catechism, and in such other useful learning as will be profitable for them in their condition and to establish them in the true principles of the Church of England.[15]

Dr. Bell's advocacy of the monitorial system, whereby the schoolmaster supervised the monitors, who drilled their pupils, by rote learning and repetitive exercises, appealed to the educational planners who looked for a simple method which was cheap to implement. Winchester was one of the first cities to set up central schools for boys and girls. It was especially unusual for such provision to be made for girls.

For the attainment of the objects of this Society it is expedient that a school for girls be established in the City of Winchester for the united purpose of education of the children of parents of all denominations and instructing future teachers for other parts of the Country.[16]

A room at the *Bell* inn was engaged as a temporary school for the girls at 10s. 0d. per week. On the recommendation of the Ladies' Committee, Mrs. Churcher was appointed as schoolmistress. Her salary was £30 per annum, together with an allowance of £10 per annum for coals, candles, and a tenement. The room over the Westgate was engaged for the boys' school. The master, Mr. Miles, was paid £50 per annum and £10 in lieu of a tenement. By 17 February 1812 the Central School had opened with 100 boys under the superintendence of Mr. Miles, who had been educated at the Barrington School, Bishop Auckland, founded by the Bishop of Durham to serve as a model school for the training of teachers according to Dr. Bell's system.

An excellent report in April 1812 concerning the Winchester central schools referred to them as a 'perfect specimen of the new plan of education', and this would seem to be confirmed by the National Society report in 1813, which with reference to the training carried out at the central schools of the dioceses noted that 12 masters and one mistress had been trained at Norwich, and 20 masters and five mistresses at Winchester.[17] The period of training, however, was not extensive.

As very considerable expense has been incurred already by the payment of 12s. 0d. per week for the board and lodging of persons sent to the central school to be instructed as teachers in the new system, it is proposed that such allowance should not be granted beyond three weeks, in which time it is presumed, if the persons are competent, to the appointment, they may acquire sufficient knowledge of the method to be pursued in the conduct and management of a school.[18]

There we have the first teacher-training scheme in Winchester, lasting three weeks, costing £1 16s. 0d., plus overheads, and thought dear at the price. Small wonder then that the strain on the schoolmaster of running both a school and a teacher-training institution must have proved too much. A complaint was made that on 1 July 1813 the schoolmaster had been guilty of disorderly and riotous proceedings in a public house in Winchester, but had expressed contrition for the offence. The Chairman of the Management Committee wrote to him:

It is the opinion of this Committee that your behaviour has been so far reprehensible on a late occasion, that the Clergy are induced in consequence of your promise of future amendment in regard to general conduct to pass over the present fault, yet may deem it necessary that you should present a written memorial signed by yourself, promising to abstain in future from all riotous and disorderly behaviour, as well as from frequenting Public Houses, and make expression of contrition for being concerned in the late affray.[19]

The central school had also made provision for the teaching of the cathedral choristers, but they proved as uneasy an appendage to the central school as in the early 1840s they were to prove to the Diocesan training school. On 17 October 1816 it was resolved

. . . that all measures hitherto taken in regard to the Choristers having proved totally ineffectual, the Committee finds itself compelled to request that the Dean and Chapter would have the kindness to remove them from the Central School with as little delay as possible on account of the influence of their irregular example to the children in general.[20]

The Hampshire Society continued for nearly forty years to show concern for the schools in the county by raising and distributing funds, by exerting direction, through management and through exhortation, and by maintaining a supply of teachers, trained, however inadequately, through the central schools. The role of the Society was superseded by the formation of the Winchester Diocesan Board of Education, whose first action was to found a commercial school in Southampton, and whose second was to review the position with regard to the education of the poor throughout the diocese.

The whole population of Hants and Surrey may be taken at 780,000; of these it is considered that two-thirds (520,000) are in a condition of life requiring cheap education; of these one-seventh (74,285) are between the ages of two and seven years, and one-eighth (65,535) are between the ages of seven and twelve; leaving a total of children under twelve, 139,830.

To meet this want, it appears there are now in the course of education, in daily schools, under the superintendence of the Clergy of the Diocese, 37,644, leaving a deficiency of children under daily instruction of 102,176. Nor will this large amount be greatly reduced by taking into calculation the number of Sunday scholars, reported to be 40,989, leaving a deficiency of 61,187 destitute of Church education, among the classes requiring cheap education.[21]

The bishop noted with pain, at the meeting of the Board at Farnham Castle in February 1840, what scant improvement there had been in the education within the diocese since his Visitation in 1833, and with reference to the parochial schools recalled remarks he had made in 1837:

I think a higher standard may be introduced with advantage. The education need not be solely elementary, at least in towns, reading and writing, and reading and writing only; we must extend and improve our machinery, or continue to live in the centre of an ignorant and reckless population—reckless, because ignorant; we must go among them with the Bible in one hand, and the book of useful knowledge in the other.[22]

A higher standard was not to be achieved without a radical review of the organisation of schools, and a training programme for teachers which afforded an education as well as a professional training. The Board undertook to reform the school system by urging all parishes to provide funds for their schools, to seek union with the National Society, to secure inspection by a representative of the Committee of Council on Education, and to enlist the support of the landowners to help found new schools and improve the old ones. Above all, there was the hope that a steady supply of well-trained teachers, schoolmistresses from Salisbury, and schoolmasters from Winchester, would bring enlightenment to the 'ignorant and reckless population'.

In such a rural county as Hampshire, however, there were deep-seated prejudices against bringing enlightenment to the poorer classes. The social unrest of the 1820s and 1830s which had led to such 'reckless' action by the agricultural workers, was accounted for by some as the result of too much, not too little, education.

> It was argued that the populace have in many cases been excited to tumult by the dissemination of seditious publications put into their hands, or read to them by others—a circumstance which could not have taken place if none of the lower orders had been possessed of the advantages of education, and thus prepared to look into questions far above their comprehension.[23]

The chairman of the Winchester magistrates, not such a backwoodsman, took a different view when, on 26 October 1829, the Court was opened in the County Hall for the purpose of hearing appeals and the trial of prisoners, 50 in number.

> The Chairman remarked that the prisoners for trial were more numerous than usual at this season of the year. He could not avoid noticing with regret the frequent occurrence of assaults upon females, and hoped that the effusion of education among the lower orders would have a tendency to repress these outrages in future.[24]

A clear picture of the state of education in the Hampshire parochial schools before the middle of the 19th century can be gathered from the reports of the inspectors acting on behalf of the Committee of Council on Education. The inspectors were chosen by the committee, but approved by the Archbishop of that province in which the inspection was to take place. The role of the inspector was carefully circumscribed, and the reports were submitted to the Privy Council, the Archbishop of the province, and the bishop of the diocese in which the parochial schools lay. The 1840 Report of the Winchester Diocesan Board of Education includes under Appendix No. 13 an account of the visit of the first inspector, Rev. Edward Feild, to schools in the Salisbury diocese. (See Appendix III.)

In the early 1840s the Rev. John Allen, a chaplain of King's College, London, inspected schools in Hampshire and Surrey on behalf of the Committee of Council in two successive years, 1843 and 1844. 'The great want', he writes,

> is that of properly-trained teachers; and to secure these, we must not only extend and improve the efficiency of our training schools, but we must also with earnestness supplicate the landowners to make sacrifices for the payment of proper salaries to

teachers. The cases where the landowners have exerted themselves to provide fit education for the children of their tenantry, in the parishes I have visited, as at Elvetham, Hursley, . . . East Stratton . . ., are, as I hope, indications of a state of feeling that will be found to spread throughout all our agricultural districts.[25]

The landlords of the three parishes mentioned were, respectively, Lord Calthorpe, Sir William Heathcote, and Sir Thomas Baring. All had suffered disturbances on their farms at the time of the Swing Riots (1830), and all were now generously devoting their time and money to improving the educational conditions within their own estates and also, through the Diocesan Board of Education, more generally through the counties of Hampshire and Surrey. They were among the first to send on some of their more promising youngsters to the new Diocesan Training School in Winchester. The first Students' Register, which records the names and details of all students entering the training school from its opening in August 1840, until January 1872, lists William Stuart as the second student to be registered. He was nearly fifteen, and was recommended by the Rev. John Keble, the vicar of Hursley. Henry Potter was the fourth student to be registered. He was 16 years old, recommended by Sir Thomas Baring, whose school at Stratton he used to attend as a monitor, where his father was the schoolmaster.

To press home his point about the poor remuneration of the teachers, Allen details the salaries of those in Hampshire. Of 39 schoolmistresses, 4 received less than £15; 15 between £15–£25; 9 between £25–£35; 10 £35–45; and only 1 £45–55. Of 14 schoolmasters, 6 received £25–35; 2 received £35–45; 6 received £45–£55. 'The scanty salaries', he comments,

> that are offered to masters and mistresses meet one at every turn in the endeavour to put things on a better footing; but as soon as it is felt by the owners of property in this country that the wages of one who is fit to teach the children of the poor ought not to fall below those paid to a humble mechanic, this blot on the face of our social condition will be got rid of.[26]

The Inspector regrets that:

> many promising youths are lost to the calling of a schoolmaster from the difficulty of finding employment and maintenance for them from the usual time of leaving school till the age of sixteen (when they might be admitted into a training establishment), which shall not interfere with their intellectural culture. The poverty of the parents makes them anxious to send out their children into the fields as soon as they can earn more than the additional wear and tear of clothes caused by out-of-doors' work; and too many of the farmers are more ready to employ children than lads, as procurable at a cheaper rate. A general system of paid monitors might keep under tuition the promising children until they were old enough to be admitted to the Normal School.[27]

Allen, drawing on his experience of inspecting schools in many of the industrial parts of England, records that many clergymen would advocate legislation, similar to that which affected employment of very young children in the cotton factories, which might be enacted for the protection of the children of agricultural labourers.

On the one hand Allen is prepared to support the paid monitorial system as a means of keeping on at school potential teachers, but on the other, he is critical of Bell's long-accepted system.

> I have been long desirous to get rid of the use of monitors, except for such parts of school discipline as approach to what is purely mechanical, and to see only small school-rooms erected; for example, such as would accommodate 100 or (in the case of infant schools) 140 children. The advocates of the monitorial system of instruction remind us that it is not their plan that one ignorant child should teach another, but that the schoolmaster should diligently prepare his monitors; and that these when instructed by him should become so many channels through which the teaching derived from him as the source should be carried over the whole school. But if it be granted that in ordinary cases the master has the energy enough to do intellectually for his monitors what is needed, the most important question still remains, as to the power of moral training which such instructors are likely to exercise over their pupils.[28]

In the Rev. Edward Feild's report[29] the teaching in the schools was confined to 'reading, writing, and arithmetic, with the Church Catechism'. Allen's reports on the Hampshire schools three and four years later praise the teaching of scripture at Alresford, the music at Longparish, the marching and singing at Ropley, and at Bishopstoke, we read:

> Master trained at Winchester; appears quiet, painstaking. His school much improved since the last visit. His boys are taught the Holy Scriptures well; read with intelligence; are exercised in composition; writing and arithmetic good. Some knowledge of geography and grammar. Discipline satisfactory.[30]

To extend the children's reading the inspector recommends

> ... fitting secular reading-books. The Society for Promoting Christian Knowledge has published several good ones; and a penny biographical series of remarkable cheapness, commencing with extracts from Izaak Walton's Life of George Herbert, is now in course of publication.[31]

Practical advice that would have been well taken by the teachers with an interest in local personalities. The curriculum of the parochial school at Cross in Portsea, however, gives rise to some reservation on the inspectors' part:

> Besides needlework, girls are taught to wash, iron, and clean knives. The boys plait straw. Mistress bears an excellent character. Instruction, perhaps, might be enlarged, without interfering with the industrial teaching.[32]

Allen is particularly impressed by the instruction given at King's Somborne school, a village school eight miles west of Winchester. Here the farmers were at first strongly opposed to the endeavours made to raise the standard of teaching:

> The school was built for 112 but is always overfull, the average number found being 130; it is attended at varying payments by the children of all classes, from the substantial farmer to the poorest labourer.[33]

The unusual mixing of classes, variation of payment according to means, and the community's access to the clergyman's lending library led the inspector to include as an appendix to his report a letter from the incumbent, Rev. R. Dawes, on the general running of the school. It is a blunt, humorous, compassionate record of a rural school, giving instances of 'dense, stolid, bucolic, Hampshire-hog ignorance, in which education must have done good'. Dawes expresses concern for the lame, whom he would not have 'thrown upon the parish', but speaks of his 'working up the cripples into schoolmasters'. He then speaks of his lending library:

> . . . which I still continue to keep at my house, but which I hope to transfer to a book-case in the contemplated class-room . . . the number of books from 1st January, 1845, to 29th December, is 540 volumes, and of these nearly 300 were taken out the first six months, and about 240 the last. This difference arises principally from the harvest of corn and potatoes, etc. falling in the last half of the year.
>
> Of the usefulness of this there can be no doubt; and although the actual reading is confined, or nearly so, to those who are or have been at school—in fact very few of the others can read—yet, through the children's reading to the parents, it is a source of instruction both to young and old.[34]

Such were the schools which provided the first students for the Winchester Training School, and such the schools which received them after their training.

The First Students and Staff

The training school opened on 15 August 1840. Who were the first students? Their names are given under Appendix No. 4 of the first report of the Winchester Diocesan Board of Education, together with their age, date of admission, and also the name of the person who recommended them. The Students' Register gives fuller details. The Register's first part contains an alphabetical entry of all students joining the training school from 1840–1872; the second part lists the 'Daily Pupils' in 1841; the third part offers a periodical table of the student's progress. A double page is allocated to each student: on the left-hand side details may be given of name, age, former occupation, station in life, residence of parents or friends, by whom recommended, and on what terms admitted, what schools previously attended, and acquirements on admission. On the right-hand side details may be given, alongside a date of entry, of health, conduct, attention and progress in study, general ability, temper, capacity as instructor, and peculiar talent. Under this part there is space for additional information in answer to the following questions: how and when disposed of; if as schoolmaster or assistant; amount of salary obtained.

Principal Waugh entered each student's name in the Register with a modicum of additional information. One might have wished him to have been more expansive. The first entry is of George Monk. His age and former occupation are not given, but he comes from Wonston, as an exhibitioner, and is recommended by the vicar of Wonston, Rev. A. Dallas. Monk had previously been in attendance at the Wonston National School. On admission he was 'possessed of a tolerable acquaintance with Arithmetic'. Monk left the training school on 25 March 1842, 'at the instance of the Rev. A. Dallas, in order to spend some time as assistant in the Wonston National School, intending afterwards to return to the Training School, to complete the period of his Exhibition'. This he did, for the last entry reads: 'Returned to the School Lady Day, 1843. Left the Training School finally September 29th, 1843'. Monk, then, completed a three-year sandwich course, which included a year's teaching at Wonston. This pattern was repeated in a few cases, but it was unusual. The majority of students were 15 or 16 years of age on entry, and stayed on average 18 months. There were a few older students who stayed for much shorter periods, some leaving after only three months to take charge of schools. In the first few pages of the Register the students' fathers' occupations are recorded as schoolmaster, labourer, carpenter, butcher, farmer, gardener, smith. Former occupations of the students were linen-draper, shepherd, cabinet-maker, coach-builder, 'attendant to a Public conveyance'.

The clergy and landowners supported candidates for one of the 10 Exhibitions available at the training school, or acted as patrons, or were prepared to pay in full for the students' training. Edward Bull, who was registered as a student on 25 March 1841, was 25 years of age; his father was a farmer. He completed his year on 25 March 1842, left the school and obtained a situation under the patronage of Lord Calthorpe. John Browne, registered on 13 March 1845, aged 18, of Godstone, was recommended by Lord Calthorpe, 'who pays his expenses'.

Samuel Wilberforce, through his building of his parish schools at Brighstone and Alverstoke, kept so lively an interest in education in these areas that a number of students came from schools founded by him. James Shotter was registered on 25 March 1841; 'his friends reside in the parish of Brixton (Brighstone), Isle of Wight'; 'recommended by Archdeacon Wilberforce, an Exhibitioner; attended school at Brixton for many years'. For 'acquirement' he was described as 'a good arithmetician and acquainted with Land Surveying'. He left the training school on 29th April 1843, and was appointed by the Dean of Winchester as Master of Bishopstoke National school. There is also James Hawkins, registered on 25 March 1845, aged 22, formerly a gardener, whose father was gardener to Archdeacon Wilberforce at Alverstoke.

The twentieth student to be registered was Arthur Clarke, on 21 August 1842, 21 years of age, an assistant to his father, who was by trade a shoemaker, and kept a school. He came as an independent student to stay three months 'in order to fit himself to keep a school'. His acquirement was 'Writing, and Arithmetic; but not English Grammar'. The Principal's additional comments were: 'I have been much pleased with the diligence, advancement, temper, and religious spirit of the pupil. He left (without a certificate of course) at the expiration of the Quarter, returning to his Father's'.

Arthur Clarke was not alone in being unacquainted with English grammar: such ascription by the Principal recurs most frequently among the students whose fathers were schoolmasters. Among the first 50 admissions there is only one reference to a student having any knowledge of Latin. More often the Principal writes of the student, 'his acquirements are humble'.

The requirements for admission were a certificate of baptism, and one of good character and conduct from the student's schoolmaster, or the clergyman of his parish. In addition every candidate for an exhibition had to produce

1. A recommendation from some Local Board, or member of the Diocesan Board, certifying his fitness for training, the inability of his friends to undertake the whole expense without aid from the Board, and giving guarantee for payment of the remaining £13.

2. A written statement, signed by the parent or guardian of the boy, the persons recommending him, and the boy himself, that (in the event of his obtaining an exhibiton) it is intended that he shall pursue the profession of schoolmaster within the diocese.

Further, to be eligible for one of these £10 exhibitions, the candidate

shall have attained the age of 15 years, and be able to read, write, and spell correctly; be versed in the first four rules of arithmetic, know the Church Catechism, and have a general knowledge of the contents of the Old and New Testatments.[35]

Only exhibitioners were required to show that they could read and write before entry.

All students were required to attend the service at the cathedral every morning at 10 o'clock, and twice on Sundays. The cathedral is about two hundred yards from the original site of the training school in St. Swithun's Street. On leaving the school, the student would be examined and receive a testimonial according to his attainments, which would be laid before the bishop, in order that he might receive his licence to teach. No certificate would be given unless the student had been in residence for at least six months.

The original curriculum is set out as Appendix No. 6 in the Board's 1840 Report. Wednesdays and Saturdays were half holidays. Bearing in mind the 'humble acquirements' of the students admitted, it comes as something of a surprise to see the range of subjects taught: scripture, poetry, English history, English grammar, Latin grammar, mathematics (including mensuration), writing, writing from dictation, natural philosophy, music, Book of Common Prayer, Church Catechism, arithmetic, geography, scripture history. The régime was rigorous, with long sessions before breakfast with, on most days, supervised study lasting until bed-time. To teach this curriculum there was but one member of staff, the Principal. We know little about him apart from his qualifications, his youth and energy and devotion to his work, in 1845 of his sickness, and in February 1846, of his death. The bishop paid tribute by saying that 'to his great diligence and zeal, exerted, it is feared beyond strength, the present efficiency of the School is in a great measure to be attributed'[36] Such a curriculum as outlined, set in so relentless a time-table, might well have proved a killer.

The committee whose responsibility it was to look to the affairs of the training school had been circumscribed in its planning by the St. Swithun's Street site, and by the substitution of the junior department for the original intention of annexing to the training school a commercial school for the practice of teaching. This comprised 30 pupils: 26 made up of college choristers and cathedral choristers, and four boys of Christ's Hospital,

Winchester, who like the cathedral choristers were day boys. The junior department did not prove satisfactory. In 1843 Winchester College removed its choristers to No. 5 College Street, a building which then backed on to Cheyney Court in the Close. William Whiting, an exhibitioner from the training school, was at the age of 17 appointed their master. The reason given for the move, in the Winchester Diocesan Board of Education Report for 1843, was on account of 'great practical difficulty owing to the different hours of attendance of the Cathedral and College Choristers'—a practical difficulty which might still elicit sighs from the present headmaster of Pilgrims' school, where once again both groups of choristers are brought together for their education. In the following year, 1844, the Dean withdrew the cathedral choristers from the training school to extend 'its benefits to other classes of persons than those destined for the scholastic profession'. Within three years of opening, therefore, the training school had lost its choristers, and with them the built-in teaching practice opportunities. The committee overseeing the affairs of the school, in its recruitment of pupils not looking to a career in teaching, marked its anxiety about sustaining numbers for economic viability. At the same time they knew that the lease on the premises in St. Swithun's Street had less than three more years to run.

The staff of the training school had at the outset consisted of the Principal, the Rev. D. I. Waugh; Mr. Moody, who had been master of the college choristers, and who was now responsible for the conduct of the junior department, and Mr. Long, the deputy organist of the cathedral, who was responsible for the instruction in church music. From the training school's foundation until the present day there has been an unbroken link between the training institution and the organist or deputy organist of the cathedral.

Mr. Benjamin Long, the deputy organist at the cathedral, was elected organist at Winchester College in 1849, and effected some improvement in the singing of the college choristers whose role for many years had been that of errand boys and fags to the scholars. Mr. Long is referred to warmly in the examination reports on the training school pupils, to one of whom each year he invariably awarded a prize for outstanding musical achievement. He died in November 1850, and was succeeded in his work at the training school by Dr. Samuel Wesley, the newly-appointed cathedral organist.[37]

In 1840 Robert Moody had been responsible for the college choristers, of whom there were traditionally sixteen. When he took charge of the junior department of the training school he added to his charge the 10 cathedral choristers and the four Peter Symonds' Christ Hospital boys. Before 1840 the college choristers had received their schooling at the Free School in the Chapel of St. John's Hospital. For three years they were taught as part of the junior department of the training school, and in 1843 they were removed from the training school and housed in No. 5 College Street, which for this purpose was extended through the High Wall into Cheyney Court within the Close. At this stage Robert Moody must have resigned, for, as mentioned before, the master who moved with the boys to the new premises was William Whiting, who had entered the training school on 25 March 1841 from his Clapham home, and had distinguished himself in examinations. On entry Whiting had been described as 'an excellent arithmetician', and his 'general information' was considered 'very respectable'. He was appointed Probationary Second Master at the training school, where his duties were largely with the junior department, on 25 March 1842, at a salary of £50 per annum, and in 1843 (although there is conflicting evidence that he might have moved in the autumn of 1842) 'he was transferred to the Mastership of the College Choristers School in Winchester at the same salary, £10 per annum being afterwards added by the Governors of Symonds' charity for the instruction of four boys in their foundation'.[38]

Although the training school records have nothing further to say about Robert Moody, there is mention in the Diocesan Board of Education Report, 1842, of Vincent Moody, perhaps Robert's son, who entered the training school on 25 January 1841 at the age of 14, under the 13th rule of the school which was that 'Boys of good and eligible character, on leaving the junior school, may be received at once, though under age, as boarders'. Vincent Moody had attended the Cathedral Choristers School for four years. Principal Waugh, according to the entry in the Students' Register, was clearly impressed: 'Acquirement: rather good, considering his youth—advanced in Arithmetic as far as decimals'.

There appears to be no record of Principal Waugh's salary on appointment. The earliest balance sheets of the Winchester Diocesan Board of Education, made out by the Treasurer, Dr. Moberly, account for the overall expenditure on the training school, without a detailed breakdown of individual items. On Principal Waugh's death in 1846 an advertisement appeared in the *Hampshire Chronicle* on 28 February announcing that there would be 'an election of a Principal of the School on Thursday the 12th March next. The Principal must be in Priest's orders. Salary of £200 p.a. and other advantages . . .'. It might be assumed that Principal Waugh himself was appointed at this level. Principals' salaries must, however, have varied considerably. The Principal of the Chester Diocesan College, on taking up his post in 1840, was paid £500 per annum plus a capitation fee of £3 for each student and £2 for each day scholar.[39] This capitation fee would have enhanced the Chester Principal's salary very considerably, as well as encouraging him to keep recruitment buoyant. The different dioceses, in securing principals for their new colleges, were invariably looking for Oxford or Cambridge scholars in holy orders, who with minor ancillary support would have to bear the main responsibility for teaching the students. The calibre of principal might not be that of a College Fellow whose salary in the 1850s would have been about £200 per annum with attractive perquisites. The public schools were in keen competition for the outstanding scholars among the College Fellows. For instance, when in his early twenties, Edward White Benson, a Fellow of Trinity College, Cambridge, was offered a post at Rugby of assistant master with special duties in the sixth form at a salary of £900 per annum. At the time that Principal

Waugh took up his post at a salary in the region of £200, the schoolmaster and schoolmistress at Fordingbridge would have been earning £50 and £20 per annum respectively, and the farm labourer in Sir Thomas Baring's estate would have been receiving a weekly wage of nine shillings.

The early reports of the Winchester Diocesan Board of Education refer frequently to the shortage of funds to meet their third and fourth aims: developing parochial schools, and rewarding masters and mistresses, and deserving scholars. The major expenditure was taken up by the training school. Initially, the founding of the commercial schools at Southampton, Portsea, and Dorking made severe inroads into the funds, but within a few years these schools, through their fees, became self-supporting. A typical disbursement of funds is exemplified in the balance sheet Dr. Moberly drew up for 31st December 1843:

The Treasurer in Account with the Diocesan Board of Education, December 31, 1843

DR	£	s.	d.	CR	£	s.	d.
Balance at the last Account ..	161	0	4	Expenses of the Diocesan Training			
Donations and Subscriptions received in 1842	671	13	5	School	674	17	1
				Southampton Church School ..	275	13	6
Sale of Exchequer Bills	937	14	8	Dorking School	200	0	0
Interest on ditto	51	3	9	Portsea School	100	0	0
Received from Pupils at the Training School	161	15	0	Grants paid to Parochial Schools ..	140	0	0
				Collector, Salary and Expenses ..	55	6	2
				Stationery Depot	50	0	6
				Other Expenses	55	18	2
				Balance	431	11	9
	£1,983	7	2		£1,983	7	2

A centrally-controlled stationery depot was now making, for the first time, teaching materials available to the parochial schools which had been in this respect lamentably under-provided. The training school was as poorly provided with teaching aids as the schools. There was no library, geography was taught at first without maps, and text books were at a premium. The difference that the acquisition of a library made to the learning of the pupils is reflected by the Principal's comments in 1844:

'I can discern a considerable improvement in information among the pupils this quarter . . .' and the Board Secretary continues 'an improvement attributable not more to the recent establishment of a library in the Training School, than to the accession of a race of young persons more accustomed than their predecessors to intellectual pursuits.'[40]

It was very largely the fear of a national system of education being imposed on the country if the Church of England failed to fund its own educational initiative that helped maintain the Church's role in the founding of teacher-training colleges, and middle and parochial schools. But even in the early 1840s many Churchmen must have realised that, with the great increase in population, with many urban areas untouched by the parish churches and parochial schools, with a growing understanding that sounder education could only be achieved through a more costly system of teacher-training, resulting in higher status and salary for the teachers, sooner or later the Church would have to cede to the State the major responsibility for the nation's education. Members of the Winchester Diocesan Board of Education viewed the State system of education, 'as being not simply hostile to our ecclesiastical institutions, but ultimately subversive of Christianity itself'.[41]

When, in the 1843 Report, note was taken that the training school more than exhausted the annual subscriptions, the question was put, 'Is it a time to halt, or to go back from a position thus acquired?' The answer came as a rallying call to the diocese from the Secretary of the Board, the Rev. Philip Jacob, a canon of Winchester and rector of Crawley:

> The institution of Diocesan Boards, in connection with the National Society, presents not only a protest against false systems of education, but an efficient substitute for them. In their Training Schools there is a protest against ignorance, or mere fact knowledge, or mechanism in the teacher. The great aim is to bring the man, the Christian instructor with all his awful responsibilities, and warm sympathies, and glorious hopes, into close contact with the mind of youth, and this Christian man not simply learned, but, by a sort of apprenticeship to the art of teaching, learnt theoretically in the Training School, and practised in Model Schools, made 'apt to teach'. By providing better and more extensive means of instruction for that great division of the community which, as lying between those brought up at our universities and old classical schools, and other similar establishments, and those who avail themselves of our national and parochial schools, are justly called the middle classes, the Diocesan Boards claim to consider themselves engaged in an object of national importance, as well as of vast private benefit. And in days when there is too little communication between two classes, when 'not perhaps the feeling but the expression of sympathy between rich and poor', the higher and the middle classes, more personal communication is required, these institutions of Diocesan Boards, representing as they do the Charity of the Church in the love of all her members one towards another, may justly be held to be a practical expression of that enlarged sympathy.[42]

As funds were flagging it is understandable that Canon Jacob should appeal directly to the 'higher classes' to assist in an endeavour to train teachers drawn from the middle classes, whom he here identifies as 'poor'. His appeal was not in vain and, although the parochial schools drew less support from the Board's funds, the training school, at least on financial grounds, was not seriously threatened.

The Bishop of Salisbury had attended some of the early meetings of the Board with the intention of hearing discussions relevant to the setting up of a Salisbury diocesan training school for masters. It was largely through Dr. Moberly's advocacy that it was decided to found a training school for mistresses in Salisbury, with the clear advantage of the men from the Salisbury diocese who wished to train as teachers coming to Winchester, and the women of the Winchester diocese wishing to be teachers enrolled at the Salisbury training school, which was opened on 15 January 1841. The Winchester diocese had founded 10 exhibitions at the Winchester training school of £10 each, and for Salisbury three exhibitions of £8 each. Whereas at Winchester the charge for each student was £23 per annum 'for his board, instruction, and lodging, including washing, to be paid on the quarter days in advance', for Salisbury it was £15 for the first year and £14 for the second and subsequent years. The requirement for the women students was more extensive than for the men:

> Previously to admission, they will be examined in reading, writing and spelling; in the first four rules of arithmetic, simple and compound; in the history of the Old and New Testatment, and in the Church Catechism—without a competent knowledge of all which they will not be admissible. An elementary knowledge of grammar and geography will be generally expected; and they will be required to be well skilled in plain needlework and in knitting.[43]

Martha Gibson, aged 17, from Godstone, Surrey, was the first Winchester exhibitioner; and Harriet Baker, from Brighstone, Isle of Wight, sponsored by Archdeacon Wilberforce 'at the entire charge of her friends', was the second student from the Winchester diocese to enrol at Salisbury. The women students were allowed six weeks' holiday 'at harvest time and one week at Christmas; though at the latter period pupils are not required to leave the Establishment: and every Saturday will be a half-holiday'.[44] The régime is even more rigorous than for the men:

> All pupils are to bring with them two pairs of sheets and six towels.
>
> All pupils are to assist in doing the work of the house, as the governess shall direct.
>
> The pupils are not to be visited by any persons but near relations, and by those only at a fixed time, and with the sanction of the governess.
>
> The dress of the pupils is to be most plain and economical . . .[45]

Deviation from such a régime, as is illustrated in the case of Hardy's Sue Bridehead, resulted in harsh penalties and possible dismissal.

The early history of the two training schools at Winchester and Salisbury, founded for the same purpose, and sharing the same ambitions and anxieties from their inception, makes it more poignant that the opportunity to unite as one college was given them in 1975, but not taken—a decision that led to the closure of the Salisbury college after nearly one hundred and forty years of distinguished service in the field of teacher-training.

Examinations at Winchester took place twice a year, at the very end of the Christmas and summer terms. They were conducted in the presence of the Dean or the Bishop, and usually in attendance would be a selection of the following: the Warden and Headmaster of Winchester College, the Warden of New College, Oxford, the Archdeacons of Winchester and Surrey, the Secretary of the Board, Canon Philip Jacob, Chancellor Dealtry, Rev. John Keble, members of the Diocesan Board of Education, and subscribers to the work of the Board. The examinations were conducted orally and from 1843 were spread over two days in the summer term, lasting seven hours in all. It was customary for there to be bursts of applause from the audience at the conclusion of batches of questions and answers on particular subjects. In later years musical interludes were interjected. The audience was certainly larger than the number of students being grilled. The range of examiners in the first few years comprised the Dean, Dr. Moberly, the Archdeacons, Rev. John Keble, the Chancellor, Canon Jacob, Canon Vaux, and in 1845, and for a few years following, J. D. Walford, mathematics master at Winchester College. A reporter from the *Hampshire Chronicle* was invariably present, and the event was recorded as front-page news, giving an account of those present, an outline of the subjects examined, the response of the students, and the congratulatory comments of the examiners, which included commendation of the Principal and his method of training. It became a tradition for the Dean to present books to two or three prize-winners, and for the music master, Mr. Long, also to present a book to the student who gained the highest mark in music.

The very first examination was conducted on Boxing Day 1840, and was reported as follows:

> On Saturday last, previous to the Christmas vacation, the young men of the Diocesan Training School, who have been under the charge of the Rev. D. Waugh, M.A., preparatory to their being employed, when qualified, as schoolmasters, underwent examinations before the Very Rev. the Dean, the Rev. Canons Vaux and Jacob, the Rev. Dr. Moberly, the Head Master of the College . . .

The report lists the subjects examined as 'Sacred History, especially the Gospels and Acts of the Apostles, the History of England to the close of the reign of Queen Elizabeth, Grammar, Geography, and Elementary mathematics'.

> Besides the general accuracy of the answers, showing much diligence and serious study, the temper and spirit evinced in the manner of the replies to those questions which were of a religious and moral character were most satisfactory.

Then follows the gratuitous advertisement.

> Four exhibitions of £10 each, for a period not exceeding 3 years, for young men of this diocese, are not yet filled up. Independent pupils, intended as well for commercial as for parochial schoolmasters, are admitted into the training institution, provided a guarantee is given that this diocese shall have the prior claim to their services, when they are declared competent to become assistants or schoolmasters themselves. The whole expense of such pupils does not exceed £23 per annum. This feature in the Diocesan Training Institution is well worthy the attention of those parents who, with limited incomes, are intending to bring up their children to the scholastic profession.[46]

In the five years that followed the students were divided into separate classes for examinations according to the date of admission. In 1841 there were two classes, and in 1845 three classes. Only seven pupils were examined in December 1840, but by December 1845 there were 18 pupils in training. The maximum accommodation of the St. Swithun's Street site was for 19 pupils. The range of subjects during this period, extending with the developing range of the pupils, was as follows:

English History to the present time—Chronology—English Grammar and Parsing—
Euclid 1st Book—Elements of Mensuration—Land surveying and Solids—Latin
Grammar—Latin Delectus—Geography of Europe—Algebra—First four Rules and
Fractions—Arithmetic—To Double Rule of Three—Compound Multiplication and
Division, to Single Rule of Three—Latin—Caesar—English Grammar—Parsing and
Etymology—English History—Henry VIII to George I—Geography—Europe and
America—Euclid—Books 2 and 3—Arithmetic and Vulgar Fractions—Latin—Virgil's
Aeneid—Algebra—Quadratic Equations.[47]

The examining of music is always given separate mention in the Minutes of
the Board of Education. The teaching of singing followed the system set down
by Mr. Hullah, who, at the instigation of the Committee of Council, had
travelled abroad with Kay-Shuttleworth to observe (particularly in Paris) the
methods of Wilhem. The new emphasis given to singing, which Mr. Long so
ably promoted, was, according to Kay-Shuttleworth, to encourage the natural
genius of the English for choral singing—Kay-Shuttleworth cites the Lancashire
and Yorkshire weavers' enthusiasm for the choral works of Handel and Haydn—
to improve congregational singing as had been done by the Lutherans of
Germany and Holland, and to preserve for the peasant, through song, the
traditions of his country's triumphs, and inspire him with confidence in her
greatness and strength.[48]

Such reasons account for the reports on the music examinations being
accorded almost as much prestige as biblical studies. Considerations were
not merely educational, or even imperial, but also industrial. Kay-Shuttleworth
had been influenced in his advocacy of music as being of great importance in
elementary education by his belief 'in the greater contentment of children and
young men and women employed in the manufactories of large towns (singing)
during the hours of labour, the psalms and hymns which they (had) learned
in the Sunday-schools.[49]

The strain on the Principal and the pupils of these public twice-yearly
examinations must have been very considerable, especially as the curriculum
was steadily extended during the first six years. This extension reflected both
the progress of the pupils within their course and also the improved quality
of the pupils admitted. Certificates, signed by the bishop, were issued to a
small number of pupils after each examination. This certificate became their
licence to teach, and as they took up their posts some had as many as 200
children to look after. Among the first prize-winners were William Whiting
and James Shotter. The Warden of Winchester College appointed Whiting
to take charge of the choristers; the dean appointed Shotter to take charge
of his school at Bishopstoke, the village in which the dean had his private
residence.

As he inspected the National schools within the diocese, H.M.I. Allen
was asked by the Diocesan Board of Education to report on those former
pupils of the training school now teaching in the schools. We have already
heard what he thought of Shotter at Bishopstoke (p. 18). Extracts quoted in
the 1845 Report of the Board read:

(1)   'gentle and pleasing—scripture knowledge satisfactory'.

(2)   'Master apparently respectable and painstaking'.

(3)   'The teacher appeared to me to be very serviceable'.

(4)   'Master full of spirit and intelligence, very anxious to do his work well, takes pains throughout his school'.

(5)   'School lately open, under a young master, who will, as I hope, prove efficient'.

(6)   'Master Intelligent'.

(7)   'Master not long at his post, gentle and promising'.

The inspector is clearly not giving much away. All his remarks are cautiously commendatory, but we may take them as true to his own observation of the teachers he had seen. His extensive reports are illuminated by his penetrating and discriminatory powers, and he was not the man to edit a report to curry favour with a local Board.

The posts to which the first students were appointed in so large a diocese were not all in rural areas such as Bishopstoke. The 1846 Board Report, which records that 25 former pupils had been appointed to school posts, lists the places to which the most recently-certificated students had been assigned.

> Portsmouth, Havant, Croydon, Stratfield Saye, St. Nicholas, Guildford, Bishop's Waltham, Alverstoke, Westmeon, towns and villages above the ordinary importance. Young men, full of spirit and well directed energies, are thus brought to bear upon the masses of our population. What may we not expect, under the divine blessing, from such efforts.[50]

As the students were going from strength to strength, the Principal's health was failing. The first hint of this is a notice in the *Hampshire Chronicle* in November 1845, which stated that as the Principal was unwell the Principal's curate and assistant, the Rev. J. Huston, would be acting, in a temporary capacity, as the superintendent of the training school. The reference to the Principal having a curate and assistant would refer to the Principal's appointment in 1844 as Chaplain of the Hospital of St. John the Baptist, where some of the students assisted with Sunday school and with the singing of psalmody.[51] For a short time the Principal had had Mr. Kemm as an assistant in the training school after William Whiting had left and before the dean withdrew the cathedral choristers. At their withdrawal Kemm was deemed redundant and appointed as schoolmaster to a National school in south Hampshire[52] Kemm's resignation left the Principal with the teaching of a time-table from 6.00 a.m. to 9.00 p.m.; Wednesdays and Saturdays were half-holidays, with a full day on Sunday of services and sermons. It was virtually impossible for the Principal to have any time for rest or relaxation during these long days. He himself had to teach the different classes of which there were two after the first year, and subsequently three (see Appendix IV). In addition, since the defection of the choristers, the Principal had been left in sole charge of the domestic arrangements, including the supervision of the boarders.

By the end of January 1846 it became clear that the Principal's life was ebbing away, and on 12 February he died. A week later the 18 students of the school, along with relatives and Board representatives, attended the funeral service. At the time of the Principal's death, the Rev. J. Huston was still acting as Principal, and so he was asked to continue in office until a new Principal had been appointed. The Board acted expeditiously and, from a list of 16 candidates, appointed the Rev. John Smith, M.A., of Magdelen College, Oxford, who, on 12 March 1846, a month after David Waugh's death, took up his duties.

The Rev. John Smith is described as 'a gentleman long engaged in tuition'.[53] He was to need all that experience to inherit the Principal's teaching and supervisory duties, to develop arrangements for a model school for his students, and, above all, to brace himself for the major upheaval of moving the training school from St. Swithun's Street to Wolvesey Palace.

On 3 December 1846, at a meeting of the Board of Education,

> . . . when the Secretary announced the approaching termination of the lease of the premises hitherto used as the Training School in St. Swithun's Street. His lordship stated that he had watched over the rise and progress of the Training School with great attention, and had found in it an instrumentality fraught with good, by God's blessing, to the diocese; he therefore desired to place the Palace of Wolvesey at the disposal of the Board, free of rates and taxes, as the future Training School.[54]

The Board, not wishing to wait for the termination of the lease, decided to transfer the students to Wolvesey at the earliest possible date.

> The removal was made in Easter week. The old premises inconveniently accommodated 19 pupils. The present will comfortably receive 50.[55]

The modest and cramped quarters of St. Swithun's Street gave way to the spaciousness of the Bishop's Palace. The training school was making a fresh start in a prestigiously historical setting, with a new Principal, who within a year of his appointment, found himself virtually master of Wolvesey.

CHAPTER THREE

WOLVESEY, 1847–1862

The Palace

THE FIRST MENTION of a bishop's palace at Wolvesey is made as early as the turn of the 10th century. Henry of Blois, Bishop of Winchester (1129–71), built it anew. Water was brought to the palace by a system of lead pipes and stone chambers, still in working order. Henry of Blois's palace was pulled down by Bishop Morley in the 17th century. Morley had been in exile with King Charles II, and when, at the Restoration, the king set Sir Christopher Wren to plan and build a royal palace in Winchester where the old castle stood, Bishop Morley followed suit by directing Wren to build a new bishop's palace. Both king and bishop died before their palaces were complete. Bishop Mews, who succeeded Morley, called a halt to the building when he realised there was no longer any possibility of the royal court being held in Winchester. Wolvesey was eventually completed in Queen Anne's time by Mews' successor, Sir Jonathan Trelawney.[1]

In the 18th century, however, there was no obligation, even less tradition, for the bishop to live in his Winchester palace. Indeed, Bishop Hoadly in the 27 years of his episcopate (1734–61) never once visited Winchester. The bishops habitually lived in their palaces in London or Farnham which they found more convenient and more healthy. Bishop Sumner (1828–69) was the first Bishop of Winchester for three hundred years to be enthroned in the cathedral, but like most of his predecessors he did not live at Wolvesey.[2] Indeed, it was not until 1927 when the huge diocese of Winchester was divided into the three diocese of Winchester, Guildford, and Portsmouth, and when Farnham Castle was therefore no longer within the Winchester diocese, that the Bishop of Winchester once more took up his abode at Wolvesey.

Bishop Sumner's generosity in allowing the training school to use Wolvesey, free of rates and taxes, was warmly acclaimed by the Diocesan Board of Education for a variety of reasons. Their funds were low; the training school had been absorbing the whole of their income, leaving nothing for the other objects of the Board: the promotion of middle schools; assistance in the primary establishment of schools; and inspection of schools, connected with rewards to masters and mistresses and deserving scholars. The Board's Report

31

of 1847 stresses the need to establish more schools within the diocese and especially in Winchester for the education of the children of the labouring classes. They also note the inspector's report on one of the schools that the children had been reclaimed from a wild heath. It was hoped that with some of the costs of the training school alleviated by the move to Wolvesey, more money might be released for improving and building new schools within the diocese, especially in Winchester.

There were even weightier reasons why the Board was delighted to see the training school transfer from St. Swithun's Street to Wolvesey. The Committee of Council on Education had indicated to members of the Board that the St. Swithun's Street premises were quite unsatisfactory for a training school wishing to secure the official inspection of the Committee of Council and consequently a share of the generous State grants made available by the Privy Council Minute of 1846.[3] The Board's Report for 1847 refers to 'the large benefits derivable under those Minutes' and also details at the end of its Report the payments that were to be made to pupil teachers and the benefits which were to be derived when these pupil teachers were recruited for training as Queen's Scholars.[4] The pupil teachers were to receive a stipend from £10 at the end of their first year to £20 at the end of their fifth. They could then become candidates for a Queen's Scholarship and, if successful, secure a place at a training school, which would receive £25 per annum for each Queen's Scholar. Every master leaving the training school with a certificate of the first degree of merit (the lowest) was entitled to a grant of £15 or £20 per annum; of the second degree of merit to a grant of £20 or £25 per annum; and of the third degree £25 or £30 per annum. This was on condition that the trustees or managers of the school, of which he had charge, provided him with a house rent free, and with a further salary equal to twice the amount of the grant. The teachers therefore instead of being assisted by monitors whose age varied from nine to 13, might now have pupil teachers aged from 13 to 18 who were paid more substantially for their work and who, if successful as Queen's Scholars, had a sure future. If they were unsuccessful in securing a scholarship the government were to offer alternative employment in the public service.

School teachers were allowed one pupil teacher for every 25 children. For instance, a master or mistress in charge of 150 children would be paid for the six pupil teachers in his care £21 in addition to his regular salary, for his supervision of the pupil teachers and for the tuition he gave them before or after normal school hours. In addition arrangements were made for teachers' pensions to be two-thirds of their annual salary. This was for those who had served for not less than fifteen years. Such a pension scheme did not, in fact, materialise. But the other provisions within the Privy Council's 1846 Minute did, and the Winchester Board, in response to the Minute, made official application for inspection on 4 November 1847. No Privy Council funding appears in the 1848 accounts, but in 1849 the Privy Council paid £70. The sum steadily increased year by year until in 1860 the sum received was £718 10s. 0d.

The Privy Council measures brought an immediate improvement in the recruitment of teachers for training. St. Swithun's Street premises would have been unable to accommodate greater numbers, but Wolvesey had space for fifty.[5] The absence of a trust deed, however, proved a difficulty which the Committee of Council was prepared to treat sympathetically. The Board was clearly anxious that its application for inspection should succeed.

> It is impossible that the Board should not take a deep interest in the result of this application, seeing that in a well ordered Training School (besides the after benefits to masters who had been treated therein) half the expense of the pupils' training, and in the case of the Queen's Sholars a still larger proportion, will be borne by grants from the public purse.[6]

Although the grants from the public purse were made to the Winchester Diocesan Training School during 1848 and 1849, full inspection was not undertaken until 1852. During the year 1847–48 a preliminary inspection was made, and the Board was informed that the training school 'was not sufficiently organised to be fitted to complete the Queen's Scholar'. In consequence the Board appointed two additional masters. On 30 September 1852 Her Majesty's Inspector of Schools, the Rev. Henry Moseley, accompanied by a fellow inspector, the Rev. W. H. Brookfield, spent two days at Wolvesey. On the first day they attended the lectures delivered to the students, and on the second day they examined the students orally. Moseley describes the site as follows:

> The building is the ancient palace of the Bishop of Winchester, called Wolvesey Palace. It is the property of the bishop, who has granted it for the use of the school, *during the term of his episcopacy.* A portion only of the original palace remains, but it includes the chapel, a suite of apartments used as classrooms etc. by students, and a range of dormitories. It affords ample accommodation for fifty students. The site covers apparently five or six acres. It includes a large garden, pleasure grounds, and a plot covered by the ruins of a more ancient palace; affording to the students space for exercise. The whole is surrounded by a high wall. It is situated near the banks of the river Itchen, and is within the city of Winchester, communicating by a gateway with the cathedral close.

The report gives an account of the salaries received by teachers leaving the school, noting that no teacher leaving in 1852 received more than £50 per annum, with a house. Receipts of the training school are detailed, among which is £82 17s. 4d. 'by fees of Yeoman's School', an indication of a subsidiary use of the Wolvesey premises. As a result of the inspection the Yeoman's school was discontinued. Staff and their training qualifications were noted. There was the Principal, Rev. John Smith, the Vice Principal, Mr. John Blain, a certified schoolmaster and former student at Battersea, and Mr. Edward Sheppard,[7] also a former student at Battersea, now acting as 'industrial master and assistant teacher'. In addition there was Dr. Wesley, the cathedral organist, who taught vocal music, and Mr. Weaver, 'a scientific gardener' employed by the Warden of Winchester College, whose garden adjoined. Mr. Weaver instructed the students in horticulture.

A brief account is given of the occasional lectures delivered by a variety of the local clergy, among whom are George Moberly and Chenevix Trench. The scope of the curriculum covered religious knowledge, English grammar, arithmetic, history, geography, vocal singing, horticulture, and elements of of Latin and Greek. The teaching practice school of St. Michael's was praised as a good example of a national parochial school. The students attended St. Michael's every Monday from 2-4 p.m. Students in their last four months at Wolvesey attended every afternoon.

The general tenor of the report is supportive and commendatory, but the living conditions at Wolvesey leave something to be desired.

> A portion of it remains yet unfurnished; and furniture, fittings, and apparatus are but sparingly provided for the rest. The rooms are of a good height, but apertures are needed for ventilation in the ceilings of the dormitories, and in the passages which lead to them.

The Board's accounts for 1853 reflect their ready response to Moseley's criticism of Wolvesey's deficiences:

Lee, Carpenter (1852) ..	..	..	..	..	..	..	..	5	17	0
Ditto (1853) ..	..	..	..	..	..	..	..	3	3	3
Still (iron work for dormitories)	..	..	..	..	..	..	20	15	9
Wall (furnishing ditto) ..	..	..	..	..	..	..	93	3	10

Despite the national trend, there were only 13 students at Wolvesey at the time of Moseley's inspection, and this small number was reflected in the need the Principal felt for maintaining fees by running the Yeoman's school. Following the inspection, receipts for 12 Queen's Scholars were set at £255, and the allowance by the Committee of Council for 12 certified pupils was set at £110. With such additional income the carpenter's, iron-worker's and furnisher's bills could be met with confidence.

The Committee of Council's conceding institutional approval to the Winchester Diocesan Training School had come about through the training school taking measures to meet the stringent requirements of the committee. The move to the larger premises at Wolvesey was vital in this respect, as was the appointment of two additional members of staff. The absence of a trust deed was a serious setback only temporarily solved by the bishop making over Wolvesey to the training school for the period of his episcopacy and undertaking payment of rates and major structural repairs. The record of former students would not have been an insignificant consideration in leading to approval. The 1847 Report gives a detailed account of H.M.I. Allen's report of such teachers' performance within the diocesan schools, and it further emphasises the involvement of the training pupils in the parochial Sunday schools of Winchester, at a time when Sunday school teaching was the only teaching many children received.

The Committee of Council had insisted on the training school's pupils having regular access and teaching experience within approved practising schools. At

Winchester St. Michael's was used for this purpose. The rector of St. Michael's was the Rev. N. Midwinter, a member of the Winchester Diocesan Board of Education and himself a regular visiting lecturer at the training school. Indeed, facilities for teaching practice were considered so high a priority that the training school put by a special sum for the building at St. Michael's of an additional classroom for teaching practice purposes. Mr. Mason was the master at the school responsible for the training school pupils. He himself had been trained at St. Swithun's Street, and joins, with William Whiting, that long line of former students who have given back to the college the benefits of their training and their further experience.

In 1847 the new Principal, at the instigation of the Winchester Board, had visited St. Mark's and Battersea training schools, from which he had derived 'several useful hints'.[8] He was in search not only of additional staff but of standards of comparison which would enable him the more readily to raise the quality of the training provision at Winchester. Training schools approved by the Privy Council were now to be compared publicly and it was important for Winchester first to meet the conditions of approval and second not to be a laggard when the annual national report on the approved training schools was made. With approval the Winchester Board cast a wider net for its training school pupils. There was no longer a requirement that they should be drawn from the Winchester and Salisbury dioceses only. In addition the Board looked to a better class of candidate for admission.

With the growth and development of training schools throughout the country, some of them directly associated with diocesan initiatives, such as at Chester, Exeter, and Durham, some established, or at least supported, by the National Society itself, such as St. Mark's, Whitelands, and Battersea, and the Home and Colonial Training College in Gray's Inn Road, which had been founded by Evangelical churchmen in co-operation with dissenters,[9] Winchester was unwilling to be left behind. In other parts of the country colleges were being built anew. The move from St. Swithun's Street to Wolvesey had ensured the survival of the training school and had materially increased its chances of securing the approval from the Privy Council, but there was no question of there being a purpose-built college at that stage in Winchester. Wolvesey was a prestigious building for the training school, but being both inadequately furnished for the prospective 50 pupils, and lacking a trust deed, could not secure the future of the training school. There were, however, compensations: the building was spacious, the grounds extensive, and the distinguished site encouraged the wide-ranging and gifted clergy of the diocese to proffer their services as visiting lecturers and examiners. Now in addition to John Keble, George Moberly, Richard Dawes, and the Archdeacons, there was the Rev. Professor Richard Chenevix Trench, whose series of lectures to the students on 'The Study of Words' and 'English Past and Present' were published and gained wide acclaim. The Principal delivered a series of lectures on chemistry and supported the efforts of Mr. Weaver, 'the scientific gardener', to the point of encouraging G. W. Johnson, who was the editor of *The Cottage*

Gardener to examine the students in 1850 in natural philosophy and agricultural chemistry.[10] The urgency of the times was not forgotten when in 1855, in the midst of the Crimean War, students were encouraged to hear Mr. Mason lecture at the Mechanics' Institute on 'Russia and the present War'.[11] The Winchester Diocesan Training School at Wolvesey may not have been numerically the most flourishing teacher-training establishment in the country, but its curriculum and the range of additional lectures given by visiting clergy and laity bore favourable comparision with what was happening elsewhere.

The Curriculum

'It is by attending a school, seeing what is going on there . . . that teachers are to be formed, and not by lectures and abstract instruction.'[12] The words are Dr. Andrew Bell's, but they might equally have been Joseph Lancaster's. The two initiators of the monitorial system laid down rigid rules for teacher-training dependent on neither intellectual attainment nor acquirement. Their systems of mechanistic drilling, abhorred by the inspectors in the 1840s, had a profound influence on the curricula of the training schools founded in that period. A mass of teachers was required for the poor schools, the ragged schools, the parish schools, the commercial schools, and the middle schools. A mass-produced method was called for. It produced ignorant teachers but competent drillers. The few months spent at Battersea or Borough Road compared unfavourably with the three-year period of training existing in Germany, but the pattern of Continental training was condensed into the shorter period. R. J. Bryce's view of teacher-training taking place within a university department of education with a model school attached found no favour with Oxford and Cambridge. London and Durham were too newly formed to contemplate such innovation. In any case the need for teachers was essentially for the children of the poor, and it was generally accepted that their curriculum would not extend beyond holy scriptures, the Catechism, reading and writing.

At both Battersea and Borough Road the régime for training the teachers who were to drill the monitors to drill the children was rigorous in the extreme. Books were scarce; teaching was done orally for long stints at a time broken by organised walks or gardening activities.[13] The Battersea pattern in particular was to influence the curriculum within most of the early Church of England colleges. It certainly influenced Winchester's. Kay-Shuttleworth's main aim at Battersea was 'the formation of the character of the schoolmaster'. He was much more concerned with character than learning. His greatest fear was that even a little learning might puff up a student inordinately 'a young man barely (if indeed at all) instructed in the humblest elements of reading, writing and arithmetic . . .'. With such a fear shared by the Winchester Diocesan Board of Education, a fear that the poor and ignorant might through a little learning challenge the class structure, the report of the inspectors following the summer examinations of 1857 must have been especially consoling: 'What higher praise can be given, than that the students appeared humble, conscientious, painstaking, remarkably simple and unaffected in manner . . .'.

That the students should be humble appears to be the first criterion. If this can be achieved through the same diet of holy schipture, reading, writing and arithmetic as might obtain within a National school, what need was there for more? In 1847 the Rev. John Smith, the new Principal, visited both Battersea and St. Mark's College in search of an answer to that question. The Board was anxious that with the move to Wolvesey the staffing and curriculum of the training school should reach the desired standard that would merit inspection by the Committee of Council. Battersea and St. Mark's had hitherto been most favoured by the inspectors' reports and subsequent funding. But in ethos and curriculum the Principal found St. Mark's a very different place from Battersea. St. Mark's Principal was Derwent Coleridge, the son of Samuel Taylor Coleridge. Like Kay-Shuttleworth he believed that teacher-training should be conducted within a residential community 'devoted to unremitting endeavour, and dedicated to Christian aims'.[14] But unlike Kay-Shuttleworth he believed that the primary purpose of a training college was to nurture educated and cultured persons; and to this end he wished to create for his students, through the buildings in which they worked and worshipped, and through their curriculum, an environment that might foster gracious living.

The dilemma of the Winchester Principal on his return to Wolvesey was apparent. On the one hand he was returning to a palace which, if appropriately furnished, might through its chapel, its spacious accommodation and elegant grounds afford the proper environment in which to implement Coleridge's ideas about a training college. Furthermore, Winchester, standing at the centre of a very large but mostly rural diocese, was required to make provision not only for teachers for the parish schools, but also for the middle schools, that is, for some of the better provided among the middle classes who might in their turn wish to become teachers in such schools. For such schools there was a clear need to widen the curriculum, and this need would have to be reflected in the extended curriculum of the Diocesan Training School.

On the other hand the Principal was keenly aware of the Board's wish that students should not be educated beyond their station in life, and that the Board looked more to the Battersea character-training than the St. Mark's gracious living. In any case there was no possibility of following the St. Mark's pattern in a pathetically underfurnished Wolvesey. It is therefore not very surprising to find the Principal of the Battersea Training School assisting at the Christmas examination of the Winchester students in 1848. By this time Mr. Gyles, formerly of Battersea, had been engaged as second master, and the Board noted with pleasure 'his great ability and skill in teaching'. At Battersea Mr. Gyles had obtained a certificate of merit of the second division of the first class. He was an accomplished teacher of mathematics. The Battersea influence was further felt when in the early 1850s as mentioned earlier two other former Battersea students were appointed, John Blain as Vice Principal, and Edward Sheppard as industrial master.

The traditional appointment of Oxbridge Principals to the Training Schools tended to harden the division between professional training and academic study. Apart from the appointment of its very first Principal, a Dublin graduate, Winchester was squarely within this tradition. Class and culture differences were reinforced in the distinction drawn between 'academic' and 'professional', distinctions that have not yet entirely disappeared. The academic teaching was undertaken by the delivering of lectures with the students taking as full notes as possible. The lack of books and the examination requirements, which initially were entirely oral, led the students to memorise their notes and respond to the questions according to their memory recall. The professional training was undertaken, during the Wolvesey years, at St. Michael's National school, where all students attended from 2-4 p.m. on Monday afternoons. Students during the last four months of their course were required to attend every afternoon.

The instruction in professional training was given largely by Mr. W. G. Mason, a former pupil of the training school. William Drewett, a student of 1860, 64 years later recalled his impressions:

> Of Mr. Mason, our Method Master, I could say much, for I knew him officially at Wolvesey as well as apart from office, for my brother lived with him, and I was ever welcome at his home in Kingsgate Street. Mr. Mason was Headmaster of St. Michael's Day School (mixed), to which was attached a boys' school of higher grade, attended chiefly by sons of citizens engaged in trade. He also assisted the Rector of St. Michael's in the tuition of his private pupils. He was well equipped for the work attached to his Wolvesey appointment, but 'rode high in the stirrups'. His attitude to the students was unbending, and never did he enliven a lecture with humorous or witty remarks. As he sat in front of us, doling out his instruction, he had a habit of moving the scalp of his head in quite an uncanny fashion, and his lectures were delivered with a solemnity almost funereal. When giving a lesson to the upper classes of the Model School, which he occasionally did for our benefit, he was seen and heard at his best; and his criticisms of our lessons to the boys were always restrained and free from excessive severity. I still have a book which he gave me on leaving College, with a flattering inscription therein, a gift possibly also as a reminder of many hours spent pleasantly together in 'recreation'.[15]

In the Board's accounts for the year ending 31 December 1857, we see that the practising master, Mr. Mason, is paid £10. This would, of course, be in addition to his salary as headmaster of St. Michael's. Also in these accounts is a payment of £150 to 'Macklin, bricklayer, on account for Model School'.[16] A Macklin built the college chapel in 1880, and the firm of Macklin still undertakes considerable building and maintenance work for the college. The payment in 1857 was towards 'an additional school-room adjoining St. Michael's schools, at the cost inclusive of apparatus of £493 2s. 11d., towards which the Committee of Council voted £221, and the Trustees of St. Michael's school £56 19s. 1d.—leaving £215 3s. 10d. to be paid by the Board'. The suggestion that the work of the training school would be improved by such an addition had been made by H.M.I. Temple, later to become Archbishop of Canterbury. At a conference with the Board after the 1857 midsummer examination he had stressed that the theory and the practice of the art of teaching would benefit by the regular use of such premises by the staff and pupils of the training school. Temple's requirements had been that there should be 'practice under careful supervision, the study of good models, and sensible lectures both on the principles of the art and on the application of those principles'.

In the three months following the completion of the building the practice adopted was that lessons were given by four students to a class of children, usually drawn from a variety of Winchester schools. The Principal, Vice Principal and Practising Master were present together with other students observing and taking notes. An hour was then given to criticism of these lessons, each being commented on by two students called on incidentally, and by the three members of staff. In addition a lecture was given to all students each week on the general theory and practice of school management and a further hour's lecture on a Saturday devoted to specific methodologies. On one morning in the week the pupils were divided into five unequal sections through the Winchester schools. The Principal attended one section and gave a lesson before them on Holy Scriptures or the Liturgy; the Vice Principal attended successively two sections, criticising the work individually; and the Practising Master gave model lessons to the sections attending his school. The Board noted that the following of the inspector's advice had increased considerably the duties of the Principal and Vice Principal and thanked them for the way they had given themselves to the work 'with cheerful alacrity, and in the full conviction of the utility of the course prescribed by Mr. Temple'.

In its 1857 Report the Board had referred to the St. Michael's *Schools*. The inspector's report for 1860[17] gives details of the organisation of the school into three divisions under the headmastership of Mr. Mason. The lowest division was composed of mixed infants and was conducted by a qualified mistress and one female pupil-teacher. This division was open for the students' observation so that they could see how the very young were being taught, but they very seldom practised in it. The middle division was a mixed school, in charge of Mr. Drewett and one male pupil-teacher, but was superintended and partly taught by the headmaster. There was constantly one student practising in this section. The upper division was composed entirely of boys, who were taught by the headmaster and one male pupil-teacher. Here also one student was always teaching; and it was in this section that the criticism lessons were given. As each division of the school was organised as though it were a distinct school, the student teaching in it was expected to 'hold himself responsible for its discipline and working during the time of his practice'.

The curriculum for the pupils at the training school was conditioned by the advice of the inspectors, the array of visiting examiners, but above all by the full-time and part-time staff. The Principal for the first 11 years of the 15-year stay at Wolvesey was the Rev. John Smith, of Magdalen College, Oxford, described as a fanatical scientist but who, in his routine teaching in 1851, was responsible for the teaching of scripture, English history, Shakespeare, Milton's *Paradise Lost* (for paraphrasing and parsing), Greek, Latin, the geography of Palestine, Articles of the Church, natural philosphy (text book: *The Chemistry of the Creation*), and teaching (School Organisation—Moral and Intellectual Training—Subjects of Instruction—Methods of Teaching—Notes of Lessons).[18] The Vice Principal's lectures were all in mathematics: arithmetic, Euclid, algebra, industrial mechanics, mensuration, plane trigonometry, spherical trigonometry, differential calculus. The Vice Principal at this time was Mr. Gyles, who in December 1851 left to prepare himself for entry to Cambridge university. He was replaced by Mr. Blain, who took over the lecture programme in mathematics and served as Vice Principal for five years, when he, too, left to read for a degree, but this time at Trinity College, Dublin. In 1860 the Vice Principal, still in charge of the teaching of mathematics, was Mr. Johnson, a Cambridge graduate who took holy orders soon after his appointment.

The students who attended the Principal's and Vice Principal's lectures and who were commended by the examiners are scarcely within that category described by Kay-Shuttleworth as stemming 'from the common drudgery of a handicraft . . . barely instructed in the humblest elements of reading, writing, and arithmetic'. Here we have in 1851 students Peake and Covey who have studied two hundred lines of Homer's *Iliad*, Book II, and selections from Horace's *Satires*; and Targett, who is reported as having read the first four chapters of Snowball's *Spherical Trigonometry*; viz., those on General Formulae connecting the sides and angles of Triangles, Gauss' Theorem and Napier's Analogies, Solution of right-angled, quadrantal, and oblique-angled Triangles. He had also read the whole of Professor Hall's *Treatise on Differential Calculus.*[19] Text books are clearly now available for the students and by 1851 neither teaching nor examining is wholly done by oral means. One of the examiners, the Dean of Hereford,[20] reported to the Board that his papers on geography and astronomy have been better answered by the students than in the previous year.

In November 1850 Mr. Long died. He had been appointed in 1840 as the training school's instructor in church music. He had examined the students annually and it had become a custom for him to award a prize to the most able student musician. He had combined his training school work with that of cathedral organist. Dr. Samuel Wesley succeeded him in both roles and left a formidable impression on the students:

> To engage such a giant in musical knowledge, as was Samuel Sebastian Wesley, to take a lot of young fellows through Hullah's Course was like setting up a Nasmyth steam-hammer to crack nuts. The Cathedral organist was more at home with the Second Year men, who took theory; but it was droll to see him, seated at a small harmonium, guiding us through two-part vocal exercises.[21]

The move to Wolvesey in 1847 had not only made available much larger premises for the training school; it had also provided gardens, and, in the person of Mr. Weaver, the Warden's gardener, an able instructor in horticulture. Pestalozzi had strongly advocated that the training of teachers should be associated with a residential community that contributed to its own well-being by agricultural and industrial activities. Kay-Shuttleworth had himself been impressed by Pestalozzi's theories and practice. The Committee of Council was concerned that the training of teachers should strengthen not weaken the ties between the teacher and his agricultural or industrial background. As evening schools developed it was thought that the apprentices who attended should be taught by schoolmasters themselves trained and skilled in practical work. In 1857 H.M.I. Temple wrote:

> For every kind of reason it is an advantage to a schoolmaster that he should not be totally helpless in handling any tools besides those of his profession. He is unquestionably better fitted for many a contingency if he has some skill in gardening, carpentering, bookbinding and printing. Several attempts are made to teach gardening which of all of these is the most useful. At Winchester the instruction in gardening is particularly good, and includes a most useful branch of the art, the pruning of fruit trees.[22]

The Board's support for Mr. Weaver's work was reinforced by their inviting Mr. G. W. Johnson, the editor of *The Cottage Gardener*, to examine the students on the way they had maintained their allotments in the course of the year. Dunkerton proved to be the most successful gardener and was presented with the first edition of *The Cottage Gardener*.[23]

The local gentry were just as keen as the inspectorate in nurturing among the students and teachers a practical knowledge of everyday things. In 1855 Lord Ashburton offered £60 in prizes, £30 for male winners and £30 for female winners. Individual prizes were of £5 and £10 value, and in the following year a prize of £8 was offered to a student competitor. The awards were made 'to those parties found to possess pre-eminence in the knowledge of common, practical, and familiar things connected with daily life, and the phenomena of nature around us, as related to health, shelter, food, cooking etc., and all things that conduce to the comfort and usefulness of life'. The competitors were to produce a written response in which they could show that they knew enough to teach the 'Knowledge of Common Things'. To give better guidance to the candidates H.M.I. Brookfield produced in 1854 a pamphlet entitled *Elementary Instruction of the poor in the Knowledge of Common Things*.[24]

Associated with their gardening activities the students received lectures on and were examined in agricultural chemistry. Mr. G. W. Johnson was the invited lecturer. The Principal also lectured on chemistry. But there were other visiting lecturers in this field. The Rev. G. A. Seymour delivered fortnightly lectures for the greater part of 1848 on Chemical Combinations and the Chemical Constitution of Plants; the Rev. W. Williams had lectured weekly on physical science; and the versatile Rev. C. Walters, F.S.A., had lectured on pneumatics, archaeology, astronomy, as well as the connection of Anglo-Saxon with our present language. Such a programme of science lectures, regular not spasmodic, indicates that the training schools were among the first educational institutions to attempt organised science teaching. For instance, Dr. Moberly at Winchester College was adamant: 'It is plainly out of the question that we should *teach* chemistry'.[25] But as early as 1849 the Winchester Diocesan Board was congratulating the training school on the high standards of its scientific teaching due to the appointment of Mr. Gyles as second master.

H.M.I. Moseley questioned the value of the lengthy oral examinations every summer of students in each area of their curriculum. He suggested that the oral examinations should be limited to those subjects that the students would be required to teach when they became masters. The written examinations at Christmas were more appropriate for testing the broader curriculum. He laid down what he thought was 'proper and basic' to the teacher-training course: scripture, English history, teaching and school management, vocal music, and model drawing. He advocated less geography and history and more arithmetic and English, with especial attention being given to the religious and moral elements within the curriculum. Health education he also stressed with the effect that there was an increase of time allocated to football and cricket for the male students at Winchester and a coresponding increase for the female students at Salisbury in walking in crocodile.

In 1855 H.M.I. Moseley was asked by the Committee of Council to construct a three-year syllabus for the training colleges. The syllabus was approved and published and put into effect directly. The syllabus comprised religious knowledge, reading, penmanship, arithmetic, English grammar, geography, English history, physical science and vocal music. Candidates were also to be examined in either classics or higher mathematics.

The model drawing which Moseley had personally advocated but which did not find a place in the national syllabus until later was at Winchester taught by the cathedral architect, Mr. J. Colson. As a basis for his lessons he used to take the students on detailed guided tours of the cathedral. It was this Mr. Colson, who after visiting a number of newly-constructed training colleges was to submit and have accepted a plan for the new college to be built on West Hill.

Mr. Sheppard, the third master, had travelled extensively as a merchant seaman. From a good deal of personal knowledge he lectured in geography: mathematical, physical, descriptive, and British colonies. He also lectured in astronomy. Moseley, reporting on his work to the Committee of Council in 1852, wrote:

> We heard the third master deliver a lecture on the geography and history of the United States, which showed a very complete knowledge of the subject, and considerable power and judgement in treating it . . . The experience of this institution, as of others, appears, indeed, to show that the best officers for training schools will eventually be found among the men who have themselves been educated in them.[26]

Of the many gifted part-time lecturers perhaps the most outstanding was Richard Chenevix Trench. In 1847 he became an elected member of the Board and in 1849 when Professor of Divinity at King's College, London, and also rector of Itchenstoke, he delivered at the training college a series of fortnightly lectures throughout the year on ecclesiastical history. In 1851 he gave a further series of lectures on 'The Study of Words'. These lectures were printed, and he gave a volume to each student in the college. Later in the decade he lectured on 'English Past and Present'. This volume of lectures was also published, and in the preface Trench identifies the audience he is addressing:

> . . . a body of young Englishmen, all with a fair amount of classical knowledge . . . not wholly unacquainted with modern languages; but not yet with any special designation as to their future work; having only as yet marked out to them the duty in general of living lives worthy of those who have England for their native country, and English for their native tongue.

Surely Trench would have known his Winchester audience well enough not to be deceived in their academic capabilities and their professional expectations. Yet his lectures, all of them delivered in the evenings, as were all the other extra-curriculum lectures, when the students might have been nodding at the end of a relentlessly time-tabled day, were packed with scholarly, encyclopaedic detail, fluent, fascinating, profoundly erudite. Trench was one of the foremost lexicographers of the age, and the students were greatly privileged to have benefited from his long and close assocation with the college. As Dean of Westminster he maintained this association, and on his appointment as Archbishop of Dublin he bequeathed an annual prize of books to the value of £1 for the student who produced the best paper in English at the midsummer examinations.

The distribution of students' time is given in Appendix V. In 1853, exclusive of Sundays, 88½ hours were given to work, including worship, walking, washing and dressing, and the rest, 55½ hours, to meals and sleep. On Sundays the students had a scripture lecture from 7.30 to 8.00 a.m. They attended at least one cathedral service, and usually assisted with one of the city's Sunday schools. Of the 88½ hours the largest section, 14 hours, went to mathematics; 8½ hours was devoted to scripture and liturgy, and 7¾ hours to history, grammar and Milton. The Principal argued: 'That a smaller aggregate of time is given to this (scripture and liturgy) than to mathematical studies results from the fact that every person, considered as a proper candidate for admission to the school, must possess much previous acquaintance with these subjects'.[27] He later clarifies the juxtaposition of Milton with grammar. 'The parsing and paraphrasing of Milton, though difficult to attain without a competent knowledge of Latin, are yet justly made by Privy Council the test of a schoolmaster's acquaintance with his own language'.

The time-table for 1851, set out in Appendix VI, extended daily from 5.45 a.m. until 10 p.m. On Wednesdays and Saturdays there were half-holidays, but on Wednesdays work recommenced at 7 p.m. On Saturday students were required to attend evensong in the cathedral. This routine time-table was varied by the evening lectures, many of them open, delivered by invited speakers, by the twice-yearly examinations, by special excursions, such as a visit to the Dean's garden at Bishopstoke, and by the students entertaining at Wolvesey at an annual festival all the children educated at Church schools in Winchester.

The occasion of examinations continued to be an event of entertainment for the subscribers. In 1849 as many as sixty attended the winter examinations. The visitors far outnumbered the students. The oral examination lasted two and a half hours and was followed by presentation of prizes by the Dean and Mr. Long, and concluded by a stirring harangue from one of the cathedral clergy, Canon Woodrooffe.[28] The summer examinations comprised written exercises and in 1851, for example, lasted a week and were followed by oral examinations. There were invariably musical interludes and the Principal and his mother usually 'entertained the company with a hospitable luncheon'.[29] With regard to the mode of questioning, just as within the set syllabus Milton was used as an adjunct to the study of English grammar, so when Dr. Moberly questioned the students on Shakespeare's *Henry V,* he called upon them 'as they read aloud, to paraphrase sentences, and explain their historical and grammatical meaning'.[30] During the course of the examination proceedings the Secretary of the Board, Canon Jacob, the rector of Crawley, would read out reports sent to him by the managers of schools, in answer to inquiries as to the character of those masters who had trained at the college.[31]

In 1848 the Dean of Winchester invited all the students to spend a Monday at his residence at Bishopstoke. The students, who then numbered over thirty, took the train from Winchester to Bishopstoke station. They had a short walk to the Dean's house where the Dean gave them a conducted tour over his parterre, which was celebrated for its exotic plants. The students were then permitted to play cricket on the lawns. At one o'clock they retired to the Dean's summer-house where they partook of a 'sumptuous collation'. After lunch the students entertained the Dean with their singing, concluding with the national anthem. Cricket rounded off the day's excursion, and each student was presented with a small bouquet, and one was sent to the Principal, who had not accompanied the students.[32]

Wolvesey became the ideal rendezvous for the Winchester church schools' children's festival. This usually occurred at Whitsuntide and in 1849 almost 1,400 took part. The day began with a service in St. Thomas's church. At two o'clock in the afternoon the children with their clergy and teachers assembled in the open spaces around the church. Each school had its own flag and marched under it through the streets of the city to Wolvesey Palace. The students were responsible for the organisation of events at Wolvesey which consisted of a massive tea-party and the subsequent supervision of the children's recreation. Then, joining with the choristers of the cathedral and Winchester

College, they sang together many of Mr. Hullah's songs, ending with a special song about the old Wolvesey Castle.

Such then were the staff, such the students, and such the curriculum, which were inspected by H.M.I.s Moseley and Brookfield in 1852. It was an intensely busy, hard-working, many-sided community. Humble students were being taught and examined by some of the country's most eminent scholars. It is not then too surprising to read Moseley's summary of his report to the Lords of the Privy Council.

> My report to your Lordships on the application of this College for inspection, and for the appointment of Queen's Scholars, having been printed in the present volume (page 242), I need not further advert to it than to point out the excellent way in which its students passed the Christmas examination. Those of no other College obtained a like proportion of certificates, as appears by the Table (page 264). This success is as remarkable in what are called the higher subjects of instruction as in those which are proper to elementary instruction. The results of the examination of this College, and of those at Durham and Exeter, are the more worthy of observation, as there were no Queen's scholars, or, I believe, pupil teachers, included among the candidates. They justify your Lordship's decision to admit these lesser Diocesan Colleges to a full share of the privileges offered by your Minutes of 1846.[33]

The Students

The most puzzling discrepancy is the humble unlearned origin of the students set against their distinguished examination success in so broad a curriculum.

The Committee of Council's 1846 Minute inaugurated the system of paid pupil-teachers, established Queen's Scholarships which paid for the best part of the students' fees, and through a system of certificate examinations at the end of the first year (1st Class), second year (2nd Class), and third year (3rd Class), brought incremental funding to the training schools (£15 or £20, £20 or £25, £25 or £30 respectively). In addition the salary of some qualified lecturers was augmented by the Council by as much as £100 a year. Kay-Shuttleworth's intention was clearly to raise the character and position of the schoolmaster. The pupil-teacher was a stipendiary monitor beginning his apprenticeship at 13, and, after five years, entering the training school at eighteen. It became possible for him to subsist without a great deal of additional support until the age of 18 on his apprenticeship payment and during his training school years on his Queen's Scholarship grant. Once he was established as a schoolmaster at, say, £50 a year with a house, he would receive additional payments for the pupil-teachers in his care, and sometimes the 'children's pence', the payment made for attendance. The measures not only raised considerably the average age of students attending the training school. It raised their expectations also. They stayed for longer periods and left with better prospects.

H.M.I. Moseley had advocated that first class certificates should not be awarded to students unless they had successfully completed their examinations after a full 12-month stay at their training school. He further opened up the possibility of schoolteachers who had not been trained, or who had left prematurely, to have the opportunity of securing their certificates and consequent payments by sitting the yearly examinations at the training school. He further urged at a later stage that, to ensure the professional application of the training course, certificates should be granted only after the teacher had completed two full years of teaching. His intention was to avoid rewarding academic attainments until it had been supported by professional efficiency.

The Winchester Diocesan Board of Education expressed its confident response to the 1846 Minutes of Council in the following terms:

> It is acknowledged that the standard of qualifications fixed by the Minutes of Council for teachers and stipendiary monitors, and still more for Queen's Scholars, is high. But the past attainments of the masters sent forth from the Diocesan Training School, and their character for efficiency, as tested by the Inspector of Schools during the past three years, offer the best assurance of future and higher excellence; and more so as it may reasonably be expected that a better class of candidates for admission into Training Schools than those which have hitherto presented themselves, may be expected to arise under the encouraging stimulus of the Minutes of Council.[34]

From H.M.I. Moseley's 1852 report on the students it would seem that the Board's 1847 hopes for a better class of student had been fully achieved. They were certainly older. In the years 1840–46 many students were admitted who were between the ages of thirteen and sixteen. From 1847–62 relatively few students entered below the age of eighteen. Most of those entering at 18 had served for five years as a pupil-teacher. Many entered over the age of 18 who had matured in their experience of life as carpenter, footman, gentleman's servant, assistant schoolmaster, chandler, tailor, or bricklayer.[35] Through their past occupations many brought a useful craft that enhanced their teaching in industrial schools. Some came with a quality of learning unrecorded in the earliest pages of the Students' Register. George Lloyd was admitted in January 1847, at the age of seventeen. He had previously assisted his father who owned a dairy in Gillingham, Dorset. He was recommended by the vicar of Gillingham and granted an exhibition by the Salisbury diocese. About his 'state of acquirement on admission' the Principal writes: 'Arithmetic to Barter. Some knowledge of Grammar—and took his place in a class beginning Caesar. He had wrought Algebra to Simple Equations some years before'. Of James Burr, who was admitted at midsummer 1847 at the age of 15, we read that his father was a gunner and that the son's accomplishment extended to having read five books of Virgil, four of Euclid, and algebra 'through Simple Equations'. Burr showed 'remarkable talent for discipline and teaching'. Within 1848 he was placed in charge first of the Salisbury National school, and then of the school of industry in the Isle of Wight. After Christmas 1849 he was appointed master of St. Maurice's School, Winchester, but he continued to lodge at Wolvesey becoming responsible for the departments of English and history in the training school.

The Principal's comments on the students' acquirements on admission during the Wolvesey period are more positive, less dismissive, indicating a broader range of achievement in mathematics, grammar, classics, and often, chemistry.

The rising class of the students is to be seen from a selection of their fathers' occupations: coastguard, superintendent of the Dungeness lighthouse, spirit merchant, lawyer, missionary, gentleman's servant, maltster and postmaster, army officer, servant to H.R.H. Prince Albert. Many students without exhibitions or Queen's Scholarships were supported in their studies by payment of their fees by local clergy such as Charles Kingsley, Richard Dawes, and the Dean of Winchester, or by local gentry, Sir Thomas Baring, or the Warden of Winchester College. Some students who lacked such support had to work their way through college. Henry Targett, whose father was the postmaster in Kingsgate Street was admitted in June 1849. It is recorded that 'he lived with a Hatter'. He was then 18 years old. He had spent five and a half years at Mr. Bentham's private school in North Walls and then became a 'daily pupil' at the Wolvesey Yeoman's school. His limited means 'made it expedient for him to devote some time to tailoring in the Commercial School'.[36]

The training school education helped many students to rise, if not meteorically, at least a grade or so above the level of the class, or socio-economic group, into which they were born. Many in this 1847–62 period took posts of schoolmaster at a salary of about £50–£70 a year with a house. This salary was augmented by their various certificate awards and sometimes by the children's payments. Many entries record that, where a house was provided, school appointments were made of the student and his sister, who would act as housekeeper, sempstress, and teacher. Better remunerated were those such as William Targett, William Hoskins and George Howell who became teachers in the prison service at Parkhurst or Portland with considerably higher salaries. Edwin Biddick's career after leaving the training school was master of Farnham National School, master of method in the York and Ripon training school, Vice Principal of the York and Ripon training school, Principal of Trinity College, Carmarthen. While at York he was ordained by the Archbishop of York. He had entered the Winchester training school in 1850 at the age of 19, and he died in 1870.

Some of the most successful students, however, moved away from teaching. One was William Drewett (1860) who made his way as a bookseller, who recalled in the 1924 *Wintonian* his one year at Wolvesey so vividly. Another was William Henry Long who was admitted in January 1858 at the age of eighteen. His father was coachman to Sir R. Simeon on the Isle of Wight. Long failed his exams at the end of his first year and 'left for want of friends'. He set up as a second-hand bookseller in Portsmouth. He wrote books on the Isle of Wight dialect, naval and army medals, and the memoirs of Emma, Lady Hamilton. Recent interest in 'militaria' have led to two of his books being reprinted. Long, who was forced to leave the college because there was no friend to pay his fees, died aged 56 in 1896, an author of some merit, noted by an obituary in *The Times*. George Long, a pillar of our present maintenance staff, is a direct descendant.

During the Wolvesey years there are very many entries by the Principal which refer to the frail health of the students. Their studies are often 'impeded by reason of ill health' or they suffer 'an alarming attack of epidemic illness', or they are 'absent for change of air'. Of John Robinson in 1849 we read 'This pupil's attention to the sick and his self-denying exertion have been exemplary', and later, 'this kindness and exertion have since been shown in a more trying illness'. This last would seem to be a reference to William Thomas's death at the training school on 13 October 1849.

During the autumn of 1849 an epidemic of cholera had struck Winchester. There were many deaths at Winchester College, and the training school was not exempt. The epidemic in the city lasted for 66 days and caused 36 deaths. By 15 November the ravaging disease had abated and the Queen ordered that a thanksgiving day be observed. For the training school, however, the following 10 years were to continue to take their toll of the students' health and sometimes of their lives. Alfred Freedgard died in July 1852 after constant nursing by the Principal and his mother, and in September 1853 William Doling died. Doling was from Bridport, 'a Gentleman's Servant', aged twenty-four. By 1857–58 the incidence of the sickness was so severe that the closing of the training school was seriously considered. William Rowden in 1857 'removed to Cheltenham Training College believing that at Winchester to be abandoned'; and in 1858 George Coombs, for the same reason, 'removed to Battersea Training College'. The illness was identified as typhus and some students, such as Alfred Hammond, were taken home to die.

Planning a Move

The Board of Education was bound to investigate the sanitary conditions of the training school. In 1858 there were 38 students in residence of whom 10 for health reasons were obliged to leave, seven of whom were unable to present themselves for examination in December. Even the Principal's health was affected. The Committee of Council, on hearing of the unsatisfactory sanitary state of Wolvesey, ruled that 'Wolvesey would not be permitted to be used for the nightly domiciling of the students, though no objection would be made to the temporary use of it in the day-time for lectures and meals'.[37] Consequently the students were lodged in a house in St. Peter's Street, but spent their days at Wolvesey. The Board had to decide whether to abandon Wolvesey altogether. It was recognised that about £500 would be required to repair the building to a satisfactory health standard. Uniting with the Chichester diocesan training school was seriously considered, but the overwhelming view was that a new training college should be built in Winchester, and the Bishop appealed to the diocese to support a new and permanent college. The Bishop divulged that the Dean and Chapter had offered a suitable site of two acres of land 'in a most eligible situation, and the sum of £500 in furtherance of the object'. The Bishop himself offered a further £500.[38] The subscription fund was thus established and the Queen herself headed the list with a donation of £100. The work of the training school was to continue, with the students sleeping at the house in St. Peter's Street, but studying at Wolvesey, until the new premises were ready to receive them.

The Principal, the Rev. John Smith, had resigned on his appointment to the rectory of Little Hinton in Wiltshire. The announcement had been made in October 1858, and the Board, in view of the doubtful future of the college, paused before appointing his successor. The new Principal, the Rev. Charles Collier, M.A., was appointed in February 1859. He had been second master of the Sheffield Royal Free Grammar school and an assistant curate of the parish church of Sheffield. Soon after a new Vice Principal was appointed, Mr. J. W. Johnson, B.A., of Trinity College, Cambridge.

The new Principal, like his predecessor, was to take responsibility for the college in its transition from one site to another. But Charles Collier had the added difficulty of supervising the lodgings at St. Peter's Street, the curriculum work at Wolvesey, and to participate in negotiations relating to the building of the new college on West Hill. He is described by the *Hampshire Chronicle* as

> . . . one who was senior wrangler of his year, and also one of the Committee of Management of the York Training College . . . some of the most efficient masters of the West Riding had been trained by him for their office . . . His published works and lectures are some index of his range of study—Monasticism in England previous to the Reformation—Poetry in Virgil—England in Past and Present Times . . . But his chief praise is that few men possess in a higher degree the faculty of influencing the conduct as well as training the intellect of young men and, whilst being a devoted churchman, and anxious to carry out on all occasions the directions of the Church of England, he is singularly free from party spirit, and eminently endowed with the manners and kindliness of a Christian scholar and gentleman.[39]

The new Principal, as his predecessor, became the chaplain to St. John's hospital. His lectures and sermons were well received. The students did him much credit in the summer examinations of 1860, and in November the Principal was honoured by the Lord Lieutenant by being appointed the Honorary Chaplain of the 1st Hampshire Volunteer Rifle Corps, which carried with it a commission. In a remarkably short time Mr. Collier had gained the admiration and confidence of his students, colleagues, fellow citizens, and the Board.

It was at this stage, in November 1860, that, in accordance with advice from the Committee of Council, the Diocesan Board of Education ceded its authority over the training school to a Committee of Management by a deed of conveyance of the site for its new premises. The Bishop was President of the Committee and the other members, lay and clerical, were annually elected from among the subscribers to the college. The control of the building programme remained in the hands of the Board, and it reported that it was Mr. Colson's plans that had been chosen from the 11 submitted in competition.

Mr. Colson was the cathedral architect; the pseudonym he had chosen in submitting his scheme was 'Spes'. He, perhaps more than his unsuccessful competitors, knew a great deal about the building requirements of a training college. He had taught drawing at Wolvesey for 12 years, and before submitting his drawings he had visited a number of the new training colleges. The builder who won the contract was Watts of Southampton, for £7,450, the building to be completed by Michaelmas 1862. The diocese was to pay £5,180; the Committee of Council £2,000; and the National Society £500. It was estimated that a further £1,000 would be needed for furniture and for laying out the grounds, which by this stage the Dean and Chapter had increased to five acres. The ceremony of laying the foundation stone was planned to take place in the spring of 1861, and it was hoped H.R.H. the Prince Consort would be the principal guest. The prince, however, was in declining health. The foundation stone was laid instead by the Lord Lieutenant, Viscount Eversley, on 5 April 1861, and very fully reported in the *Hampshire Chronicle*. The streets of Winchester were gaily decked. The day began with a special service in the cathedral at which the Bishop preached the sermon. The Dean then entertained a large number of clergy, gentry, and their ladies to lunch. He threw open his gardens to the public who were there entertained by the band of the Rifle Depot Battalion. After lunch a great procession made its way to West Hill in the following order:

Volunteer Rifle Corps and Band; choristers; training pupils; schoolmasters, Principal, Vice Principal and staff; Mayor and Corporation; clergy (in gowns); Board of Education and training school committee; Warden and Fellows of Winchester College; members of the County and City; Archdeacons, Dean and Chapter; High Sheriff; the Bishop; Viscount Eversley; carriages.

The route taken was along St. Swithun's Street, up St. James's Lane and so to West Hill. The houses along the route were decorated with banners, streamers and flags of all kinds. Even evergreens were strewn across the road 'with effective taste'. At West Hill Viscount Eversley in his speech referred to the time not so long ago when teachers were selected for the profession because of their infirmity or deformity. More recently he had marked how education had benefited by the qualified teachers that the training college had been producing. At the conclusion of his speech and the Bishop's prayers the stone was lowered into position. It was reported that 'in a cell formed in the understone was placed a glass bottle containing a copy of the trust-deed and the dedication . . .'. Lord Eversley, having struck the stone with the gavel, declared the foundation stone of the building laid. The Bishop pronounced the Benediction. The national anthem was sung and the bells of the cathedral rang out.[40]

The new college was to accommodate 56 students with residence for the Principal, Vice Principal and the matron. There were two classrooms, a lecture hall, and a dining hall. On the ground floor there was to be a waiting room, a students' sitting-room, a master's private room, kitchen, stores, and offices.

On the first floor there were to be dormitories, two sick rooms, and the staff quarters. Gas and water were laid on. Each student 'will have a separate stall in the dormitories, and each stall will have a window, water, basin and tap'. Whereas the Principal was provided with a hall, three sitting rooms, six bedrooms and two dressing rooms, kitchen and offices, the Vice Principal and matron were each to have a sitting room and a bedroom.

As the building neared completion arrangements were made for the bishop to open the college at a ceremony to be performed on 13 October 1862. A service in the cathedral was the first event, at which the Bishop of Oxford, Samuel Wilberforce, preached. The ceremony at West Hill followed when the Bishop of Winchester formally opened the buildings of the training college in the presence of many distinguished clergy and gentry, including Lord Palmerston, the prime minister.

The year 1862, however, was not one of much rejoicing in educational circles. The Newcastle Commission had made its report in 1861 and Robert Lowe, the Vice President of the Committee of Council on Education, decided to act on its recommendations in the following year. Severe measures were taken to reduce government spending on education. Grants to schools were to be paid in proportion to the attendance of individual pupils, and the success of these pupils in an examination of the elementary subjects. Payments to apprentice teachers, teachers, and lecturers were to be curtailed; the Revised Code withdrew from the training college lecturers the annual grants of £100. The 'Hallelujah Chorus' may have been sung in the cathedral on the morning of 13 October by full choir, but on the morning of 14 October the Principal, staff and students of the Winchester Training College knew they were facing a winter that would blow bleakly on educational endeavour.

CHAPTER FOUR

WEST HILL (1862-80)

The Revised Code and the 1870 Education Act

IN 1856 THE GOVERNMENT had established the Education Department to act as the administrative instrument of the Committee of Council. The Department was committed to 'the extension of sound and cheap elementary instruction to all classes of people'.[1] A number of Educational Bills between 1847 and 1857, seeking to extend school opportunities to those most deprived, were fiercely opposed, whether by Dissenters or Anglicans, and defeated on denominational issues. In 1858 a Royal Commission was set up under the chairmanship of Henry Pelham, Duke of Newcastle, 'to inquire into the present state of popular education in England, and to consider and report what measures, if any, are required for the extension of sound and cheap elementary instruction to all classes of people'.[2]

While the college on West Hill was being built, members of the Commission were carrying out their inquiries into the education of poor, vagrant, and criminal children. They investigated the school supported by the army and the navy, and the widest spectrum of other schools throughout the country. Matthew Arnold was detailed to report on schools in France, French Switzerland and Holland, and Mark Pattison on schools in Germany. The Commissioners' report, which was published in 1861, endorsed the work of the Committee of Council, made no attack on the denominational bodies responsible for most of the country's schools, nor urged central control of school management. Their main proposals related to a change in the method of paying grants to schools. They advocated new payments from local rates. In the event the only recommendation which was implemented by government was that of payment by results.

Robert Lowe, Vice-President of the Council, in his Revised Code of 1862, set up a system of dispensing central government grants to the elementary schools, according to the inspectors' reports on the children's attendance and level of performance. For instance, each child over the age of six was to earn the school a grant of 4s. on the basis of attendance, and 8s. subject to examination: of this 2s. 8d. was forfeited for failure to satisfy the inspector in reading, 2s. 8d. in writing, and 2s. 8d. in arithmetic.[3] Children were to be presented to the inspector in six standards. Those under six were not examined, but they earned 6s. 6d. each for the school, subject to the inspector finding their general education satisfactory.

The effect of the new code reduced public expenditure in the mid-1860s from £800,000 to £600,000. It ended grants augmenting teachers' salaries and training college salaries, it ended grants to pupil teachers and specific grants for school maintenance. Payment of grants was made direct to school managers and not to teachers. The managers were thus in a position to negotiate teachers' salaries on an individual basis. Such deleterious effects on the schools were felt directly by the training colleges. Numbers of pupil teachers fell, the benefits of Queen's Scholars were removed, staff salaries were severely reduced, and the curriculum which had been broadening was in danger, as in the schools, of being driven back to the acquisition of mechanistic tricks to drill the teachers to drill the pupils to produce the right answers in reading, writing and arithmetic to earn thrice 2s. 8d.

The Revised Code which was formulated in 1862 was not put into operation until August 1863, such was the fierceness of the opposition and the pressure for amendments. The Principals of the training colleges were forthright in their condemnation. Bromby of Cheltenham College claimed that 'by destroying the pecuniary value of a teacher's certificate without attending a normal college, the Code had lowered standards and dealt the training colleges a deadly blow'. Secondly he declared that 'a system which made grants dependent on success in reading, writing and arithmetic would undermine the position hitherto occupied by religious instruction, lead to the exclusion of other subjects the skilled mechanic has learned to value, and produce an inferior race of schoolmasters'.[4]

The correspondence between the Winchester Training College and the Secretary of the National Society, Canon Lonsdale, reflects sharp anxieties about the implementation of the Code. Writing on behalf of the college are the treasurer, Rev. G. H. Sumner, and Principal Collier. The Code laid down that no payment should be made for its students until they had completed two years' training and had remained in post in the same elementary school for a further two years. Sumner, writing from his father's residence at Farnham Castle on 17 January 1863, refused to sign a memorial contingent upon the operation of the Code, and wrote to Lonsdale as follows:

> My dear sir,
>
> I regret that I cannot sign the proposed memorial in reference to the draft Minute on Training Colleges. Paragraph two on the second page seems to me worded in such a manner that Government might fairly reply that the object of the Training Schools was not the welfare of the schools to which they sent their masters, but solely the obtaining of the Government money wholly irrespective of the fitness of the trained student for the post in which he has been placed.
>
> This paragraph seems to me so objectionable that I must beg to decline signing the memorial.
>
> Believe me, Yours faithfully,
> George Henry Sumner
> Treasurer Winchester Training School.[5]

Sumner was not alone in objecting to the draft Minute from the Committee of Council on Education. On 23 December 1862 the Principals of the Church of England training colleges met in London at the rooms of the National Society. This may have been the very first of such meetings, and the occasion was clearly to draw up a concerted plan in opposition to the draft Minute. Principal Collier was present.[6] A memorial addressed to the Committee of Council was drawn up and directed to the Council through 'her Majesty's Inspectors of Training Colleges'. The gist of this memorial, signed by Collier and included in Appendix VII, compares the generous propositions of the Newcastle Commission with the niggardly consequences of the Revised Code. It underlines the main point made by Sumner that the Code holds out inducements to students to leave the college after one year's training whilst under the draft Minute no payment will be made to the college for any student not remaining two years. There is an inducement for the colleges to keep in residence over two years students whom otherwise they would have encouraged to leave earlier. Furthermore 'each second-year student will see that he . . . is worth £100 . . . to the College, and also, that, unless the College is to suffer loss, all the students, whatever may be their character or conduct, must be retained for the two full years, and be appointed to schools under inspection; so that in fact the authorities will, to some extent, be in the power of the students'.[7]

It could happen that an unsatisfactory student might be placed in a school, where he might well prove to be an unsatisfactory teacher. But the Code's condition that no payment should accrue to the college until the student had completed two years' teaching at the same school until certificated placed 'the managers of the Training College in a false position with respect to the managers of elementary schools'.[8]

The government, however, were firm in making payments to colleges 'for those only of its students who are fairly launched in their professions as teachers' The college was so concerned about this possible loss of revenue that it made a requirement of all students entering in January 1863 to sign the following declaration:

> We do hereby sincerely declare that it is our intention and our desire, if admitted into the Winchester Diocesan Training School, to continue our period of training in that Institution to the end of the second year; and thereafter mindful of the advantages conferred upon us in our Training to follow the profession of a Schoolmaster at least until we have obtained our Certificate.

This declaration appears on the very last page of the first students' register. The words 'at least until we have obtained our Certificate' are written at a later date and in another hand, reflecting that payment was made by the government to the college only for those students who had completed their certificate by two years' service in the same school following their two-year college course. A college whose students failed to become teachers would gradually lose its grant. (See Appendix VIII.) Thus the demand for trained teachers would in time regulate the sum which the State would pay for its training colleges. Moreover, the grant was made in respect of students in residence so that government would not be making large grants to empty colleges.[9]

The college on West Hill had been built for 56 resident students, but Principal Collier's returns to the National Society show 21 students in 1862, 40 in 1863, and 34 in 1864. In every college numbers dropped. At Borough Road, which had accommodation for 100, student numbers in 1866 were only sixty-eight. Some colleges, Highbury and Chichester, for instance, were forced to close.[10]

The Winchester Training College had been particularly fortunate in completing its new buildings before the Revised Code was put into operation. But just as the teachers in the schools soon adjusted their teaching techniques to meet the requirements of payment by results, so the colleges, for their very survival, adapted their management skills, curriculum, and teaching methods to meet the new economies. The Archdeacon of Winchester, Philip Jacob, who for its first 20 years had been secretary of the Winchester Diocesan Board of Education, in his address to the clergy in 1863 even spoke in favour of the Revised Code in so far as it brought a new standard in literary and scientific subjects.[11] In 1864 he revealed that in the case of the Winchester Training College the government, realising the financial difficulties, 'had showed some commendable toleration of the position by releasing the college temporarily from the normal computation systems', and thus reducing the burden on private support for the first few years after the great effort to build the new college. Without this special treatment the college, he claimed, could not have survived.[12] Yet by 1866 the Principal was reporting to his management committee that 'a considerable lump sum' had been deposited in the bank, as the foundation of a special reserve fund.[13] Later in the year the Archdeacon in his annual charge congratulated the college's treasurer on his book-keeping and made it clear that the diocesan educational funds were no longer *in toto* devoted to the college.[14]

The college's new academic year, which began in January 1863, brought with it a new syllabus. The purpose of change was twofold. Firstly, 'the excision of the more ambitious parts of the original scheme', and secondly, 'the insertion of some particulars which will more specially require cultivation of the power of memory, facility in mental calculation, a close attention to English composition and some knowledge of economy, political, social and sanitary'.[15] The Revised Code was thus quick to have its effect on the curriculum.

The inspector throughout this decade most associated with the college was the Rev. B. M. Cowie. In his 1863 report to the Committee of Council he complained of the shortage of pupil-teachers and of 'the lachrymose and peevish tone of many elementary schoolteachers', due, he claimed, to the new financial regulations. He noted a steady demand for teachers, but the pupil-teacher shortage caused him misgivings for the continued existence of some training colleges.[16] In 1866 he complained again about the shortage of pupil-teachers, and at the instigation of the Bishop of Winchester, the secretary of College's Governing Body, the Rev. T. Bacon, circulated to all the church schools in the county an inquiry into the standards of trained teachers, compared with those of untrained teachers. The results, which clearly vindicated the expense and time spent on training, were appended to Mr. Cowie's report to Council.[17] Thus the Revised Code's loophole for the untrained teacher to secure certification came under close scrutiny.

Mr. Cowie had noticed that pupil-teachers were turning aside from teaching to more lucrative professions, but others attained too low a standard to pass their examinations. In his report to Council of 1864–65 he criticised the training colleges' curriculum generally. Religious instruction, he not unreasonably maintained, should be taught to be understood. Physical geography would benefit from the use of maps. Text books were better aids than lecture notes. He recommended good blackboard work, perpetual examinations and clear arrangement! He was clearly a man after Robert Lowe's heart. His report on Winchester commended the repairs made to the building to prevent the recurrence of the damp patches he had seen previously, and he affirmed that the low average cost of each student was principally due to the low salaries of the staff. The students were healthy, well-conducted, and well-cared-for, and the time-table, apart from too much drawing, was suitable. Many students augmented local choirs on Sundays, and some performed as organists. Several were Sunday school teachers. College worship was at the cathedral on Sundays and at Christchurch on Friday mornings. He recorded the staff as comprising the Principal, the Vice-Principal (Mr. B. T. P. Tennear), Mr. Broomielaw, the method master, Mr. Colson, the drawing master, Dr. Wesley and Mr. Carter for music, and Mr. E. S. Sheppard, geography.[18] Mr. Cowie thought that the students were left for too long periods at the practising school at St. Michael's without sufficient supervision by trained staff. He did, however, commend the employment of the students on the West Hill site in levelling the college grounds, making terraces and undertaking the gardening.

In his charge of 1869 Archdeacon Jacob, referring to parliamentary activity in the field of education, said 'each new bill was pregnant with consequences'. The Clarendon Report of 1864 had reviewed the funding and the course of studies of the leading nine public schools. The Taunton Report of 1868 had reviewed the funding and the course of studies of the endowed schools, those not included in the scope of the Newcastle or Clarendon Reports. In 1867 the Second Parliamentary Reform Act enfranchised a large proportion of working men in the towns. Hitherto government funding had gone to those richer areas where voluntary funds had already been raised in the cause of education. The inner city areas and remoter country districts were left untouched by the country's general educational advance. The Dissenters had bitterly resented the compulsion put upon their children, that if they attended a Church school they were also required to attend the Established Church on Sundays. The Church had stoutly maintained its right to give religious instruction according to the formularies of the Established Church. It had contested State organised secular education, whether at school or teacher-training level. Now with

1. (*left*) No. 27, St. Swithun's Street. The original site of the Winchester Diocesan Training School, 1840-1847.

2. (*below*) Wolvesey Palace, where the Winchester Diocesan Training School was housed from 1847-1862.

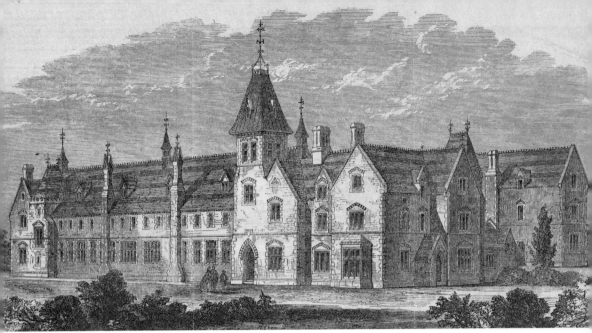

3. The Diocesan Training College, West Hill, opened on Monday 13th October 1862 by the Bishop of Winch[

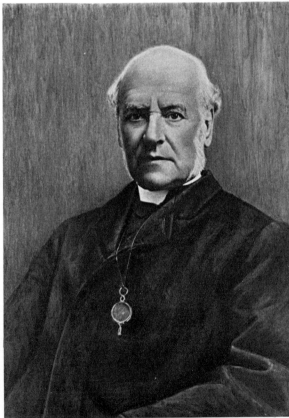

4. The Founder, Charles Richard Sumner, Bishop of Winchester, 1827-69.

5. The Rev. Canon Charles Collier, Principal, 1859-78.

6.   The College buildings, 1870.

7.   The College Chapel interior, 1900.

8. Henry Martin, Honorary Canon of Winchester Cathedral, Principal 1878-1912, seen here in 1900 as Major of the 1st Hampshire Volunteer Corps.

9. H. W. Padwick, student 1874, Tutor 18 1917, Secretary of the Winton Club.

10. The first committe Winchester Reunion Cl l. to r.: Coombes, Stree Smith, Tuck, Flux, Bru

11. Samuel Wilberforce, Bishop of Winchester, 1869-73.

Edward Harold Browne, Bishop of Winchester, 91.

13. C. E. Creese, student 1899-1900, Secretary, London Winton Club.

14. William Smoker, 1902-1904. Each student in the first term of his course was expected to join 'B' Company of the 1st Hampshire Rifle Volunteer Corps.

15. Bernard Goddard, student 1897-1900, Tutor 1900-1934, Secretary of the Winton Club.

16. Ernest Wainwright, Honorary Canon of Winchester Cathedral, Principal 1912-1933.

G. H. Barker, M. C., student 1900-1902, tor (P.T.I.) 1913-1927.

18. Herbert Jarman, Tutor 1911-1951, Vice Principal 1936-1951.

19. Winchester Training College, February 1920.

"Winchester Training College"
February 1920.

20.   College Principal and Tutors, 1922. Front row, *l. to r.*: Pells, Lockton, Wainwright, Davis, Burfitt; Back row, *l. to r.*: Jarman, Barker, Goddard, Mackie.

21.   Principal Wainwright, Vice Principal Lockton and chapel choir, 1930.

22.   Student Group, 1919-1921.

23.   St. Luke's Night, 1928.

24. Muffs and Duffs, 1929: an annual sporting event for those less enthusiastic about team games.

25. The Rev. R. C. White, Principal 1933-1945.

(*right*) William Parker Dickinson, Principal
6-1958.

. (*below*) West Hayes, purchased in 1946.

28. The Principal, John Stripe, with Vice Principals, Hugh Humphrey and Robina Macintyre, 1961.

29. Sherard Falkner Allison, Bishop of Winchester 1962-1975.

30. Holm Lodge, purchased in 1926, used as the Principal's residence since 1928.

31. Beech Glade, the Vice Principal's residence built in 1968.

32. (*above*) Degree Ceremony, 4 Novemb[er] 1978. The first conferment of C.N.N.A. degrees to K.A.C. students. The Bishop of Winchester is conferring the first B.Ed. degree on Jane Yelland. (*Photo*: Tony Lee[

33. (*left*) The Bishop of Winchester and Lord Briggs at the opening of the new Library, 1978.

34. Martial Rose, Principal, 1967-

35. Photograph of the College, 1980.

36. (*right*) Winchester
Diocesan Training College
football team, 1899-1900.

37. (*centre*) Cricket at
Bar End playing fields,
purchased by the College
in 1935.

38. (*bottom*) Chilbolton
Court, Day Students'
residence, 1980.

government having completed its comprehensive review of education—even Oxbridge was investigated in the 1850s—there was an overwhelming drive towards universal elementary education in which the State, delicately poised between Churchmen and Dissenters, was to advocate a secular system of schooling in which religious education was to be taught on a non-denominational basis.

The 'pregnancy' referred to by Archbishop Jacob resulted in the birth of the 1870 Elementary Education Act. Under this Act every district in England and Wales was empowered to set up school boards, directly elected, and to raise a rate to meet the educational needs of their district. The right of withdrawal from religious instruction on grounds of conscience in all public elementary schools, including those run by the churches, was guaranteed. Although voluntary schools were to receive a 50 per cent. maintenance grant from the Education Department, the building grants came to an end.[19] The school boards operated in those areas where there was a gap in the provision offered by the voluntary schools. The voluntary sector was given a six-months' period of grace before the needs of each school district was surveyed. On the part of the Church of England this led to a feverish building period. In Winchester, however, there was no such need. The city was by now well stocked with Church schools and, with some relief, the operation of a school board was considered superfluous.

The establishment of the State system of elementary school education inevitably led on to speculation about State secondary education and a State system of teacher education. Each year the Church College Principals were requested to inform the Secretary of the National Society of the employment of their leaving students. Collier's letter of 11 April 1877 reflects his anxiety about the State's encroachment into teacher training:

> In reply to your queries I beg to say that all my students who left at Xmas are provided with situations—and that I have no candidate of any kind for a mastership.
>
> I had, up to Xmas 1876, more applications for masters than I could meet—but not near so many applications as I had in the corresponding period of 1875.
>
> I think it of the greatest importance that Church of England Training Colleges should be ready to meet *every* and *any*, demand for schoolmasters, if only to render the foundation of secular Training Colleges unnecessary.
>
> Sincerely yours,
> C. Collier.[20]

In Collier's view, if the Church training colleges were to meet the growing demands of both Church and Board schools, they should not only be fully recruited but on a path of expansion. Collier became Principal when, because of illness, college numbers fell below twenty. Even when the new college was built on West Hill with accommodation for 56 students, numbers remained in the 20s and 40s, and it was not until 1873 that all 56 places were furnished in anticipation at last of a full college. And full it stayed until Collier retired in 1879. The new Church schools, it was said, were created to prevent the election of school boards in hundreds of districts.[21] In the long run the Church neither had the funds nor the political power to prevent the spread of secular schooling. The voluntary religious colleges, however, continued to supply teachers to both Church and Board schools without any competition from State-founded colleges until the 1890s.

The Church colleges were being criticised for the weakness of their work in secular subjects. They were sharply aware that despite the primary attention to be paid within their curriculum to religious instruction, they had to broaden their curriculum or face being overtaken by the foundation of State training colleges. The difficulties they encountered were considerable. At Winchester, for instance, the Revised Code in 1863 brought about a restriction rather than a broadening of the curriculum. Furthermore, the adverse conditions for pupil-teachers lowered both quantity and quality of entry. However, later in the 1860s, there was some welcome relaxation in administering the Code which had beneficial effects on teacher training. Within the schools specific subjects might be examined as well as the three Rs, and the proficiency of classes was assessed rather than each individual child being examined. This was a mercy for the inspector as well as for the staff and children. At Winchester part of each Saturday morning was taken up with the examination of the students, and the twice-yearly public examination of the students had become a city spectacle. In 1876 the inspector, the Rev. T. W. Sharpe, inveighed against the over-examination of the students, and urged that staff, including the Principal, should be relieved of their intolerable burden of marking, so that they might have more leisure time.

The relentless time-table of the 1850s was extended into the 1860s and 1870s, with the Principal maintaining responsibility for the teaching of Holy Scripture (6 hours per week), the Book of Common Prayer (1½ hours), English grammar and Latin (4 hours), economy (1 hour), reading and repetition (2 hours), a total of 14½ hours per week; the Vice-Principal was the mainstay of the mathematics teaching with 16 or 17 hours' teaching per week.[22] In the 1870s, with a larger staff, French was taught. Music and drawing grew in popularity and claimed a larger share of the time-table. The inspectors strongly commended the daily gardening, the attention to health and recreation, and, in 1876, suggested that the students should be given more time for private study. 'Sanitary Economy' is the title of a lecture given to the students in 1863 by Mr. J. B. Yeo, house surgeon of the County Hospital. The Wolvesey era of sickness and death was not far behind. In 1871 the inspector was at pains to praise the college's physical facilities and physical activities of the students. The field below the college (the dytche) had been acquired on a yearly rental, and there the students did their drill. Perhaps the most significant broadening of the curriculum during this period was in the field of science.

The industrial growth of the nation was epitomised in the Great Exhibition of 1851. Prince Albert's royal patronage of industrial development, which was itself dependent on scientific and technological advance, affected more directly the curriculum in the training colleges than the public schools and the older universities. The publication in 1859 of Darwin's *Origin of Species* set the Churchmen new problems for their constituents in pew, school, and training college. In the Winchester Diocesan College the problems both of preparing teachers for the greatest industrial nation of the world and of helping them through their Christian training to face the growing scepticism of accepted doctrine of the creation of the world and the origin of man were, in the context of the times, squarely dealt with. The Winchester students, apart from their 'scientific' gardening, were set to study heat, light, and acoustics, and were examined in these subjects. Many special lectures were arranged on current scientific issues, especially when scientific discovery seemed to challenge traditional belief. In 1864 Canon Carus lectured on 'Science, its Failures and Successes'. The lecture was delivered in college, but open to the public and attempted to show 'the plausibility of the new sciences of geology when seen in the light of the Scriptures, just as in the past had happened to astronomy'.[23] Later in the same year Archdeacon Utterton spoke on 'The Sceptical Tendences of the Age', urging the students to hold fast to their faith and Christian principles against the attacks of the infidel. A few weeks later the college treasurer, the Rev. G. H. Sumner, lectured in the city on 'The Bible and its Relation to Science'.[24] In February 1870 Bishop Sumner, recently retired, paid for all the students to be present at two lectures, one on the 'Moon', the other on the 'Sun', which were part of a course given publicly by the vicar of Romsey, the Rev. E. L. Berthon.[25]

The Department of Science and Art in South Kensington sent speakers to the training colleges to acquaint the students with the work undertaken by the Department and with the possible benefits which might accrue to the students. Since 1859 it has been possible for teachers to qualify in art or scientific subjects by sitting either an examination in subject knowledge only, or one for the award of a certificate of competency to teach the subject. Candidates were given their rail fares and an allowance of 10s. a day for subsistence. On 26 May 1866 Mr. J. C. Buckmaster addressed the Winchester students on behalf of the Department of Science and Art, stressing that teachers who qualified by passing the Department's examinations would be able to teach science or art to classes of students at evening schools, and so earn between £40 and £70 in addition to their normal salaries.[26] The government's concern to promote both art and science education in the schools and colleges was prompted by the needs of an intensely industrialised economy. The Winchester students who followed these extra courses were finding that teachers' salaries which in 1860 had averaged £50 a year with a house by 1874 had risen to £100 a year with an additional £70 or £80 a year to be earned by taking evening classes. The status of the teacher was changing.

Founding the Winton Club

In 1870 the formation of the National Union of Elementary Teachers, later to be called the N.U.T., was brought about with the intention of promoting the status of teachers and of protesting, with a united professional voice, against the Revised Code. In Winchester there had been earlier moves towards forming a professional association. In 1853 Mr. Mason, the former student of the college who had become the head of St. Michael's School, held a meeting at his house at which the Winchester Church Schoolmasters' Association was established. Rules were drawn up and officials appointed. Mr. Blain, the Vice-Principal, was elected president, and Mr. Mason was elected secretary. The Association had a social as well as political function. It was to hold meetings fortnightly to hear speakers on a variety of educational topics followed by discussion. Members formed a library to which generous contributions were made by Dr. Moberly, J. D. Walford, and W. Gunner.[27] There would appear to have been some uneasiness felt by the Winchester Diocesan Board of Education at the formation of this professional Association and in April 1854 the Hampshire Church School Society was formed which had a wider brief and a wider membership than the Association 'to promote unity and sympathy among the friends, promoters and teachers of the Church Schools in the Archdeaconry of Winchester'.[28]

No doubt the majority of the teachers who were members of the Winchester Church Schoolmasters' Association or the Hampshire Church School Society comprised former students of the Winchester Training College; but it was not until 1874 that the former students of the college set up their own Re-union Club. On Friday, 28 August 1874, the club's first meeting was held in the college. Its purpose was 'to meet together occasionally, and thus, by mutual intercourse, preserve old friendships and show a more real appreciation of their place of education'. The pattern of the re-union took the form of divine service, followed by a business meeting, and then dinner, which in 1874 was 'a cold collation' at the *Old Market* inn. Some excellent addresses were given and many toasts proposed, including 'the Board of the College', 'the former Principal', 'the present Principal', 'the Masters of the College', 'Success to the Winchester Training College', and 'Success to the new Club'. The evening ended with glees being sung by club members and students present.[29]

Thus was established the society of former students which in later years was named the Winton Club. Branches were established in many different parts of the country wherever Wintonians were gathered together in sufficient numbers. As most clubs, it offered fellowship and support to its members. In addition there were shared memories of a hard, vigorous, and dedicated training.

Personalities

An especially large gathering of former students attended the 1878 annual reunion of the Winton Club. The Press had been politely excluded from the event because of its private and domestic nature. Principal Collier attended with his wife, son and daughter, and, because he was resigning his post as Principal of the college, was presented with a 'handsome centre piece of solid silver, with accompaniments of the same metal, in a case, accompanied by an address, beautifully illuminated'.[30] Collier had taken up his post in March 1858 at the age of forty. He took up residence at Wolvesey at that most difficult time of sickness and death. He helped plan the new college and most certainly was the prime contributor to its academic attainment and professional standing at a time when the Revised Code not only threatened other institutions but brought about their demise. In 1878 he accepted the living of the parish of Andover, and eight years later moved to the rectory at Chilbolton. He was made a Canon of Winchester Cathedral, and died in 1890.

He was remembered for his physical and mental vigour, for the range of his intellectual interests which encompassed history, archaeology and science, for his services within the various chaplaincies he held, at St. John's hospital, the Winchester Corps of the 1st Hants. Administrative Battalion of Rifle Volunteers, and the new Royal County hospital. He frequently attended the Volunteer camp, and was especially remembered for preaching from a pulpit of drums. In Winchester he had promoted the work of the Mechanics Institute, the Penny Readings Society, and the Winchester and Hampshire Scientific and Literary Society.[31] When, in April 1864, Garibaldi visited England, the Principal was invited to accompany the mayor, as chaplain and friend, to greet the great general. Collier received one of the four autographs given to the mayor by Garibaldi. The Winton Club held him in great affection and would willingly have subscribed to the sentiments expressed in his obituary:

> . . . he was a man of very considerable mental power, acquired knowledge, force of character, a personal influence and a way of imparting his own gifts to those who looked up to him, which exercised the happiest influence over them at the very crisis of their lives. Thus, hundreds of young schoolmasters, though under his immediate direction only a couple of years, never failed to turn to him for sympathy and advice in after life.[32]

During this period some of the distinguished founder-governors of the college died. John Keble, for more than thirty years vicar of Hursley, and for most of that time an examiner at the college, died in 1866. George Moberly resigned his headship at Winchester College in 1866 and was appointed to the living of Brighstone, Wilberforce's living in the 1830s. However, he maintained his examining role at the college until 1869 when he was appointed Bishop of Salisbury, where he was able to support and supervise the work of the Diocesan Training College for Women, which he was instrumental in founding.

The founding bishop, Charles Richard Sumner, retired, after serving for 41 years as Bishop of Winchester, in 1869. When he died in 1874 he must have had the satisfaction of having seen the college he had founded, funded, and fought for, firmly established and highly esteemed. It was to Charles Richard Sumner that the five-acre site (see Appendix X) on West Hill was legally conveyed in 1860 by the Dean of Winchester, Thomas Garnier, himself a founder-governor of the college. Garnier died in 1873, in office at the age of ninety-seven.

Samuel Wilberforce, too, died in 1873. In 1839 and 1840 he had acted as the bishop's chief agent in founding the college. He had assiduously built schools at Brighstone and Alverstoke and supported a number of students from his parishes or, later, archdeaconry, during their time at college. As Bishop of Oxford (1845–1869) he had been the prime mover in founding Culham, and on his translation to Winchester he was a frequent visitor to the college, constantly exhorting the students in their vocation. When riding near Winchester he was thrown from his horse and killed. In him the college lost a redoubtable champion.

Two students in this period were appointed to the staff of the training college. Thomas Archard entered college in January 1869, at the age of nineteen. He had been a pupil-teacher at St. Thomas's National School, Winchester. His father, who lived at St. Cross, was gateman on the railway. He came as a First Class Queen's Scholar and was a prize-winner at college. On leaving he became schoolmaster at Overton, Hampshire, at £50 a year with half the additional government grant and a house. Subsequently in 1876, as third master at the college, he taught arithmetic, drawing, and reading. At that time Arthur Butt, a fellow former student, was also on the staff of the college. Butt registered in January 1871, and on leaving taught in a National school in Great Yarmouth before joining the Principal, the Vice-Principal, who was then George Cowfield, B.A., and Thomas Archard. Butt taught music and English.

The Students' Register for this period shows a number of students, for instance, Thomas Luffman (1863), Henry Woodman (1864), Thomas McLean (1865), training for the priesthood after leaving college. Social betterment and status seeking might have been motives, but that a number of former students became missionaries in deeply troubled parts of the world shows more positive qualities at work. Such qualities were certainly fostered by the devotional life of the college and the dedication of the staff.

The Building of the College Chapel

The new Principal, the Rev. Henry Martin, formerly Vice-Principal of Cheltenham College, took up his post in August 1878. It was at this stage that Canon G. H. Sumner resigned both his posts as treasurer and secretary to the college, in the belief that it was proper and timely for the new Principal to be supported by new officers. John Utterton, now Bishop of Guildford, referred to Sumner as 'the motive power of the Committee for these seventeen years'.[33] It was Bishop Utterton, too, who distributed prizes at the examinations in December 1879. Three days later, while administering Holy Communion in Ryde church, he died.[34]

The bishop in his address to the students 'not only expressed his earnest desire that there should be a chapel for divine service on the premises, but promised to use every exertion among his friends to interest them in the erection of such a building'.[35] Following his death, therefore, his friends thought that a fitting memorial to him should be the building of a chapel for the Winchester Diocesan Training College. With this aim in view advertisements appeared in the 10 April and 17 April 1880 issues of the *Hampshire Chronicle* announcing the project and asking for subscriptions. The point was made that although plans for the West Hill college had included provision for a chapel, shortage of funds had precluded its building.

> It is, therefore, proposed to erect, on the site originally marked out for the purpose, a small chapel, in which an inscription might record the fact that it was 'erected in grateful and loving memory of John S. Utterton, D.D., Bishop of Guildford, who, during the service of Holy Communion in Ryde Church, suddenly fell asleep in Jesus, 1879'.[36]

By May £592 had been raised. Later that month design plans were published, beginning, 'The new chapel will be built to harmonise in design with the school, of which it will be a continuation and to which it will be attached at the western end, and by it, accommodation will be provided for a congregation of a hundred persons'. The architects were Messrs. Colson and Son of Jewry Street. The builder was Mr. H. Macklin. On 2 February 1881 the consecration ceremony was conducted by the Rt. Rev. H. E. Browne, Bishop of Winchester. The chapel had been erected entirely by private subscription, costing something in excess of £1,000. The building, in late Decorated style, was able to accommodate one hundred and fifty. The walls were substantial, the sanctuary roof was close-timbered and panelled, with moulded ribs. The choir stalls were of oak, as were the pulpit, credence table and altar. Two windows had stained glass; the other six were glazed with cathedral tinted glass. Under the south window in the sanctuary was placed the brass plate dedicating the chapel to the memory of Bishop Utterton.[37]

The chapel was largely furnished by gifts. The S.P.C.K. presented the service books, a double set for the communion service, and a bible. The brass lectern was given by the students of the years 1880 and 1881; the oak desk, pulpit and two small stained glass windows by old students; a handsome set of markers worked and given by the Misses Carey; the brass pulpit desk by the Vice-Principal, the Rev. J. Haworth, and friends; a beautiful altar-cloth, the work and gift of Mrs. Martin, the Principal's wife; a set of mats and kneelers and the oak choir stalls by the Principal and friends.

The Bishop of Winchester, assisted by the Principal, conducted the service, and took as the text for his sermon St. Matthew 5 v. 14: 'A city that is set on an hill cannot be hid'.

CHAPTER V

CONSOLIDATION (1880–1914)

The Volunteer Company

IN 1859, IN RESPONSE to a circular letter from the War Office to the Lords Lieutenant of the various counties of England, the Volunteer Force was raised on a local basis. The force at Winchester was called the '1st Hants Rifle Corps'. Principal Collier had taken a great interest in this development and had, from its inception, been appointed Honorary Chaplain to the Corps, an appointment which he held until 1889. During the years 1860–1874 a few of the training college students joined the Volunteers and formed a sub-division of the Corps. When, however, the Principal's son, C. D. Collier, was gazetted Sub-Lieutenant in 1875, there was sufficient enthusiasm to form a College Company, which in December 1875 was authorised by the War Office. The Company was officially called 'The Winchester Diocesan Training College Corps' or the '24th Hants Rifle Corps'.

The Rev. R. A. Thomas, Vice-Principal of the college (1905–1910), in his history of the Volunteer Company,[1] describes the uniform of the Company as at first light grey with green facings and black braiding. The men were armed with muzzle-loading Enfield rifles, which were replaced in 1871 by Sniders, the first breech-loading rifle of the British Army.

In December 1875 Captain J. C. Moore, a retired officer from the Rifle Brigade and then living in Winchester near the training college, was gazetted first Captain of the Company, and took command. Drill was carried out in the college field (the dytche); musket practice took place on Teg Down; and annual camp was usually held on Hayling Island or Barossa Hill, near Camberley. In 1877 the uniform was changed from grey to national scarlet, with black facings which two years later were changed to white, the same as the regular battalions of the Hampshire Regiment.

When Principal Collier retired from college, his son resigned his commission. Soon after his appointment, the new Principal, the Rev. Henry Martin, was gazetted Second Lieutenant and posted to the Company which from 1880 became known as 'I' Company of 1st Hampshire Rifle Volunteer Corps. The battalion was then about 650 strong, comprising 10 companies. The College

Company mustered the entire student body of 56, together with a number of staff and former students. In 1881, for instance, when the Principal had been promoted to Lieutenant, and the Vice-Principal, Rev. J. Haworth, gazetted as Second Lieutenant, the Company at camp in Windsor Park comprised one officer, three sergeants, and 56 rank and file.

The summer camps, lasting usually about a week, were enjoyed with the rest of the battalion. They included exercises, manoeuvres, parades, an annual inspection, musketry drills and competitons, and regular sporting events.

From 1886 until 1899 the chief inspector for training colleges was H. E. Oakley. On each visit to Winchester he not only examined the students on their academic attainment and professional training, but also on their military turn-out, drill, and exercises. In 1886 he writes: 'The students form a very good company in the local volunteer corps. They presented a very smart appearance and went through the manual and platoon exercise extremely well'.[2] His predilection for this part of his duty is explained:

> I had great pleasure in inspecting the drill; the young men of much the same age and in the prime of youth presented a very smart appearance, and reminded me of the 1st Company of the Cambridge University Volunteers of which I had the honour to be captain in the early years of volunteering.[3]

In later years he notes that the local volunteer corps was stated by several papers to be the best regiment at the July Review, and that the training college Company were very fine marksmen.[4] In 1892 the adjutant told Oakley that the Company was the best within the volunteer corps and, in 1893, they possessed the best marksmen.

George Sampson, the author of the *Concise Cambridge History of English Literature,* was a student at the college, 1892–1894, and during his first year he acted as sub-editor, and during his second year, as editor, of the college magazine *The Wintonian.* These are the earliest copies of the magazine available, and in both there are references to the activities of 'I' Company. In 1893 Captain H. Martin (the Principal), and Lieutenant D. J. Thomas (Vice-Principal), Pte. Cole (the new physical training instructor), and 11 others made up the shooting team. On 9 November the gallant 'I' Company protected Winchester from an enemy attack coming from the north and south, Lieutenant Thomas being in command. Although the weather was very cold, the exciting attack, and the drill that followed, kept the men sufficiently warm.

In the 1894 *Wintonian* George Sampson describes a day's shooting at Bisley. He reflects, too, on his first being issued with his uniform. He covered it with his overcoat and 'slunk upstairs by an unfrequented route', and buried it deep in his box. Each night, however, he took it from its hiding place, 'and by dint of wearing it for five minutes each day in private . . . grew accustomed to its martial glare, and finally conceived quite a sneaking fondness for it'.

Notable occasions in which the Company participated were as guard of honour at Micheldever station on 22 June 1883, and at Winchester station on the following day, to receive the Prince of Wales; and also at the Queen's Jubilee in London in 1897, and in the same year two members of the Company were part of the guard of honour when the Queen's train stopped at Winchester.

By 1900 the Company numbered as many as two officers and 106 N.C.O.s and men at the Bisley camp. Forty students were entering the college each September, and all were joining the Company, which was well supported, too, by former students who were teaching locally. Drilling for new recruits was strenuous. From the second week in September, in the midst of a bewilderingly busy time-table, they were drilled twice a day, 2-3 p.m. and 5-6 p.m. Once credited with 30 drills, the pace relaxed. Particular enthusiasm was shown for the cyclists' section, which in 1906 undertook special 'Cyclists' Manoeuvres'.

The staff's enthusiasm for, and support of, the Company was a spur to the students. The Principal was promoted to Major in 1900, and to Hon. Lt.-Col. in 1902. He retired from the Volunteer Force in 1904. In 1908 the Territorial Force was formed and the Volunteer Force came to an end. The College Company continued as 'B' Company of the 4th Territorial Battalion of the Hampshire Regiment. But the students were no longer enrolled, they were enlisted. Few students did not join, but the Territorials expected and demanded a more rigid discipline than the Volunteers. The training was more thorough and the men were subject to military discipline at all times when on parade. There were aspects of the professionalism of the Territorials which did not appeal to all the students.

At the outbreak of war in August 1914, 'B' Company was enjoying its annual camp at Bulford on Salisbury Plain. The Company comprised 104 men, 40 of them second-year students. As members of the Territorial Force they were all immediately mobilised and remained under canvas at Bulford for several weeks. They were joined by Principal Wainwright, who held the rank of Captain, and by Bernard Goddard, one of the tutors, who was a Lieutenant in the Company. Early in September the Company returned to Winchester and were billeted in the college buildings, the War Office paying the college 3d. a night for each man and supplying each with rations. The Company remained in college for most of the winter, and in December were sent overseas to India.

The fate of 'B' Company during the First World War will be taken up later in this history. The total college commitment to the earlier Volunteers and later to the Territorials underlines the prevailing strength of the corporate spirit. Staff and students shared both an academic and military régime that knit them close together. In action in the Far East, Middle East, and on the Western Front, it is reported, that some songs were heard across the battle lines that could only have stemmed from the Winchester Diocesan Training College.

Henry Martin

On 25 June 1912, at a meeting of the Committee of the Winchester Diocesan Training College (the Governing Body), the Principal was asked to withdraw while the chairman read to the members his letter of resignation, submitted on medical advice. The following resolution, proposed by Archdeacon Fearon, reads:

> The Committee of the Training College wish to place on record their recognition of the exceptional service of the retiring Principal during the last 34 years, and tender to him their warmest thanks for the devotion with which he has served the College. The Committee recognise that by his ability and zeal he has not only maintained and added to the reputation which the College has so long held, but has also done much to advance the cause of Education throughout the country.

Henry Martin was born in 1844 and educated at Merchant Taylors' School and St. Edmund Hall, Oxford. He became classics master of St. Elizabeth's College, Guernsey, and curate of All Saints'. His next appointment was as Vice-Principal of Cheltenham Training College, from where he moved in 1878 to take up the principalship in Winchester. He presided over many changes: the building of the chapel and its subsequent extension; the college's increased involvement in the Volunteers and Territorials; the provision of teaching facilities for physical education, music, and science; and the increased residential provision from the 56 students in 1878 to the 80 students at the time of his retirement.

An increase of 24 students in 34 years might seem insignificant. But at a time when the quality of the student reflected directly the quality of the institution that nurtured him, such growth was carefully planned and success-fully achieved. It came at the turn of the century when the first day training colleges and the new municipal training colleges threatened the hitherto supremacy of the Church colleges. Quality was maintained by careful selection of students, by the setting of a varied but intensive academic régime, by a kindly but firm religious education, and above all by Canon Martin's ability not only to extend the range of his staff but also to appoint men who them-selves were to make a mark in the field of education. No less than five of his Vice-Principals became Principals. Towards the end of his principalship there was the Rev. D. J. Thomas, 1889–1896 (Principal of the Home and Colonial Training College), his brother, the Rev. R. A. Thomas, 1905–1910 (Principal of Chester Training College), and, of course, the Rev. E. G. Wainwright, 1903–1905, who succeeded Canon Martin at Winchester. In addition, the Rev. H. Searle, 1879–1903, was appointed Vice-Principal of the Home and Colonial Training College. Searle had taught mainly science and music. One of his successors was H. Morrell, B.Sc., and when Morrell left in 1911 to take up a post at Chester Training College, the Principal appointed Herbert Jarman, B.Sc., who was to give 40 invaluable years' service to the college. There is no doubt that Principal Martin chose his staff well. By Jarman's appointment, in his last full year of office, one can see that his judgement was not failing.

In November 1898 the Principal was installed as an Honorary Canon of Winchester Cathedral. The event is solemnly recorded in *The Wintonian*, December 1898:

At the ordinary four o'clock service the Bishop of Guildford (the Rt. Rev. G. H. Sumner) read the first lesson, and then proceeded to the Chapter Room: from thence he returned leading the new Canon by the hand to the gate of the Choir, which was locked. Here the Bishop's mandate was read, the gate unlocked, and the Principal was led to his seat by the Dean. The Magnificat (Richardson in F) was sung, and Canon Martin read the Second Lesson. The ordinary service was then continued. All the staff and students were present.

So, like his predecessor, he received this honour, and, like his predecessor, his son served as an officer in the Hampshire Volunteers. In 1905, however, a double sorrow struck the Principal. In January his wife died after a long illness, and in May his eldest son, Lionel, died in West Africa where he had been serving in the Army. The college was deeply affected by these events because of the close association of mother and son with the life of the college. From the diary of W. E. Smoker (1902–1904), writing of the Principal, we read:

His pleasant mien promoted respect and obedience on all occasions. We had sympathy for him too, seeing his ailing wife daily enjoying the warm sun, in a sheltered corner of the terrace.

In the following year, however, Canon Martin remarried. The ceremony was performed at St. Cross and conducted by the Dean.[5] His retirement in 1912 was the occasion of a special Winton Club presentation on 13 May 1913:

. . . all those Wintonians concerned with the presentation to the Rev. Canon Martin, late Principal of the Training College, assembled in the Hall, and the Principal, the Rev. E. G. Wainwright, having briefly stated the object of the gathering, called on Mr. S. Tompson ('96–'98), Secretary of the Portsmouth Winton Club, to address those present. This he did in a most happy manner, and asked Canon Martin's acceptance of the painting which the Rev. E. G. Wainwright then unveiled. Other gifts, consisting of a small replica of the large portrait, a set of pen and ink drawings in an artistic triptych frame, a photographic group of those present at the last College Re-union, and an album containing their autographs, were then handed to Canon Martin who then thanked all concerned . . . and then the Senior Prefect asked Mrs. Martin's acceptance of a gold bracelet watch, engraved with the College arms and motto, as a small memento of her association with Canon Martin at the College. The Proceedings terminated with three cheers for the late Principal and Mrs. Martin.

Among Canon Martin's many interests was mountaineering, and this became his chief recreation. He was a member of the Alpine Club and, in times when climbing aids were less sophisticated, was one of few to have reached the summit of the Matterhorn. In July 1919 he went as usual to Vevey in Switzerland and on Sunday, 27 July, while at service in the village church, collapsed and died. His wife was with him when he died. She decided not to have his body taken back to England, but to have it buried in the country he loved so much. When the news of his death reached Winchester, the bells of the cathedral and the college chapel were rung.

William Smoker, who entered college in 1902 at the age of 21, had taught for nearly five years as a pupil-teacher in an East London dockland area school. He spent half of each day at the school and the other half at the Woolwich Pupil Teacher Centre. His religious education had, however, not received the same attention as those pupil-teachers serving in Church schools, and on entering college he encountered some difficulties. Recollecting some of these difficulties in 1966 he wrote:

> The Prinny was most assiduous to us in his twice a week Divinity lectures. I had not been apprenticed in a Church of England School, and although I never appeared before the Principal for a breach of College rules, I was interviewed by him twice for my failing in Prayer Book history and for my inability to answer such Catechism questions as, 'What did your Godfathers and Godmothers then for you?'
>
> Although I have long since discarded many of my College-time books, I do retain a little volume on 'Companionship' in which Canon Martin has written, 'To William Smoker, In memory of Sunday, March 24th, 1903. Winchester. "Be thou faithful unto death " '.

A service to dedicate a memorial erected by past students of the college to the memory of Canon Martin took place in the college chapel on 4 March 1922. The dedication was performed by the Archdeacon of Winchester, Canon Daldy. The memorial consisted of two oak stalls, harmonising with the oak panelling placed round the walls as a memorial to the students who fell in the Great War. The inscription on one stall (Decani) was 'In grateful memory of long and faithful service, Henry Martin, M.A., Hon. Canon of Winchester, Principal, 1872-1912', and on the other (Cantoris), 'Other men laboured and ye entered into their labours'.

College Life

College life was to a great extent conditioned by the premises in which the students lived. The following account is derived largely from the diaries and recollections of C. E. Creese (1892-1894), E. G. Leggett (1902-1904), and W. Smoker (1902-1904).[6] The east end of the main building looking towards the city was the Principal's residence; the south-west corner next to the chapel was for the Vice-Principal, who had a study on the ground-floor and a bedroom above it. The main entrance on the terrace was not to be used by students, nor were they allowed to use the main driveway to the college from Sparkford Road. Students were required to approach the college from lower down the hill and enter through the west door near the Vice-Principal's study. When on the terrace they might walk on the gravel, but the turf was preserved for the staff. On either side of the main terrace entrance was a stone sphinx which received festal paint at frequent intervals, and as frequently both were removed to surprising parts. An early copy of *The Wintonian* comments, 'a concrete stand and iron band now fix them firmly to the land'. But not firmly enough, for they finally disappeared altogether. Inside this entrance was a room used mainly by Mr. Searle, the music and science lecturer, and opposite his door was the entrance to the dining-hall and adjacent was a green baize door leading into the Principal's house. On a small shelf outside this door was a small hand-bell which had to be rung before passing through the baize door to the Principal's study.

In the opposite direction were the doors leading to the three classrooms. The one nearest the Principal's study was the senior room; the one to the west was the junior room; and the one in the middle was the library, described as 'an absolute misnomer, for the only books there were the students' text-books'. By 1902 the library and reading room had been placed northwards into the quadrangle, and the two lecture rooms had been extended to meet at the mid-point.

At the instigation of the visiting inspectors a student common room had been built to the north of the chapel. This is now the main music room. South of the common room was the armoury, where a seasoned retired soldier kept the rifles cleaned and oiled and also stored the Vice-Principal's sword.

On the first floor adjacent to the Principal's wing and under the tower was the hospital, smelling of cabbage from the kitchen fumes that wafted up from below. The three students' dormitories were called in 1892 the Cocks (1902 Paradise) because of the proximity of the cisterns directly over the kitchens, the Longs facing south over the terrace, and the Blacks, over the armoury and common room. In 1892, Mr. Germain was the tutor whose bedroom was strategically placed on the landing by the steps which led to the tower, but this proved no hindrance to the students getting on to the roof to smoke after bedtime.

Bernard Goddard had been a student at the college (1897–1900) and had been one of the first to stay on for a third year to gain his B.A. He was then appointed as junior tutor. His study was next to the common room and his bedroom above his study. Goddard had large ears and was affectionately known as Loppy. In 1913 Goddard, then senior tutor, asked the Governors if he might marry and move out of residence, but it was felt that such action 'would be detrimental to the discipline of the College to depart from the rule that there shall be three unmarried tutors in residence'.[7] Smoker recalls the evening of 7 July 1904 after the certificate examinations had just been completed, when the Principal told the 1902–1904 group that they were among his most loved students. He gave the students a marvellous feast in the dining-hall. This was followed by prize-giving and speeches, and the Principal announced amid 'uproarious cheers that Mr. Bernard Goddard had been awarded an M.A. degree. We did not retire to bed till midnight'. Another student of these years, E. G. Leggett, in commenting on the staff, puts Goddard first, saying, 'he was to all past students the personification of Winton. His association with the College as student and then resident master for over sixty years coupled with his astounding memory of faces and names meant that he knew all who went back to Re-union'.

Goddard's study was set between the common room and the lavatories and baths, described by Leggett as crude and without any privacy. A music room was set within the quadrangle. Here C. F. Creese found himself for the first time in 1894 confronting Sir John Stainer, H.M.I., who was to examine him in music. Up the hill to the west of the common room was the science laboratory. In 1910 an iron building upon concrete and brick foundation to serve as a gymnasium was erected on the north side of the dytche for £367.

To the west of the dytche was the Principal's kitchen garden and piggery. Leggett described how although this area was out of bounds to the students they were frequently called, in an emergency, to round up the Principal's pigs, this happening once in the middle of a chapel service. Tennis courts were to one side of the dytche, leaving room for football or cricket, although when playing visiting teams games fields were hired at Bar End.

Both Leggett and Smoker stress the importance of the training they received as pupil-teachers before they came to college. The age at which a pupil-teacher might be apprenticed to a school rose from 14 to 15 in 1879 and to 16 in 1900. They both comment somewhat wryly on the post-graduates who undertook a one year's training at one of the new day training colleges as entering their first appointment with minimal professional experience. They describe how they, as potential King's Scholars, applied for a place at Winchester. The examination, although common to all colleges and set under the auspices of the new Board of Education, was taken at the college of the student's choice with an H.M.I. in attendance. Smoker describes his first acquaintance with the college

> In my journey through London to Waterloo Station . . . I bought a watch for 6/6d. the better able to gauge my time in answering papers. The fare from Waterloo to Winchester return was 10/6d. . . . and the time of the journey 75 minutes. The exam lasted from Tuesday till Friday. Two senior prefects directed us, and the College asked a modest 10/- only, for our board and bed. About 50 of us sat. I was one of the successful, being 9th on the list. I remember two details of that week. One was the question: 'Draw the position of a sheet of metal weighing one pound and suspended from one corner, when a 2 lb. weight is attached to an adjacent corner. The other was an evening chat I had with a kindly invigilating H.M.I., when we discussed why so many cities like Winchester grew up in such damp and water-logged hollows.

Smoker took his entrance examination in December 1901 and entered college in September 1902. When Creese entered for his Queen's Scholarship in July 1891, the college year, as it had done since 1840, ran from January to December. The academic year changed to September–July in 1895. Candidates for a Church college place spent an extra day on examinations because they were required to take the Archbishop's entrance examination in religious knowledge. This put the pupil-teachers from the board schools at some disadvantage. Creese tells of how, early in December 1891, he received from the Principal a list of articles he was required to bring to college the following January. This included sheets, pillow-cases, towels, all to be plainly marked; but first on the list was 'one silk hat'. He recalls on arrival seeing each new student carefully carrying his hatbox or actually wearing the silk topper. On the first Sunday they all sallied forth in their top-hats, but scarcely used them again during their course. He noted that at this time the boys at Winchester College were required to wear silk hats. In town the training college students wore school-caps which they had to doff to any member of staff they met. Another feature of the first week was joining the Volunteers, which was a condition of acceptance to the college. On one evening during the private study the Principal accompanied by the sergeant instructor paid a visit to the junior room. All stood and took the oath of allegiance to Her Majesty, Queen Victoria. They were later as members of the college 'I' Company issued with their uniforms—'fitted out' would not be the right expression because they inherited the uniforms of the last group of leaving students. The tunic was scarlet with white cuffs and collar and needed pipeclay as did the white belts. The trousers had a thin red stripe down the seams. Each man was issued with a spiked helmet and a glengarry, a greatcoat and bayonet. These items had all to be kept in the student's cubicle and most of them, apart from the spiked helmet and bayonet, were usually placed under the mattress. Each was given two pouches of ammunition and a rifle which was kept in the armoury, along with the white rifle sling. Each former student reported with pleasure the shooting practice, sometimes on Teg Down butts (now the golf course), and the annual camps.

The weekly routine at the turn of the century was less severe than in the earliest days of the college. On weekdays reveille was sounded by the bell-monitor at 6.15 a.m., making his way through the dormitories, ringing a hand-bell. A cup of cocoa stood ready for students at 6.30 in the dining hall, and roll-call, taken at 6.45, was followed by an hour's lecture. Then came morning service and afterwards breakfast at 8.30 a.m. On Mondays, Tuesdays, Thursdays and Fridays lectures lasted from 9 a.m. until 12.50 p.m., with a break from 10.45–11 00 a.m. Lunch was at 1 p.m., and at 2 p.m. on the above days there followed a 1½-hour art lesson or psychology or hygiene or criticism lesson. This still left time for football, cricket, or tennis on the dytche before tea at 5 p.m. From 7–9 p.m., commencing with roll-call, all students undertook private study in their appropriate lecture room, either junior or senior. A member of staff supervised in one room and a prefect in the other. Evening chapel was at 9.15 p.m., followed by supper at 9.30—then to bed, with lights out at 10.30 p.m.

On Wednesdays and Saturdays the time-table was varied to allow for set matches being played. The selected teams were excused study at noon, while the rest of the students did Swedish drill or company drill with small-arms under the company officer, or rifle-cleaning and 'brassing-up' of accoutrements in the armoury. On these two days the whole afternoon was free until 7 p.m., when debates or smoking concerts would be held in the 'frame-building' on the mound by the science laboratory.

On Sundays, Holy Communion was optional at 7.45 a.m. There was no roll-call until 9 a.m., which was followed by an hour's scripture study in preparation for the Archbishop's certificate. Mattins with sermon was at 11 a.m., and lunch at 1 p.m. The afternoon was free until the 7 p.m. evensong. Seniors were allowed to absent themselves from this service on the understanding that they attended a church service elsewhere in the city.

At all meals grace was sung before and after:

Before: The eyes of all wait upon Thee, O Lord, and
     Thou givest them their meat in due season;
 Thou openest thine hand and fillest all things
     living with plenteousness.   Gloria.

After: I will magnify Thee, O God, my King, and
     praise Thy name for ever and ever.
 Every day will I give thanks unto Thee,
     and praise Thy name for ever and ever.   Gloria.

On the whole, however, the students did not think they were being filled with plenteousness. In the early 1890s, as Creese records, meals were very unsatisfactory. The fare for breakfast and tea was identical: a pat of butter the size of a penny, bread cut into thick hunks, and tea served from an urn. A favoured few who provided their own oatmeal might have porridge, and those who presented their own eggs to the kitchen, with their names written on, might have them boiled. Dinner, says Creese, referring to the midday meal, always started with pudding. 'The rice puddings I shall always remember. They were a hard solid mass—very little milk was used.' On each table a joint was carved by the prefect and served with potatoes and cabbage. The cabbage for 15 students covered the pattern in the well of the dinner plate, and its division called for nice judgement. Pudding on Saturday was a good solid bread pudding. The football team had theirs in the evening. Half a pint of watered-down beer was allowed each student. On Sundays the joint was cold and served with a slice of beetroot. For supper a monitor toured the dormitories with a basket of biscuits. Students were allowed to take two each. Creese, unable to exist on this meagre diet, frequented the *Anchor* in Parchment Street after lunch for cocoa and buns. The Queen's Scholars might well have had a few pennies to spare, because a first-class man was required to pay only £10, and a second-class man only £15, for the two full years of teacher training.

In 1904, as a result of the report of the Inter Departmental Committee on Physical Deterioration, new dietary regulations came into force in the training colleges.[8] An inquiry had been conducted into why so many men wishing to serve in the Boer War had been rejected because of ill-health or physical defect. Acting on this Report the Board of Education suggested that students should have four meals a day: breakfast, dinner, tea, supper. Dinner should be the main meal, but meat, eggs, or fish should be provided at one other meal, preferably breakfast. The purpose of supper was, according to the Board, 'not so much to provide nourishment as to withdraw into the digestive area the blood from the brain excited by study'.[9]

There was consequently a significant improvement in the students' diet. Meat was served at breakfast, usually corned beef, with coffee. Lemonade was served at dinner as an alternative to beer. Rice pudding or treacle tart followed the roast. At tea, Smoker informs us, that he acted as treasurer for his table and bought tins of fish-paste for 2d. or jars of Hartley's jam for 6d. In June he would cycle to Netley and buy a peck of strawberries.

An event which rivetted itself into the minds of all Wintonians was the St. Luke's Day procession. St. Luke's Day falls on 18 October, not long after the admission of the first-year students, but perhaps long enough for their seniors to discover which of them were uppish. The senior prefect told all the juniors, just before 'Lights Out', to push their 'presses' against the doors of their cubicles so that they could peer down into the corridor below. As the dormitory gas-lights were lowered the door at the western end of the Longs opened. A dirge was being being sung by a weird and motley procession lit by the night-lights they were carrying in jam jars. Smoker, who had been told that the Principal would be in the procession, writes: 'We sought in vain for the Prinny among those dressed as bishops, priests, Falstaffs and Calibans. But what most appalled us was to see in the cavalcade women folk—some of those buxom females of the kitchen staff who were never seen outside of the dining room hatch, even in broad daylight'. The procession traversed the Longs several times, singing their dirge. The victims requiring exorcism were drawn one by one from their cubicles, charged, judged, and condemned, their punishment being ascribed a fitting pseudonym by which they would be called for the rest of their student days.

In 1892 the first college magazine, *The Wintonian,* appeared. The four officers, all London men, were- Editor, A. R. Snellgrove; Sub-Editor, A. Hollis; Manager, H. H. Jones; Assistant Manager: C. E. Creese.

Creese describes it as a very modest publication of four pages. Half the front page was taken by a large print of the college coat-of-arms. At the 1892 Re-union William Drewett (1860), who then had a printing business at Kingston-on-Thames, approached Creese and offered to take on the printing of the magazine, and this he did in 1893.

The Cross Report, which was published in 1888, led the way to establishing the first day training colleges, associated with a university or a university college. There had been much criticism of the pupil-teacher system, mainly on the grounds that it was impossible to educate a young person who spent more than half his working day in trying to educate others on too frail a basis. Creese, Smoker and Leggett would not have agreed. Leggett, in fact, paid tribute to his headmaster who tutored him before the school day's work began, The denominational system, however, escaped the Report tolerably unscathed, but greater stress was to be laid on handwriting, more practical arithmetic, more learning of poetry by heart, more varied schoolbooks and more good and economical cottage cookery. There was no support for elaborate apparatus for gymnastics, and a safe and scientific system of physical training was recommended. At Winchester and elsewhere Swedish drill was introduced in the 1890s, and at the same time Swedish methods of teaching woodwork (Slöjd). Special staff appointments were made, and the inspector commented regularly and favourably on these aspects of the college's work. In the late 1890s, at the inspector's instigation, a course of lectures on voice production was introduced. Smoker describes how an eccentric bushy-haired London

Professor of speech called out one Teucer Tibbs to recite some lines of Shakespeare. Tibbs, more Cockney than dockland Smoker, began: "Eat me these irons 'ot'.

Before H.M.I. Oakley arrived at college the students had been set certain tasks of preparation. For instance, in 1886 the second-year students had learned 300 lines from Shakespeare, and the first-year students 300 lines from Milton, Byron, or Wordsworth. They were also prepared to read both poetry and prose from certain prescribed books. Oakley inspected and reported on the masters as well as the students. In 1889, 'Mr. Williams gave a good lesson on Gray's *Elegy*. Mr. Germain lectured on problems of theoretical mechanics, but the men did not appear to have sufficient knowledge of the parallelogram of forces to be able to follow him'.[10] Oakley usually visited with a fellow inspector who examined the students' teaching at the model school. The master of method at this time was Mr. H. W. Padwick, himself a former student (1874-1876). Oakley thought Padwick's headmastership of the practising school and also his role as master of method altogether too onerous and recommended his giving up his headmastership. In 1896 he reported that the new practising school, near the College (St. Thomas's), was planned under the eyes of Canon Warburton and so served its purpose very well. Oakley is here referring to his former H.M.I. colleague who now had retired from the inspectorate, resided in Winchester, and was a governor of the college.

At the turn of the century the inspectors were advocating that the students should range further afield for their teaching practice. Two schools at Eastleigh contended to have students, and in 1913 H.M.I. Tillard was recommending to a sceptical governing body that the students should be sent to Bournemouth for their teaching practice. The custom was to pay head-teachers an honorarium for having the students. In 1913 the two heads of the Eastleigh schools received five guineas each, the headmaster of Danemark received three guineas, and the heads of Hyde and Holy Trinity, Winchester, received two guineas each.

As the day training colleges developed in the 1890s and the municipal colleges were founded in the 1900s (Portsmouth in 1907), aspersions were cast on the introverted denominational residential colleges. H.M.I. Oakley disagreed with this view, as shared by some members of the Cross Commission:

> . . . though I am very glad that day colleges are established, most excellent work has been done by the residential colleges, and the peaceful college life, the college routine and discipline, the esprit de corps, the college chapel are great advantages. Moreover, it is not generally known how good the lectures and teaching are.[11]

Canon Martin spans the whole of this period from 1880 to 1914. In 1880 he worked and planned for the college, supported by the counsel of Archdeacon Philip Jacob who in 1838 had acted as the first secretary of the Diocesan Board of Education. In 1914 Canon Martin, in the second year of retirement, could see that under the leadership of Principal Wainwright, with

William Lockton as Vice-Principal, supported by men of the calibre of Goddard and Jarman, the college could scarcely stumble. It was a consolidated institution. But on 4 August war was declared, the students were eventually dispersed to other colleges or to the battlefield, and the future looked bleak indeed for the college and for the country.

CHAPTER SIX

FROM WAR TO WAR (1914-1946)

College at War

THE GOVERNORS' REPORT on the year ending 31 July 1914 stated: 'There have been no changes in the efficient staff during the year under review, and the work has proceeded in the same happy spirit as has characterised it for so many years past'. But great changes were now imminent. The Principal became Captain Wainwright, the officer commanding the administrative centre of the 4th Hants Headquarters, Castle Hill, Winchester. His right-hand man, another Wintonian, was Q.M.S. Stanley Tompson (1896-98). During the first year of the war six second-year students and four certificate (one-year) students were sent to Bede College, Durham. In 1915 the Principal was able to visit Durham where there were then 22 Winchester students. Also in 1914 24 first-year students were sent to the Exeter Diocesan Training College, and three members of staff, Padwick, Turley, and Davis, went with them. The following year Turley and Davis were sent to Durham. Herbert Jarman joined the R.A.M.C. after spending a year at the Peterborough College with Vice-Principal Lockton, who in 1915 was sent to Saltley College. Captain Goddard was at Quetta from where he wrote to the Principal giving him an account of Wintonian activities in those far parts. His regiment was to move from Quetta in 1916 through the Persian Gulf to Mesopotamia, and in 1917 to be deeply involved in the Palestinian War which led to the liberation of Jerusalem. These were changes indeed for the staff and students of the college.

At the outbreak of war the governors had empowered G. R. Crawford, the honorary treasurer, to deal with all financial matters. There were very many additional travelling costs to be met because of the movement of students to colleges far from their homes. The governors at that stage were confident that the war would not last more than a year; but by July 1915 it was evident that the empty college would be considered for military use, as a hospital or for quartering troops. From the correspondence between the Board of Education and the National Society it became clear that if a concentration scheme were put in hand, whereby many colleges closed and students were accepted at only a few, then Winchester might possibly remain open. In the event Battersea Training College was the one chosen to stay open after 1916 and the others

77

closed. Crawford reported gloomily to the other governors that if Winchester were closed for two years it would risk extinction. No teaching, however, took place in the college throughout the war. For the first few months the College Company was billeted in the college. In January 1915 a double Company of the 1st Welsh Regiment with six officers was temporarily housed in the gymnasium and common room. From November 1915 until the end of the war the Army Pay Office of the Rifle Brigade and the K.R.R., about three hundred clerks of both sexes, under three officers were installed in the lecture rooms, dining hall and dormitories. The latter were transformed by the removal of partitions. The Principal was pleased to report that scrupulous care had been taken to avoid damage to the premises. Apart from the Principal's house, the chapel, and the library, the Army Pay Department was in control of the entire college.

Over 560 Wintonians enlisted in the course of the war: 60 lost their lives. Soon messages were being received by the Principal of casualties and deaths. Students on admission paid a £20 fee for their two-year course. The parents of those who had enlisted in their second year and had been killed received letters from the Principal with proportionate refunding of fees. There were moments of rejoicing, too. G. H. Barker (1900–1902), who had succeeded Henry Cole (1898–1900) as physical training instructor in 1913, was awarded the M.C. Both Cole and Barker had been colour sergeants in the College Company. T. E. Adams (1912–1914) was awarded the V.C. Of the many heroic exploits of Captain Goddard that reached college was one concerning a dangerous situation with the Indian troops outside Jerusalem in 1918. The Indians were in a state of nervous unrest. It was Goddard who, after his years in India, acquiring knowledge of a number of the north-west languages, was able to speak to the restless troops in Pathan and settle them down before the final assault.

In 1917 H. W. Padwick (1873–1874) resigned his post due to deafness. Writing his obituary in 1928, *The Wintonian* records his teaching at Yateley, and his headship of St. Thomas's School, Winchester, when it was first opened and known as the Higher Grade School—the name which still stands on the outside of the building. H. W. Padwick was the first master of method at the college, which he served from 1884 until his retirement to Southsea. He had been to Sweden to study the Slöjd method of instruction in manual subjects, and this method, employed at St. Thomas's and taught to the college students practising there, had been much praised by the H.M.I. During the war he taught at Exeter and Carmarthen. He was a most active Vice-President of the Winton Club.

When the governors met after the armistice they made plans for the re-opening of the college. By March 1919 the Principal reported that the staff who had served in the forces were being demobilised and would be ready to take up their posts by September 1919. A large number of student applications had been received. The Army was making preparations to move out and the War

Office was prepared to undertake certain reconditioning. Wiring for electric lights and 157 points was undertaken at a cost of £690, and central heating at a cost of £1,250–£1,500. The salary of the Principal was re-assessed at £700 a year, with house and garden, board for himself and his wife, and wages for two servants, together with payment of light, fuel and laundry. The Principal and his wife were responsible for keeping accounts and all house-keeping.

On the advice of the National Society the Principal suggested to the governors that Nonconformists should be admitted to the college as regular students. Entrance fees for students were fixed at £10 a year for two-year students, £15 for the one-year certificate students, and £7 10s. 0d. for special ex-Service students admitted to a six-months' course. Of the staff, Lockton and Jarman returned to residence: Pells (master of method), Davis (music and drawing); Goddard and Barker were non-resident. R. W. Burfitt was appointed as physics lecturer at £250 a year, and W. S. Mackie, a classics lecturer from Hartley College, Southampton, visiting twice weekly, was paid 30s., plus railway fare.

The Education Act of 1918 had made provision for continuing part-time education, but these plans were set aside by the post-war slump and subsequent cuts. However, in 1919, there was an air of optimism that, as set out in the Act, provision would be made for raising the school leaving age to 15, and, consequently, the training colleges would be required to expand. The Teachers' Superannuation Act, 1918, and the immediate post-war wave of idealism led to a high level of student application. The governors discussed links with the universities. The Board of Supervision of the Church Training Colleges thought Winchester might increase its student numbers from 80 to 100 and Mr. Cowan, the Hampshire County Education Officer, whose advice was sought, approved. The Principal, in fact, admitted 72 students in the autumn of 1919 only a week after the normal commencement of term. There had been much repair, renovation, and conversion work to be undertaken in the wake of the Army's departure. Clearly for 1920 additional accommodation would be required. 'Edgehill' (St. Swithun's Lodge) came on the market and the governors decided to buy it. In December 1919 Mr. Holland, the Secretary of the National Society, attended an emergency meeting of the governors and he warned that the college was unlikely to survive unless it was enlarged to a more economical size. He suggested 120 students. He pointed out that most of the Church colleges for women were larger than the Winchester Training College, and he also stressed the need for a closer relationship with a university, so that college residence might count as university residence. A start had been made in the case of Bede College, Durham. He urged the diocese to give financial support to the college in purchasing 'Edgehill'. The purchase was completed in February 1920 for £4,000. The college seemed set on the road of steady expansion. Among the staff and students who were to take part in that expansion were some who had travelled the world or survived trench warfare. That cumulative experience alone led to a period of profound change.

Aftermath and Change

In the autumn of 1919 of the 72 students 22 were second-year students who had completed a year's training before they had served in the forces, and 50 were first-year men. The acquisition of 'Edgehill', to be named St. Swithun's Lodge, was to increase the numbers to 120 in the following year. The Non-conformists and the Catholics were settled into the 'Lodge'. The sharpness of this denominational discrimination was not to prevail for long, but it had been part of the school experience that some of these first-year students themselves had experienced. V. C. Osborne (1919–1921), whose parents were Nonconformists, attended a Church of England infants' school in Portsmouth. His first teacher, a staunch Anglican, started each school-day with a scripture lesson, when Bible stories were read to the children and their meaning explained. On the fifth day of the week, however, the scripture lesson was replaced by religious instruction, when the Church Catechism had to be learnt by heart and a gloss given to it. Little Vernon Osborne was puzzled, when these lessons took place, by the teacher saying 'Children of wrath, stand upon your forms and face the back wall'. He did not know that unbaptised Nonconformists were 'by nature born in sin, and the children of wrath'. With the rest of the young sinners he did what he was told. He reported this to his parents, and his father, who worked in the Royal Navy shipyards, visited the school, explained to the headmistress what was happening, confronted the class-teacher, and said 'If you call my son a child of wrath you will have to deal with his parent who is wrath itself'. From that point the children of Nonconformist parents were allowed during religious instruction to bring their own picture books containing scripture stories.[1]

The story of Vernon Osborne's courageous struggle for education and degree status was not atypical of students entering college in the post-war period. He was born in 1898. In 1902 the Education Act had made secondary education more widely available. At the age of 12 he was taken to his local secondary school to sit for a minor scholarship awarded by the Joint Scholarship Board instituted by the Incorporated Association of Headmasters. As a result of his taking this examination he was awarded a 'B' scholarship. Winners of 'A' scholarships were free to take up any career they wished, but the 'B' scholarship winners were to receive four years' education at the secondary school without payment of fees on condition that they became teachers. If after leaving school at the age of 16+ Osborne broke his side of the contract, his father would have been liable for the full fees of his son's four years' secondary education. It was at this time, 1911, that the Board of Education was making arrangements for the 'Pledge' to be made for those taking the university route to teacher-training. It was not until 1951 that the 'Pledge' was replaced by a 'Declaration of Intent' to teach in maintained schools.[2]

Osborne, in September 1914, was not in a position to choose the university path to teacher-training. Instead he was appointed to Clarence Square council school as a junior assistant teacher at a salary of £26 a year. Under the head teacher's guidance and encouragement he learnt the rudiments of his profession. For the last part of the war he served in the Navy, and when he was admitted to college in 1919 he was sceptical of what further professional preparation the college might be able to offer him. His first task was to pass the Inter-mediate B.A. of the University of London. Latin was compulsory. Although he had studied Latin he had not been examined in it. The Principal, spotting this weakness, asked Mr. Goddard to test him by setting him two recent Inter Latin papers. Osborne did fairly in the grammar, rather better in the transla-tion paper. It was thought necessary that the visiting lecturer from Hartley College, Southampton, should be asked to include Osborne in his Latin group which met once a week. His other Inter subjects were English language and literature, history, French, and mathematics. At the end of his first year he passed his Inter B.A., and set himself to read for a B.A. Honours English with Subsidiary French. Mr. Goddard and Mr. Pells were his tutors respectively. At the end of his second year he qualified as a teacher, but failed his B.A. In 1921 he took up his first post as a fully-fledged teacher and pursued his degree studies; but it took him a further seven years before he secured his degree; even after that he pressed himself yet further to gain an M.A. Like so many Wintonians he had been inspired by Bernard Goddard's example and personality and established with him a deep and enduring friendship.

The college's links with universities had been stressed by Mr. Holland, the Secretary of the National Society, and had been fostered by the invitation of Hartley College staff to teach in a part-time capacity in Winchester. The Burnham Report, which was published in 1925, had outlined a number of ways connections might be established between universities and training colleges, with the intention of freeing the training of teachers from the strict limitations of elementary education. The social as well as educational differ-ences of training for elementary, as distinct from secondary, schools called for a reformed system of training. The universities were called upon to co-operate in the training colleges' examinations and to replace the centrally-operated Board of Education examination system with one by which the universities, each operating in conjunction with a group of colleges, might give to the colleges a greater measure of autonomy.

In May 1925 the governors held an extraordinary meeting to which they invited Mr. Holland, Mr. Furley, the Chairman of the County Education Committee, and Mr. Vickers, the Principal of University College, Southamp-ton. The bishop who chaired the meeting stressed that the governors had to seek ways of enlarging the college to what was considered a proper economic size of 200 students; it had also to explore the possibility of a closer association with the University College at Southampton. The Principal of the University College told the governors in confidence that the University of Wessex was unlikely to be established at Southampton in the near future. He welcomed the proposed association with the training college. The President of the Board of Education called a meeting in London in July 1926, to which he invited representative governors of the universities, training colleges, and L.E.As in the southern region. The colleges represented were Southampton R.C., Brighton and Portsmouth (Municipal), Chichester, Salisbury, and Winchester. Each was advised to approach the University Colleges of Reading and Southampton with regard to schemes for co-operation. In the meantime an approach by the Board would be made to ascertain whether the University of London might be prepared to entertain proposals for co-operation. The Winchester governors were Canon Robinson (Vice Dean) and Spencer Leeson. The governors, when the details of the meeting were reported, were more inclined to await the University of London's decision rather than initiate discussion with either Reading or Southampton. However, by January 1928, they had approved a draft scheme of co-operation with Southampton, and by May had approved the college representation on the Boards of Studies and the Board of Examinations. At this stage the Board of Education intervened. It established 11 regional groups of training colleges, each linked with a university or university college. 'Each region would have its joint examining board, which would frame and conduct examinations in academic subjects and the theory of education. The Board of Education would continue to assess practical teaching.'[3] Winchester was placed with the Joint Examining Board centred on the University of Bristol. In the later 1930s the Vice Chancellor of the University of Bristol and Professor H. W. Lawton of the University College, Southampton, were representatives on the College's Governing Body.

The relationship between the college and the universities was raised again at a meeting of governors in December 1942. The Board of Supervision was required to present evidence to the McNair Committee, which had been set up in March 1942 to investigate the sources of supply and the methods of recruitment and training of teachers. The governors set up a sub-committee. In 1944 they approved a document prepared by the Vice Chairman, Spencer Leeson, then headmaster of Winchester College. This was submitted to the Board of Supervision. It supported in general the findings of the McNair Report published earlier in the year. Points made were:

(a) the status and salary of teachers must be raised;
(b) the course should be three years and not two;
(c) the church colleges have a special contribution to make;
(d) greater attention must be paid to the meaning and scope of religious education;
(e) the staffing of training colleges needs greater thought and care;
(f) the pledge should be abolished.

The document dealt with the controversial question of whether training colleges should be grouped round university education departments or under joint boards, but it was thought no firm recommendation could be made until the government had declared its policy on the status and salaries of teachers. It was not, however, until 1947 that a scheme was proposed by the University College of Southampton for a University School of Education.

The Portsmouth Training College and the Winchester and Southampton Voluntary Colleges agreed to join the scheme.

The period between 1919 and 1939 was characterised by a go-stop syndrome in teaching-training. In 1919 colleges were asked to expand; the raising of the school leaving age to 15 and the extension of compulsory part-time education after 15 had been proposed within the 1918 Education Act. The ensuing slump brought cuts in government expenditure. By 1924 the economy axe, raised by the previous government, was suspended by the new administration. The new President of the Board of Trade, Charles Trevelyan, had endeared himself to teachers. The Board considered instituting a probationary year, following the college course, before issuing a certificate; the number of schools for 'mentally and physically defective children' increased. Provision of free meals for 'necessitous children' was sympathetically considered. School staffing improved, and for 1925 the Burnham Committee agreed on improved salaries which for men in primary schools were: Scales I and II, £155 13s. 6d.; III, £164 14s. 0d.; IV, £180 10s. 0d.[4]

The purchase of St. Swithun's Lodge had enabled the numbers to rise to one hundred. In the middle of the 1920s the college was advised to raise numbers still further. In 1924, when poised for expansion, there were 103 students in all: five third year, 50 second year, and 48 first year. The college was urged to aim at a figure of 200, but to take 150 as the interim goal. In 1926 decisions were made to purchase Holm Lodge and Christchurch vicarage (St. James's). A room at St. Thomas's School was used as a woodwork centre. New workshops were recommended by the visiting inspector in 1926 and erected on the college site. The dining hall and chapel were enlarged in 1927, and the Board of Education agreed to the college taking in a further 20 students. In 1928 a further 21 students were accommodated in St. James's, now in use, and in this year the Principal's moving to Holm Lodge released additional accommodation in the main building. It was at this point that the headmaster of Winchester College urged the governors that some means of avoiding confusion of names between the College of St. Mary's, Winchester, and the Winchester Training College might be discussed. The outcome was the renaming the latter King Alfred's College.

King Alfred's Day, 28 October, became from then a day of special celebration for the college marked by services at the cathedral or the college or the parish church of Hyde, because it was in Hyde Abbey that King Alfred was reputed to have been buried. On the eve of King Alfred's Day it became traditional for the statue in the Broadway to be decorated with ribbons. It was customary first for the Principal's permission to be obtained and then permission from the City police. Late on 27 October 1933 a most prominent Wintonian, then in his final year, was discovered by the police at the top of the ladder decorating King Alfred's statue. As he had not sought the customary permission he spent the night in the police cell, and in the morning suffered the severe censure of the Principal.

In 1930 Captain Franklin, R.N., the first bursar of the college, was appointed. With a £6,000 loan from the Diocesan Board of Finance the college planned its next phase of building expansion which was to provide for 16 more students, bringing the total to 160: a further extension of the dining hall (£600); a new assembly hall (three classrooms) west of the chapel (£2,400); a new wing added to St. Swithun's Lodge (£3,300). The idea of providing study bedrooms put forward in 1929 by the inspector, R. G. Major, was taken up in 1931. The Board of Education approved plans for a new block of 40 study bedrooms, and the conversion of the present dormitories to provide 40 more. For this work a loan of £24,000 was required from the Central Board of Finance. Just as the building of St. Grimbald's Court was beginning, a 10 per cent. cut was applied to teachers' salaries on the instruction of the Board of Education and the Board of Supervision of the Church Training Colleges.

The governors met for the first time in St. Grimbald's on 25 November 1932. It was a handsome provision of 40 study bedrooms with common rooms on both floors. They were at pains to have minuted that without such provision the college's position might have been precarious indeed.

Principal Wainwright (1912–1933), after 21 years in office, retired. In 1927, like his two immediate predecessors, he had been installed as Canon of Winchester Cathedral. His principalship was distinguished. He was much loved and respected. He had taken the college through very difficult years and must have thought that, with the completion of St. Grimbald's Court, at that time the most modern and spacious student study bedroom provision in the country, the college was secure in its accommodation, staffing and reputation to face the future confidently.

His successor was the Rev. R. C. White, a Sheffield University graduate, who immediately sought to consolidate the work of his predecessor. His salary was £750 a year, by annual increments of £25 to £1,000, but subject to the 10 per cent. deduction still in force. In 1934 he set about purchasing for the college the playing fields at Bar End. In 1935 he and the governors agreed to invite the Board of Education to undertake an inspection of the college. This had disturbing consequences. It led to the retirement of Bill Lockton, the Vice-Principal, whom it was discovered was going blind in one eye, and also to the premature retirement of R. W. Burfitt. Favourable reports were given on Pells and Laverty, but strictures passed on the inadequacy of the library, the need of an assembly hall and a larger gymnasium, with asphalt provision for outside activities. The governors' response, having taken immediate action with regard to the staffing, was no less firm and speedy in planning additional accommodation. The first-floor common room at St. Grimbald's was converted into a library. Provision was made for building on the dytche a gymnasium and a large new assembly hall.

The threat of college closure arose again in 1937. The Church of England Board of Supervision, faithful to its policy of concentration, took the initiative. Three women's colleges—Brighton, Peterborough, and Truro—and one men's—Culham—were to close. Culham alone survived because it could prove it was financially solvent.[5] Winchester had escaped the threat of closure because its finances, too, were in good trim, and its new buildings were thought attractive to recruitment. The gymnasium was opened in May 1938; its gas heating was a particular novel feature of the day. The assembly hall was delayed because of a shortage of steel, but had the unusual distinction of being successfully completed during the war (1940).

The extensive addition of accommodation had justified the expansion of student numbers to 160 at the time of Wainwright's retirement in 1933. The expectation was that with the further addition of the playing fields, the gymnasium and the assembly hall, expansion would be continued, but the number of students for both 1938–39 and 1939–40 had been reduced to one hundred and thirty-five. The great flurry of building activity, the employment of a great variety of new staff to cope with the music, art, physics, rural science, English, mathematics, and technical subjects, had been met by a falling-off in student applications. More were joining the services, and in 1938/39 there were more sombre thoughts than in 1914, when it was commonly believed that if there was going to be a war, it would be a short one.

The students' social life at college underwent a profound change during this inter-war period. The students returning from the 1914–18 war were less inclined to accept the rigid routine of roll calls, supervised private study, and severe restrictions on personal freedom. For instance, before the war smoking anywhere on the college site had been forbidden. Pre–1914 students tell of the time when in the summer the dytche was covered with tall grass. At the far west corner stood a hay-rick, and it was from this vantage point that a look-out man gave warning of an approaching prefect or member of staff, while his friends would be hiding in the grass, smoking strong ship's tobacco.[6]

After 1919 smoking was allowed in the common room. A particular feature of the students' social life was the holding of smoking concerts on Saturday evenings. Smoking, too, was an essential part of the early meetings of the drama club which later was called the Irving Club. Meetings took place in the common room; tobacco or sweets were handed round according to taste and, in a relaxed atmosphere, a play was read and discussed, but, in the 1920s, there was no great attempt at production. Music, on the other hand, was brought to performance level on many occasions: concerts in the college, in the City, glee club activities, and the regular services in which the college chapel choir maintained an exceptionally high standard, which many Wintonians recall with keen appreciation. Within the first month of the autumn term the second-years entertained the new students in what was called the Welcome Concert, and the first-years responded after some weeks with the Return Concert—feeling rawly exposed to the eyes and ears of their critical seniors, and they were at times the victims of some withering criticism in *The Wintonian*.

The St. Luke's Night ceremonies and the 'Bishop's courts' were continued, but between the 1920s and 1930s the punishments inflicted became more severe. Osborne (1919-1921) describes the 'Bishop' holding court flanked by his 'Chaplain' and other seniors. The offending juniors were brought before him two by two and commanded to sing nose to nose different songs without laughing. The intention of the seniors was to correct social misdemeanours. Gay and sombre rites developed around 'Euclid', the standard china chamber pot issued to each student in his cubicle. By the 1930s the seniors were using the slipper far more freely. In 1935 the seniors held a court in the games room and all the juniors were summoned. The senior student explained that such a court was only held if the student was letting the college down by his behaviour. One of the juniors was then accused 'of persistently consorting with various women of the city'. He happened to be a hefty rugby player, but he was sentenced to be beaten and was placed face down on the billiards-table and given many strokes with a gym shoe by six seniors. He took his punishment well, but the juniors showed nothing but revulsion for such proceedings, and later in the year went on the rampage and caused the seniors to lock themselves in their rooms, not coming out for breakfast or supper. After this the ragging was never so severe. Principal White, to the students' general displeasure, forbade any further St. Luke's Night celebrations; a 50-year tradition was broken.

Towards the end of the summer term it was customary for the Principal to choose 12 prefects from among the first-year students who were to take up their duties in the following academic year. The prefects' general duties were to sit at the head of the tables in the dining hall and, in turn, to preside over the juniors' private study in the great 'lecture room' in the evenings. The senior prefect held considerable power. He alone had power to fine other prefects, among whom was the dining hall monitor, second in command, and responsible for the service at meal times, because all college domestics kept their side of the serving hatch. Absent and late students were fined. Each student had his special seat for meals, as he had in chapel. For missing chapel a fine of 2s. 6d might be levied by the succentor. The precentor assisted the music lecturer in the choice of chapel music and was given full power to organise the musical evenings and conduct the college glee club. In the chapel he sat next to the Principal on the south side. His room was in 'Arx' dormitory. The librarian monitor controlled the borrowing of books. During evening study periods he remained in the library to supervise the study of selected students who might have been given permission to work there. There were two curators who checked the students' laundry books and collected charges for excess laundry. They also drew up a rota for the use of the bathrooms. The bell monitor roused the students in the morning, and the postman cleared the letter-box in the central tower at 6.30 p.m. each evening, but it was the junior curator who then took the mail to the nearest pillar-box. The prefects exacted fines for lateness, for absence, for smoking at prohibited times or in prohibited places. One student was even fined for wearing plus-fours. Fine money was put into the sports fund.

The sporting events from the 1870s had always been strongly supported by staff. Many a Vice-Principal became known as the backbone of the college cricket team. Jarman was more noted for his refereeing of football matches; Dane and Laverty for their tennis. That friendly spirit of co-operation was also marked on the first Monday after the seniors' teaching practice when, as in October 1926, Pells, Jarman, Burfitt, and Dane, met at Dumpers' Café (Market Street) with the whole of the senior year for tea and entertainment.

Throughout the 1930s six students each year undertook lecturing in the prison. Their task was to read the papers to the Winchester prisoners whose interest was predominantly in the football results and court cases. This service was maintained throughout the decade. Wintonians remember still the welcome reception given them by the prisoners.

When the General Strike took place in May 1926 'the Principal called all students to a meeting and told them that they were free to join the volunteer organisations set up to keep essential services running during the strike. No pressure was applied, although there is some evidence of an implicit anti-strike attitude'.[7] More than twenty, whose names were mentioned in the local newspapers, joined the Voluntary Service Corps. The first contingent was not called until the fourth day of the strike, Friday, 7 May, and then it worked in shifts through the remaining four full days of the strike, which was formally called off by the T.U.C. at 12.20 p.m. on Wednesday, 12 May. The volunteers, running the gauntlet of abusive language and truculent behaviour from the picket lines, travelled to Southampton in a canvas-covered lorry. In the docks the students were set to work unloading potatoes, onions, oranges, and bales of raw cotton. They worked on at least seven ships. They were paid sums varying from £3 to £7. Several replaced clothes ruined in the work with Oxford bags, then the rage, and college blazer. On their return to college there was some argument about strike-breaking, but no deep resentment. The students, although coming from families deeply affected by the root causes of the strike, received grants from the government and as schoolmasters in training were disposed to have a healthy regard for authority.[8]

The Winton Club

The first planned constitutional gathering of former students of the college in 1874 was called the Reunion Club. In 1881 it was renamed the Winchester Training College Club, but at the turn of the century the alternative term, Winton Club, was frequently in use. The president of the club, was, by its constitution, the serving Principal of the college; the vice-presidents were the former Principals and Vice-Principals, if still living, and senior or retired members of staff. The secretaries were until 1934 former Wintonians who were appointed to the staff of the college and so acted as a useful link between the present and the past. For the long period of the club's existence there have been relatively few secretaries. They have all undertaken their work with distinction and their record stands in the Minute Books, the Year Books, and

The Wintonian. They are: William Bright (1875); H. Searle (1876); H. W. Padwick (1874); A. Davis (1880); B. R. Goddard (1887-1900); R. G. Wing (1922-1924); and F. Wheeler (1931-1933).

The first Reunion took place in the college in 1874 and took the form of a service followed by a meal. Subsequent Reunions followed this pattern with a few additions and variations. It became the occasion of the Annual General Meeting of the club, and, when the Reunion was fixed for the first Saturday in July, light-hearted sporting events were arranged between past and present students. The club kept itself closely informed of current developments within the college and throughout its history has been significantly supportive both of the institution and of individuals within it. The Club's Benevolent Fund has assisted countless students who while at college were in particular need of financial support. It has regularly cared for, through fellowship and funding, the aged, ill, or lonely Wintonians. In addition, care has always been shown to the dependants of Wintonians, especially of those Wintonians who might have died early in their professional careers before qualifying for a reasonable pension.

By 1904 branch clubs had been established in London, Portsmouth, and Southampton. The Principal and staff, especially Padwick, Searle, Barker, and Goddard, made every effort to attend these meetings. The concerns of the college were more widely disseminated, and the club showed its support by countless gifts. The club established prizes and exhibitions for present students as well as making funds available for those in need. It enriched the chapel with memorial windows, the last of which was to the memory of Captain George Barker, M.C., and Mr. Tom Humphries. The former was joint general secretary from 1924 until his sudden death in 1931. The latter was a founder member of the London club and the first headmaster of a Home Office industrial school. One of their most generous gifts was the provision of the oak shelving for the new library in St. Grimbald's Court.[9] Also in the chapel after each world war the names of Wintonians who died were carved on oak commemorative panels.

On Saturday, 5 July 1924 the Winton Club celebrated its 50th year since its foundation. Two hundred and sixty members attended. The service was held in the cathedral. Canon N. C. Woods, a tutor in music at the college officiated; the senior students (1923-1924) formed the choir; the Principal read the lesson; and the bishop preached the sermon. Luncheon, supplied by Dumpers, was served at the Guildhall. G. W. Brunner (1873), one of the founder members of the club, was present. The roll-call was read out in years of leaving, beginning with A. Rawlins (1870). After the luncheon the mayor received the club in the banqueting hall. Tea was served at the college, followed by the Annual General Meeting. Some Wintonians had travelled thousands of miles to be present. It was a day warmly remembered by all who attended.[10]

The records of the Winton Club are contained in the Annual Report and Balance Sheet, in the college Year Book, *The Wintonian,* and the club's Minute

Books. The Report and Balance Sheet for 1913–1914, for instance, contains not merely a report on the year and a statement of accounts; it lists the club's senior officers and committee members, states the objects and rules of the club, gives a chronicle of the college, together with accounts of the college sports performance for 1913–14 and a yearly review of 'B' Company events. In addition it lists Wintonians according to their years, appending their present addresses, and concludes with an obituary list. The year books were not published regularly. After a lapse of 13 years one was published in 1949. It was a substantial document requiring much patient research in assembling the names and current addresses of Wintonians leaving college between the years 1878–1950.

The Wintonian, with an issue appearing each term, was not only a means of keeping former students up-to-date with college affairs, but it also was a means by which present students could learn something of the history of the college. Members of staff such as Searle, Padwick, and Jarman regularly contributed historical surveys of the college. Other Wintonians such as Drewett and Proctor recalled earlier days, and the obituaries told again of those days and also the later use to which the Wintonians had put them. *The Wintonian* reported lectures given by distinguished visitors such as George Sampson in 1923, when he is described as the writer of 'English for the English' and a member of the Departmental Committee (Newbolt) which presented the 'Report on the Teaching of English in England'. 'He was Senior Prefect, and the Editor of *The Wintonian* in 1893.'[11] It reported, too, lectures by Wintonians on the staff. It is clear that some of the most exhilarating lectures were given by Bernard Goddard on a wide variety of topics ranging from the 'Palestinian Campaign', and the 'Indian North-West Frontier', to 'English Folk Songs'.

The Winton Club was a means of maintaining friendships, forging new ones, giving a helping hand to students taking up their first appointments, and in particular of giving all the support it could to the Principal and staff in their endeavour, through troublesome times, to keep high the reputation of the college. Since 1937, when R. G. Wing was elected, the Winton Club, apart from a brief period in the 1960s, has been represented on the governing body.

War Again

In January 1939 the Principal reported to the governors that each student at the college had a respirator in the event of an enemy gas attack. J. Osborne, the physical education lecturer, had undertaken training as an A.R.P. warden. The Board of Education had indicated that, in the event of war, the college might have to take students, probably women, from an evacuated area. This was understood as being a reference to St. Gabriel's College, Camberwell. By June this was confirmed and the governors appointed a sub-committee consisting of the Vice Chairman (Spencer Leeson), the Treasurer (Arthur Edmonds), the Principal, and the Secretary, with full powers to act in the affairs of the college in time of emergency. All Winchester students affected by the formation of a militia had applied for postponement. A.R.P. measures called for the reinforcement of the cellars and the digging of two outside trenches. When the governors next met, 30 January 1940, the war had been raging for five months. The college had found accommodation for 19 boys from Portsmouth Grammar School, evacuated from a most vulnerable target area. Despite the lowering of the age of entry to 17, the Principal reported that entries for 1940 were low. The St. Gabriel's women had not after all come to make Winchester a mixed college. By June 1940 the government had commandeered the college for military purposes.

The permanent members of staff were to be given three months' notice to expire on 31 December 1940. The Rev. G. Suthers, who succeeded Pells in 1937 as director of training, became an Army chaplain. The Rev. K. W. H. Felstead (mathematics) went to a living in Southampton. Concern was expressed for Vice-Principal Jarman and Tom Atkinson (geography and P.T.), who as older men might find difficulty in obtaining alternative employment. The position of the bursar, Mr. Beecroft, who had succeeded Captain Franklin in 1935, was referred to the Executive Committee. The military were asked to keep the outdoor staff. A fair rent for the premises was thought to be between £1,800 and £2,000 a year.

No students, therefore, entered the Winchester College in September 1940 despite the encouragement in the brochure 'Although in a safe area there are extensive A.R.P. [Air Raid Precautions] facilities.' The War Office had made other arrangements, and the Army Intelligence Corps moved in. The Board of Supervision's scheme for the students was that the 47 second-year students for 1940–41 would go to Culham, and the 52 first-year students to Saltley; three other first-year students would be placed at Exeter. The students at Saltley were supplied with collapsible beds and special blankets for taking to ground-floor steel-strengthened air-raid shelters. The Principal started with some lecturing commitments at Culham, but relationships became strained and later he was allowed neither an office nor a bed at the college, nor allowed to see his own students. On one occasion he was escorted off the premises from the Principal's house. At Saltley he was given a flat, and circumstances were certainly easier. In the following year the Principal accompanied the students to Trinity College, Carmarthen. During the year 1941-42 there were 70 students at Carmarthen. Some students were to register for King Alfred's, but complete their training in Wales without ever setting foot in Winchester. Some, from the Channel Islands, were to register as students of King Alfred's, begin their training at Carmarthen, and then because of the German occupation of their islands, be prevented from returning home until after the war.

By June 1945, with the war coming to an end, the number of students in Carmarthen was twenty-four. In the following year the governors in gratitude for the helpful co-operation sent to Principal Halliwell of Trinity College, Carmarthen, a copy of Walter Oakeshott's *Artists of the Winchester Bible.*

In Winchester preparations were in hand for re-opening the college. In July 1945 the governors agreed that a change of Principal was desirable. After an exchange of letters between the Bishop and the Principal and a further meeting of the governors at Wolvesey on 27 August, the Principal's appointment was terminated as from 31 December 1945. The governors immediately set about the appointment of a new Principal, and at a meeting on 30 October 1945 appointed W. P. Dickinson, headmaster of Ormskirk Grammar School.

The Army were making plans to move out of the college, but the Bishop was asked to hasten them by making representations at the War Office. In the event the college was not released until July 1946. The Bar End playing fields, which had been rented out as pastureland, were prepared once more for student games. Canon Cockin, Secretary of the Council of Church Training Colleges, on a visit to Winchester, had urged expansion of the college. At the same time Alan Rannie had suggested to the governors in 1945 that West Hayes, a very large mansion in Sarum Road, which had been used as a preparatory school, would be coming on the market. Mr. Beecroft took up his post again as college accountant and helped to prepare, with the new Principal, for a new start.

CHAPTER SEVEN

FOR MEN ONLY (1946–1958)

Picking up the Pieces

W. P. DICKINSON, the new Principal, was interviewed on 30 October 1945 and his appointment took effect from 1 January 1946. He was the first layman to hold the post. He was married with two adopted children, and for the last 11 years had been headmaster of Ormskirk Grammar School for Boys and Girls, Lancashire. He had been a scholar of Corpus Christi College, Oxford, where he read natural science. Throughout his Principalship he subscribed himself 'Former Scholar of Corpus Christi College, Oxford'. He was also a qualified lay preacher. His first task was to secure the release of the college from the War Office so that for September 1946 he could enrol new students and welcome to Winchester for their second year those who, as King Alfred's College students, were completing their first year at Trinity College, Carmarthen. Apart from Principal White, no member of staff, neither academic nor administrative, had been retained by the governors. At his appointment Dickinson was faced with the probability of securing an entirely new staff. His task was daunting, and became more so as he slowly learned the true state of affairs. He kept a detailed record of the problems confronting him and much of the following is drawn from that record.

The college itself, apart from the chapel, was wholly occupied by the War Office, using it, at that stage, as the Central Record Office for the A.T.S. Despite the strongest representations from the bishop and the governors the War Office, which at first had suggested the end of February 1946 as a possible time of their withdrawal, did not leave until July 1946. As the demobilisation of the A.T.S. was then in full swing the maintenance of the Record Office in Winchester, it was argued, was essential. Holm Lodge had not been occupied by the Army, and one of the rooms there had been used as a college office, but Dickinson was unable to gain access, nor was he able to arrange a meeting with R. C. White who, technically Principal until 31 December 1945 had been appointed to the Carmarthen staff until the end of that academic year. Dickinson was thus unable to consult the students' records, nor could he discover what applications had been made for September 1946.

Canon Spencer Leeson came to his aid. Spencer Leeson was then headmaster of Winchester College. In August 1946 he resigned his post to become rector of St. Mary's, Southampton. He later became Bishop of Peterborough. For King Alfred's College he played a crucial role, as vice chairman and secretary of the governing body and chairman of its executive committee, in securing the change of Principal, in maintaining negotiations with officials of the Board of Education, the Central Council for Church Colleges, and the War Office. He was also alert to various moves on the Winchester property market which might have been of importance to the college. He had kept in touch with R. C. White. The support, therefore, he was able to give Dickinson was invaluable.

On 12 November 1945 Spencer Leeson in a long letter to Dickinson outlined the problems facing the Principal elect. Apart from the reversion of the buildings to the college and the extensive repairs that would have to be undertaken, he mentioned the need to expand the college by at least 70 students above the pre-war figure to a total of about 200; and in an endeavour to provide for these students a college which was 'a real centre of spiritual and intellectual life' the governors were looking to the new Principal to attract 'the right kind of men to the staff'. 'I hope we shall find', he writes, 'that the educational lay-out of the future provides for easy interchange between training colleges and other places of education, and also between training colleges and the parochial life of the Church. This is going to be a large matter and will take a long time'.

Spencer Leeson's concern for expansion arose from discussions he had had with officials of the Board of Education and of the Central Council for Church Training Colleges. It was confidently expected that following the publication of the McNair Report in May 1944, three months before the Education Act received royal assent, there would be a concerted drive, at the termination of hostilities, to raise the school-leaving age to 15 and to increase the period of teacher-training from two to three years. When, however, Dickinson visited Winchester in January 1946 and eventually had access to Holm Lodge, he found no details relating to the students at Carmarthen, nor to those who had applied for September 1946. Information on the former was given him by the Principal of Trinity College, Carmarthen, and on the latter by Miss Atherton, the Secretary of the Training Colleges' Clearing House. He was also to learn soon after from Spencer Leeson that the War Office would not release the college until July 1946, and this news made him contemplate the possibility of offering students a five-term course, beginning January 1947. He anticipated about thirty first-year students transferring from Carmarthen to Winchester for their second year, but both he and Spencer Leeson were anxious to make as quick and as strong a start as possible. Applications from men and women released from the forces were streaming into the emergency training colleges by December 1945 at a rate of 5,000 a month, and by 1947 fifty-five such colleges had been founded. Post-war government policy favoured the provision of new L.E.A. rather than voluntary colleges. It was apparent that unless the voluntary colleges could rapidly strengthen their position they might be considered at risk. Nineteen new L.E.A. colleges opened between 1946 and 1948. The voluntary colleges, however, although not increased in number, were assisted in expanding by receiving in government grant up to half of any approved expenditure associated with the extension or improvement of existing accommodation. Frustrated therefore in his endeavour to secure the premises and increase enrolment, Dickinson turned his attention to the appointment of staff.

Cyril Beecroft, appointed in 1935 as accountant and Principal's secretary, returned to his post on 1 March 1946. He had been extremely helpful earlier in the year in preparing Holm Lodge for the new Principal. He had maintained some link with the college during the war years, and in June 1945, with the end of the war in sight, he had written to the then honorary secretary of the governing body (1936–45), Dr. Eric James, indicating his willingness to take up his college post again, and congratulating Dr. James on his appointment to Manchester Grammar School. At the same time the head porter, Bill Gibson, and his wife also returned, but as their cottage in the college grounds was still in army occupation they were offered acccommodation at Holm Lodge.

Dickinson had received accounts of the pre-war academic staff's duties from Spencer Leeson who had asked for the information from the previous Principal. He had also written to Jarman on the matter, and had received a meticulously objective and detailed account of the staff, their role and responsibility.

In Jarman's reply to the Principal dated 3 February 1946, he described Atkinson's pre-war duties as senior tutor, director of studies, lecturer in geography, and with management of the playing fields. His own work was 'to give instruction in Physics and to lecture on the methods used to teach the various subjects of the curriculum'. This part of his work prepared the students both for their teaching and for the paper in education known as Special Course B. 'This had three sections: English; Arithmetic; and one dealing with History, Geography, Science, Music, Art, Craftwork, Gardening, Needlework. For some years this was my work. At the General Inspection about 1926 the question was raised . . . whether the respective lecturers in the subjects named ought to be responsible for the methods of teaching the subject . . . The then Principal [Canon E. G. Wainwright] thought I was doing the work sufficiently well and made no change. At the General Inspection about 1936 the question was again raised and the Principal [Rev. R. C. White] followed up the Report by arranging to share "The Method" lectures round where it could be done. Not all the lecturers had had experience in the Elementary Schools. The net result was that I continued to be responsible for the Teaching of English, the Teaching of Arithmetic, and the Teaching of Science . . . I also acted from 1937 onwards as Vice Principal.'

Jarman then mentions Laverty who 'was a part-time instructor in Craftwork and is now working . . . as a full-time instructor at Peter Symonds School,

Winchester. The Craftwork was done at College. The Art Work was carried on at the Winchester School of Art. Instruction in Gardening was in the hands of the County Council Agricultural Department. The Music Department was served by Dr. Rhodes, the Cathedral Organist, and Mr. H. Smith. Mr. Smith was also responsible for the Chapel Music . . . It has been the custom of the College that all lecturers should take part in the supervision of school practice'.

In the event Jarman, Atkinson, Baugh (English), Laverty, and Smith were re-appointed. A new chaplain had to be found; very many were recommended. The Rev. Guy Bowden, who had been both pilot and padre in the R.A.F., joined the staff and became warden of St. Swithun's. Frank Blackburn was appointed as tutor for physical education and warden of St. James's; Thomas Graty as tutor for rural science; J. F. C. Dicker as tutor for history, college librarian and warden of St. Grimbald's; Dr. Fogwell as part-time tutor in music; the Rev. K. W. H. Felstead as part-time tutor in mathematics.

When the Army eventually moved out and the Principal and his staff moved in, they were met by a scene of desolation. The college was left without equipment, almost without furniture, without even curtains and curtain rails. When the college chapel was unlocked, the staff were astounded to see the amount of material of all kinds that had been stored there, but dismayed to see the condition in which the mice and rats had left it. The college library books had suffered a fate even worse than the furniture. Bill Gibson, the head porter, who joined the college in 1908 and retired in 1955, was asked, before leaving, to contribute an article to *The Wintonian*. He vividly recalled the post-war return:

> The Army evacuated our buildings in 1946, leaving behind a shell of our former College. The first floor of the Main Building, which had once contained the students' study bedrooms, was now one long room. The period following the departure of the Forces was a busy one for all. During this period the Principal worked very hard and I remember clearly how, in charge of a party of German prisoners, he assisted and controlled the moving of furniture from the Chapel, where it had been stored, to various parts of the College. When the Chapel was cleared the floor was scrubbed by Mr. Jarman, our late Vice-Principal, and Mr. Blackburn, working on their knees.[1]

The Principal personally set about acquiring beds, bed-linen, towels, even soap, which was then rationed. The kitchen equipment was also missing, and having appointed Miss Stephenson as domestic bursar, he faced with her the task of purchasing what he referred to as 'bigger things': a potato-peeling machine, a butter-patting machine, and a mincing machine. During this period the Nissen hut, on what was formerly the Principal's tennis court, and where now the main dining hall stands, served as the emergency cookhouse and Frank Blackburn from time to time acted as chef.

For the college office there was no stationery, no typewriter, certainly no typist. However, 35 students, who had completed their first year at Trinity College, Carmarthen, were due to begin their second year at Winchester. The first-year students, who could not be accepted until January 1947, were to undertake a five-term course. During the autumn of 1946 they spent the whole of what should have been their first term at college on school practice from their home base. The second-year students who arrived in college on 5 November had spent the first half of the term in schools on the same basis. The Principal had overcome enormous administrative problems to re-open the college to these students. Before they arrived, however, he brought the staff together. That evening he wrote in his notebook:

King Alfred's Day
26.10.46

8.0   Holy Communion
9.45   Prayer

First time we have all met together in College. It has been a long time coming. Thanks for patience and help. Spirit of cooperation augurs well for the future. I want this College to be a Christian family where each works for the good of all. It is a small community and we shall all be conscious, perhaps, of each other's imperfections, but I trust we shall all respect each other and work happily together on a job which is tremendously worthwhile.

In the autumn of 1946 Spencer Leeson, who was keeping a sharp look-out for a sizeable property which the college might purchase and convert into a students' residence, abandoned the notion of buying Milnethorpe or Marfield and focused on West Hayes. Alan Rannie, the owner, who following his father had run a preparatory school on the premises, was keen that King Alfred's College should make the purchase. At the meeting of the executive committee on 4 November 1946 Spencer Leeson reported that the purchase had been agreed by the Council of the Church Training Colleges, who had offered to advance the whole of the purchase price if the 50 per cent. share from the Ministry of Education was not immediately forthcoming. The Ministry had agreed to cover reconditioning costs. The bishop had undertaken to negotiate with Sir George Cooper of the County hospital for right of way for the West Hayes students through the hospital grounds.

The first group of more than twenty students took up residence in West Hayes during the summer term 1948. The boilers had not then been installed and the supply of hot water was less than adequate, but the Principal promised the improvements would be completed by the beginning of the autumn term 1948, when more than forty students would be accommodated in the newly-acquired hostel. It was not, however, until 7 March 1949 that the governors met at West Hayes and the bishop conducted a short service of dedication. Thomas Graty, the new warden of West Hayes, and his wife conducted the governors through the new hostel.

The acquisition of West Hayes played a major role in the post-war expansion of the college. At the end of 1946 when it was purchased the Principal was already planning the conversion of the 54 cubicles in the main building into 45 study bedrooms. Early in 1947 it was clear that when West Hayes came into use there would be accommodation for 178 students, 119 of whom would have separate rooms. The governors, therefore, agreed that the Principal should recruit for a college of 180. The dining hall, however, seated only 140. Teaching space for such a number was also inadequate. Throughout his Principalship Dickinson was faced with problems of not having funds to build anew, and so having to adapt, convert, and extend premises. Meals were taken in separate areas, use was made of the army Nissen huts, some teaching (art, for instance, at St. Thomas's school) was undertaken off the college premises. The students, however, were resilient. In addition to the building changes they were beset by a change of course and change of validating authority.

Setting a New Course

'What is chiefly wrong with the majority of training colleges is their poverty and all that flows from it.' Thus the McNair Report identifies the main malaise, commenting on the smallness of so many colleges, their meagre facilities, and the general failure of the Joint Examination Boards to forge closer links between the universities and the colleges. Students in the university training departments were not in the least affected by these examination arrangements. The training college students sat the examination, but at no other level did university life impinge on them. The training of secondary school teachers was undertaken in the universities, that of elementary school teachers in the colleges. Salaries were widely differentiated; the elementary school teachers, but not the secondary school teachers, were required to serve one year on probation before their appointment might be confirmed. Sir Fred Clarke, the Director of the London Institute of Education, with four other members of the McNair Committee, advocated the setting up of University Schools of Education, rather than an extension and modification of the Joint Board Scheme. Clarke strove to elevate the study of education within the university. Sir Arnold McNair, himself Vice Chancellor of the University of Liverpool, adhered to a Joint Board Scheme. Clarke argued that universities should play a leading part in the initial education and training of teachers and, furthermore, that such training should not be viewed as inferior to education. He claimed that as the study of education, its theory and practice, was one of the proper functions of a university, there was no reason why the education and training of teachers within a university should be restricted to secondary education (non-elementary).

In the event the Joint Board Schemes were discontinued and most universities beginning in 1946 set up Schools of Education. Area Training Organisations and Institutes of Education were established, not independent of the universities but subject to senate. The new courses established under the aegis of the new Boards of the Institutes were the outcome of close collaboration between university and college staff. The assessment of the student's work was not only by external examinations but also by coursework evaluation undertaken by the internal examiner with the check of external moderation. Students were trained for the new range of schools created by the 1944 Act: primary and secondary (grammar, technical, modern). The status of the colleges improved with the government's more generous funding; a three-year course was confidently expected soon to replace the two-year; opportunities for supplementary year courses abounded; staffing ratios within the colleges steadily improved.

King Alfred's benefited from all the above national improvements. The University College of Southampton set up in 1947 a University School of Education under Scheme A (Fred Clarke's) of the McNair Report. On 25 February 1947 there was a meeting at Southampton of Sir Robert Wood, Principal of the University College, and Principal Dickinson and the honorary secretary, Dr. K. B. Hutton. Preliminary agreement was reached on King Alfred's joining the Southampton scheme. By June 1948 the final examination had taken place for the Winchester students under the Western Joint Board. By September 1948 all college courses were controlled by the Southampton University College Institute of Education. It was not until 1953 that a full university charter was granted the former University College.

The university link was strengthened by Sir Robert Wood serving on the college's governing body with Dr. Hicks, the secretary of the new institute. Dr. Hicks' wife became a part-time lecturer of French on the college staff. Dr. Hicks and university colleagues John Rushby, Ivor Pearcy and Bob Douch, were invited in these early years of the institute to lecture to the college societies on many occasions covering such topics as music appreciation, local history, and drama.

Meanwhile the college staff was not only expanding as student numbers increased, but the ratios improved in the first few post-war years from 1:14 to 1:11.5. In 1948 Harry Blamires (English), Edmund Dobson (geography), and Ralph White (mathematics), were appointed. Each had had experience of teaching in an emergency training college. They were well qualified, with the existing staff, to take the college into this new university-linked era. In 1949 a new art tutor, Wilfred Hodgkinson, was appointed. Spencer Leeson was made Bishop of Peterborough, making way for Walter Oakeshott, later Sir Walter, as chairman of the executive committee of the governing body. The governors in consultation with the Principal invited the Ministry of Education to conduct a full inspection of the college in 1951. K. J. Ritchie was the main inspector. He was accompanied by 16 colleagues. On 1 June 1951 the governors met to hear Ritchie's report. Among those present were Sir Robert Wood and Professor Wagner of the university, Alan Lubbock, Canon Stopford, and H.M.I.s Hearley and Sheppard. The Principal was highly praised, especially for his discernment in recruiting staff, and the students, too, were highly commended. It was recommended that three extra tutors should be appointed. After commenting on the need for the new appointments to be made, if possible, of a headmaster of a secondary modern school and a headmaster of a primary school, Ritchie concluded by saying that the college which had gone through exceedingly difficult times after the war was doing absolutely first-class work. The chief weakness was thought to be the out-of-date professional training offered the students. The staff whose main experience had been in grammar schools knew little about the newly-formed primary and secondary modern schools.

Following the inspection the Principal decided that each tutor should receive a copy of that part of the report which concerned his own work. He therefore cut up the report into its subject sections and pasted each section on to brown paper so that the tutur concerned would not be able to read what was written on the other side. However, it was soon discovered by the more resourceful members of staff that, by holding the sheets up to a strong light, it was quite possible to make out the print on the reverse side. Then, by putting together the information so acquired, the staff soon had a fair idea of the nature of the whole report.[2]

In July 1951 Herbert Jarman retired. He had joined the staff in 1911 and had been Vice-Principal since 1936. His academic versatility, deep professional integrity, and selfless devotion to the college were qualities which enriched the life of all colleagues and students with whom he worked. He retired to his Margate home, but maintained his contact with the college through the Winton Club. Guy Bowden, the chaplain, left the college at the same time to become a residentiary canon of Truro Cathedral. He had proved himself a first-class scholar, a most able and well-respected chaplain, and above all one who with his wife, Peggy, had entered fully into the whole life of the college. For the S.C.M. he had produced a number of plays, including 'Everyman', 'Zeal of Thy House', and 'The House of the Octopus'. Talented Winchester amateur actresses took part in his productions, among whom were Muriel Wilson and Crystal Holme.

Hugh Humphrey was appointed the new Vice-Principal. He had been a student at the College of St. Mark and St. John, Chelsea, and also at Cambridge and London Universities. During the war he had served in the R.N.V.R., rising to the rank of Lieutenant. His lecturing experience had been at Crewe and at Worcester Training Colleges. The new chaplain, Rev. H. P. Kingdon, formerly a scholar of Winchester College and of Corpus Christi College, Oxford, had for some years been Fellow, chaplain, and tutor of Exeter College, Oxford. He had also had parochial experience in the Bristol diocese, and from 1947 to 1949 was head of the Evangelical Churches Section of the Religious Affairs Branch of the Control Commission in Germany. At this time, too, Louis Grove was appointed to take charge of physics, a subject previously taught by Jarman, and, following the recommendations in the Inspectors' Report, a lecturer in education, F. R. James, and a lecturer in physical education, P. J. Chatters, joined the staff. J. F. C. Dicker left to take up a post at Kesteven Training College. Since 1946 he had been in charge of history and built up the college library. Dicker, a strong and colourful character, sometimes employed eccentric modes of teaching. 'One evening, presumably to give an extra touch of realism, he gave a lecture dressed up as Napoleon, after which he was placed in a "chariot" and coveyed along the terrace in front of the main building by an enthusiastic crowd of cheering students.'[3]

The H.M.I.'s report of the 1951 general inspection had praised the Principal's astuteness in appointing staff. During this period, 1946–58, the quality of work of the students steadily improved, due in part, no doubt, to the higher standards required by the Institute of Education, but due also to the work of a well-qualified, dedicated and accomplished group of tutors. Some were achieving success as authors: Guy Bowden's *The Dazzling Darkness: An Essay on the Experience of Prayer* was published by Longman's in 1950. Harry Blamires in the same year was beginning his distinguished record as an author with *Repair the Ruins*. When Wilfred Hodgkinson was appointed as art tutor in 1949 he had already written and illustrated *The Eloquent Silence* and *The Kingdom is a Garden*, both published by Hodder and Stoughton. The music of the college flourished under the care first of Dr. Cyril Fogwell (1946–1951) and from then under the direction of the cathedral organist, Alwyn Surplice. Both were creative musicians themselves, dynamic teachers, and insistent on high standards. Indeed, the music demands in chapel, in other choral and instrumental work, and within the curriculum course, called for an additional appointment, and in 1953 Monica Havard joined the staff as a part-time tutor of music. Sir George Dyson, Master of the Queen's Music, who lived in Winchester, gave an occasional lecture at the college. Choral scholarships at the cathedral were once again offered to King Alfred's College students. Barry Shipley replaced Mr. Dicker in 1952 as tutor in charge of history. He and Edmund Dobson (geography) were enthusiasts for taking the students on field excursions and devoted a great deal of their spare time to planning and leading such ventures. Douglas Bowers (1956) and Dennis Pass (1957) joined the physical education staff, and under Frank Blackburn's leadership the college's reputation in this field grew rapidly. *The Wintonian* during this period carries glowing reports of sports successes.

While Thomas Graty as tutor responsible for rural science led the students in the college's contribution to the national drive to 'Grow more for Britain', Wilfred Hodgkinson and Austin Laverty were extending the students' craft skills in workshops and studios scattered on and off the main site. John Duncan, H.M.I. and formerly head of Lankhills, conducted, as a part-time lecturer, a course for second-year students on 'Backwardness', and continued to make a regular contribution in this field until his retirement in 1957. Dr. Wilfred Wagland, another visiting tutor, lectured on health education and on occasion preached in the college chapel.

The governing body of such a college plays its most significant role in the appointment of the Principal. They were called on to do this in 1945 and 1958. Their chairman on the first occasion was Bishop Mervyn Haigh, and on the second Bishop Alwyn Williams. Spencer Leeson resigned as governor in 1949 to take up his duties as Bishop of Peterborough. His association with the college dated back to 1925. He had held office as honorary secretary and as chairman of the executive committee, and had even assumed both roles simultaneously at the critical time of Dickinson's appointment. His early role of secretary was when he was an assistant master at Winchester and later after his return as headmaster. Apart from his academic distinction he had the administrative experience of holding office as Private Secretary to the Parliamentary Secretary and the Permanent Secretary of the Board of Education. He had generously offered meeting facilities at Winchester College for the Winton Club during the war. He was invited to preach the sermon during the service in the cathedral, June 1949, to mark the centenary of the founding of the college. Plans to hold the centenary celebrations in 1940 had been set aside because of the war. He had chaired most of the meetings of governors and kept in touch with the Principal during the army occupation of the college. At the end of the war he had been most active in getting the college on its feet again, in dealing with the Army, the Board of Education, the Central Council for Church Training Colleges, in supervising the change of Principals, and in securing additional facilities, among them West Hayes, for the growing college. Walter Oakeshott succeeded him as chairman of the executive committee. He, too, had served previously as honorary secretary. In 1954 he resigned to take up his new post as rector of Lincoln College, Oxford, but he still maintains his interest in King Alfred's, where periodically he returns to lecture.

The Principal and staff of the college were particularly represented on the governing body by their nominee, Alan Rannie, the former owner of West Hayes. Arthur Edmonds, twice mayor of Winchester, continued in his long service as honorary treasurer at a time when critically large sums of money, such as £16,000 for the kitchen extensions, had to be found to meet Ministry requirements. In 1953 Dr. K. B. Hutton, who had followed Eric James as honorary secretary, was appointed as the first headmaster of the new secondary technical school at Hatfield. His place on the governing body was taken by Kenneth Kettle, also a Winchester College don. In 1958 Desmond Lee, who had succeeded Oakeshott as headmaster of Winchester College, became chairman of the executive committee. It was he and Kenneth Kettle, as honorary secretary, who had to steer governing body and college through another crisis.

Major Expansion Ahead

The school leaving age had been raised from 14 to 15 in 1947. This and the increase in birth-rate caused the school population steadily to rise in the late 1940s and 1950s, and as recruitment to the profession remained buoyant the government at long last acted by extending the teacher-training course from two to three years. On 6 June 1957 an announcement was made that new entrants to teacher-training in September 1960 would undertake a three-year course. This measure, the greater number of children staying on at school beyond the statutory age, and the great number of women leaving the teaching profession to marry or to start a family, called for a massive increase in the number of teachers required. On 25 October 1958, the following news item appeared in the *Hampshire Chronicle*:

> If the County Council's Finance Committee approve, representations are to be made to the Minister of Education for the provision of a new teacher training college

in Hampshire. The Further Education Committee have said that Winchester would be an eminently suitable area for the erection of such a college.

The need for additional facilities follows the assessment that 12,000 additional teachers will be needed by 1962, and in the Ministry view 9,000 places would be found by expanding existing colleges and 3,000 by new colleges.

But when this announcement appeared Principal Dickinson was no longer alive to read it. On 14 October, his body was recovered from the River Itchen at Shawford, three miles south of Winchester. The Winchester County Coroner recorded a verdict of suicide while the balance of his mind was disturbed. The coroner heard from the Principal's wife of the anxieties her husband had felt over the future expansion of the college. He had worried about the limitations of the site and the buildings. He had wondered, too, whether it was possible for two training colleges to exist together in Winchester. The Principal was last seen at the college at 10 a.m. on 14 October. The police were alerted when later that afternoon a boy fishing at Twyford Locks found a raincoat and a hat on the river bank. The coat was folded and the hat was on top. On lifting the hat he found a wallet, a diary, and a wristwatch underneath. Inside the wallet was a driving licence bearing the owner's name.

A memorial service was held in the cathedral on 22 November 1958. Friends, colleagues, former and present students filled the cathedral: the bishop asked those gathered to give thanks for the life of a deeply dedicated College Principal and a great and active churchman.

The governors had met in June 1958 and had decided that the college, if it was to survive, would have to undergo a programme of major expansion. New dining hall and kitchen premises would have to be built: those existing premises might be used for a library and tutorial rooms. There was also urgent need for additional residential accommodation. The size of the college for September 1958 was to be 235 students. The Principal, in reply to the governors' inquiry regarding the proper size of the college when running the three-year course, put the figure at about 250 students. On 9 October the executive committee had met to view the site of the college, after which, subject to the approval of the governing body, they agreed on a plan of expansion to be submitted to the Ministry of Education. Following the Principal's death the full governing body met on 25 October in St. Grimbald's Court. The executive committee was instructed to forward plans to the Ministry for a college of 400–500 men students, to purchase land necessary for this project, and to instruct the architect, Mr. Walter Chapman, to make detailed drawings. The last but most important task laid on them was to appoint a new Principal. This task they completed on 29 December 1958, when John Arthur Stripe, Deputy Principal and Warden of Residence of St. Luke's College, Exeter, was appointed the eighth Principal of King Alfred's College.

CHAPTER EIGHT

THE TRANSFORMING YEARS (1958-1980)

Mixing and Growing (1958-1967)

THERE HAD BEEN no great enthusiasm for admitting women students to the college, but with the death of the Principal, the impending retirement of Tom Atkinson, and with the executive committee of the governing body having to respond rapidly and positively to the crucial questions about the college's development, posed by both the Ministry of Education and the Central Council for Church Training Colleges, the decision was made that the college should become mixed as from September 1960. This decision was warmly endorsed by Hugh Humphrey who, on Dickinson's death, had been appointed Acting Principal. Sir Desmond Lee, chairman of the executive committee, issued to each governor a statement dated 8 December 1958, which included the following:

> The most important and difficult decision has been to accept the Ministry's view that the College should in the future accept 150 women students as part of the total of 400. But national policy and the pattern of Church training colleges throughout the country suggest that this is the right course. It is now known that there will not be a L.E.A. college in the area, which strengthens the case for admitting some women, and the Vice Principal and his colleagues believe that the future lies with mixed colleges. It seems therefore that the decision is both right and inevitable, and it has the full support of Mr. Harvey, the Secretary of the Council of Church Training Colleges . . .

Kenneth Kettle, as honorary secretary to the governing body, wrote to each member of the academic staff setting out the plans for expansion, the admission of women students, and the particular stress, and consequently workshop and laboratory provision, which was to be given to handicraft and science. Building was due to start during 1959. His letter was sent on 22 December 1958. A week later John Stripe was appointed Principal. From that moment, although he did not take up his office until the beginning of the Trinity term 1959, he was intimately involved in the building programme, the appointment of staff, and the new curriculum planning.

The main problem confronting the new Principal was making provision for the women students, appointing women to the staff as part of that provision, building new teaching and residential accommodation for a college that was nearly doubling in size, and, with the governors, having settled on building a new chapel, having to decide what to do with the old one.

An intensive building operation began on the main site in 1959. Land was bought from the hospital on which Alwyn Hall, a men's hostel for 115 students and two tutors, was erected. To the south of St. James's a women's hostel, St. Elizabeth's, was built for 54 students. The resident students from St. James's, St. Grimbald's, and the main building were to move to Alwyn Hall. The library was moved to the main building from St. Grimbald's in 1962, and a further five study bedrooms built in the available space over the present common room. The Nissen hut used for pottery, which had stood on the Principal's lawn, was demolished, and a new dining hall and kitchens started in January 1961 and completed a year later. The corrugated iron hut to the west of the chapel which had contained three classrooms separated by sliding folding partitions was demolished, and on that site and beyond was built the new science and handicraft teaching accommodation, which came into use in September 1963. The new chapel was erected south of this building. Begun in May 1963, it was completed and dedicated on 2 July 1964. There was a move to demolish the old chapel and to build on its site, but the Winton Club protested and the area was divided by an internal wall; to the west was a quiet room preserving the memorial tablets to those former students who had died in the two world wars, and to the east a small chapel with the altar, the organ, the memorial seats and windows. Holm Lodge was adapted for 11 resident students and the new bachelor Principal. An extension to the east of the 1862 building served as the Principal's office and administration centre on the first floor and as a new senior common room on the ground floor. In 1962 a new pavilion was completed at Bar End, and in 1963 permission was given for a licensed bar to be opened there, the first on a K.A.C. site.

These years not only saw the rapid increase in residential accommodation to meet the needs of a mixed expanding college, but also a sharp increase in the number of day students and students in lodgings. The close-knit small, entirely residential, community was no more. In 1957, of the 196 students, 14 of whom were taking one-year courses, 187 were resident. In 1959 of the 279 students, 146 were in residence, 87 were in approved lodgings, and 46 were day students. By 1965 of the 688 students, 296 were resident, 195 in approved lodgings, and 197 day students. This year there were 119 students on the two-year shortened certificate course for mature students, one of the largest courses of its kind in the country. They were nearly all day students. The pressure on college residential accommodation and the greatly increased number of mature students changed the nature of the college in a decisive way. Neither the students in lodgings nor the day students—and together they numbered more than half the college—found it so easy to attend morning and evening chapel, to sit with the resident students at all the usual meals, nor to participate as fully in the college societies and sporting events. Dorothy Smithson's appointment in 1963 as Warden of Students in Lodgings success-fully helped to strengthen part of the college community that was becoming fragmented. The Principal noticed the considerable improvement in the welfare of the students in lodgings, and he also noticed the relief expressed by the city landladies in having a pattern of putting first-year students in residence; in their second year they were put in lodgings in the city; in their last year they were back in college residence. Succeeding generations of students have been comfortably lodged by some of those same landladies whom Miss Smithson first persuaded to open their doors to K.A.C. students.

Tom Atkinson retired in 1959 after 32 years' service to the college. Steve Denny took his place as principal lecturer in education. Also appointed at this time were Messrs. Alves, Minty, Venables, and Venning. The appointment of the first full-time women tutors was made in the following year with Robina Macintyre, Vice-Principal, Jennifer Nias, and Pat Pemberton. With them were appointed Messrs. Foyster, Meredith, Mundy, and Watkins. Thus a greatly increased staff arrived in September 1960 at a college which was in the throes of a massive building programme. The expected new premises were incomplete, the main building itself was being converted, and the number of students who had to be catered for had leapt to 391, 53 of whom were the first women students admitted to the college. Teaching space was found at West Hayes in the common room and in the corrugated hut and, by permission of the County, at St. Thomas's school. By September 1960 St. Elizabeth's was not ready to receive the women students for whom emergency lodgings were found in the city and with members of staff. By November half the rooms at St. Elizabeth's were ready to receive the first group of women, and by January 1961 the second group moved in. Accommodation was also provided for two women tutors: Miss Macintyre and Miss Pemberton stood guard. The honour of the women students was safeguarded by more than their virtue. Miss Macintyre recalls how from surprising points of vantage she peppered with pellets from her air-gun male bottoms as she caught them in her sights climbing in or out of ground-floor women's study-bedrooms.

The Ministry of Education pressed the governors in 1960 to revise the ratio of men to women, urging them to accept 200 men and 200 women. The governors, believing that such arrangements would drastically affect staffing, proposed 240 men and 180 women, and this the Ministry agreed. Among the newly-appointed women to the governing body were Mrs. Dowdswell, Miss Roxburgh, and Miss Wayment, and in 1960 the college staff nominated Mrs. Sykes as their representative governor. Miss Roxburgh, headmistress of the Winchester High School for Girls, was elected to the executive committee.

The chairman of governors at the critical time of expansion in the early 1960s was Bishop Alwyn Williams. In the 1950s he had given almost daily support to Principal Dickinson in a worrying situation that had developed with the college chaplain. In the years immediately preceding his retirement he was to see the college grow and flourish. It was with a deep sense of gratitude that the largest hostel was named after him. In 1964 it was Bishop Falkner Allison who, as Bishop of Winchester and chairman of governors, dedicated the new chapel. Sir Desmond Lee, as Spencer Leeson nearly twenty years earlier, had led the executive committee with firmness and foresight and, in that precarious period when the college was without a Principal, had committed the college to a path of expansion which helped to ensure its survival. Reggie Harvey, the Secretary of the Council for Church Training Colleges, was at this time a regular visitor. In 1963 he told the executive committee that the college might be asked to expand to 800 'with agreed overcrowding to 1,000'. The Ministry of Education seemed likely to favour such a development. The first phase of the expansion had been undertaken with 75 per cent. of the capital expenditure being met by the government and 25 per cent. by the Central Board of Finance of the Church of England. The C.B.F. had raised a multi-million loan to support the expansion of the Church of England training colleges and, in addition, to found two new ones: St. Martin's, Lancaster, and Christ Church, Canterbury. When the governors began in 1963 to plan for a college of at least 800 there was an assumption that the C.B.F. would be able and willing to support substantially the voluntary share of capital costs which in 1966 was reduced from 25 per cent. to 20 per cent. Plans for a theatre, an additional dining hall, a large three-storey Students' Union building, a major new lecturing block, and further adaptations to the main building and the Great Hall were put in hand.

1963 was the year of the Robbins Report[1] and the Newsom Report.[2] Robbins advocated raising the status of teacher-training colleges by linking them academically and administratively more closely with the universities, which as well as the three-year concurrent certificate course would validate a four-year B.Ed. degree. The colleges henceforth would be dignified with the name 'college of education'. Independent governing bodies would be financed by earmarked grants made by a single Grants Commission. The Newsom Report recommended that the first year of full-time compulsory education up to the age of 16 should be 1969-70. This would call for a substantial addition to the teaching force. Both Reports heralded for the colleges curriculum and expansion planning. And so it was that the governors planned for a college of 800 students 'with agreed overcrowding to 1000'. This last phrase was an encouragement from government for K.A.C., and indeed many other colleges, to increase their student numbers without increasing teaching, residential, or communal accommodation, although a pro rata increase of staffing was allowed. Nationally notorious Box-and-Cox schemes were developed. At Winchester the Principal asked Harry Blamires and Harry Pratt to devise a scheme for admitting more students than the permitted accommodation provided for, so that with the least disturbance to the student's course the maximum use might be made of the college facilities. The result was the unique and ingenious Extra Entry Scheme.

The strain of expansion was beginning to tell. The bursar, Mr. Beecroft, fell ill; Mr. Simms, the accountant, took on additonal duties. In September 1963 Arnold Corkhill was appointed Chief Administrative Officer. There were many major matters calling for his attention: the completion of the first building phase in 1964; the acquisition from Mr. Rannie in 1964 of West Hayes field; the building of the P.E. lecture room in 1965; and the purchase of Medecroft in 1965. He was also concerned with new staff contracts for the many additional members who were being appointed. In 1965 Hugh Humphrey was appointed Principal of Bedford College of Education. His place as Vice-Principal was taken by Martial Rose, senior tutor and head of the Education Department, Bretton Hall, Yorkshire.

At this time the Principal himself was not well, and although he fulfilled his commitments to the utmost of his ability he began to rely more and more on his two Vice-Principals. By the Christmas of 1966 it was clear that he was very seriously ill. In February 1967 the governors gave full executive powers to Mr. Rose to administer the college during the Principal's absence. On 4 May, Ascension Day, John Stripe died at Holm Lodge. Ann Probert, the college matron, had looked after him through a long distressing illness; Christopher Ludlow, the college chaplain, had been devoted in his attendance. The college was in the grip of a great sorrow. John Stripe had brought a great healing to the college after the shock and sense of unease at Dickinson's death. He had been positive, cheerful, vigorous in welcoming the women staff and students, in making clear-sighted plans for development, in his spiritual and academic leadership. Apart from the very first Principalship, Mr. Stripe's of eight years was the shortest. Yet the college grew nearly three-fold in that time: its prestige grew at an even greater rate. At the memorial service held in Winchester Cathedral colleagues, friends, past and present students filled the nave. The address was given by Sir Desmond Lee; the Acting Principal read the lesson. John Arthur Stripe was much loved and will be long and affectionately remembered. His successor as Principal was Martial Rose.

Towards a College of Higher Education (1967–1972)

The Robbins Report (1963) had noted with regret that the links that had been established between the universities and the training colleges in the wake of the McNair Report had not been as beneficial to the training colleges as had been hoped. If teaching were to become an all-graduate profession and if, as the first move towards this goal, the establishing within the colleges of four-year B.Ed. degree courses validated by the universities were successfully accomplished, academic and administrative responsibility should then go hand in hand. The colleges, related federally to the School of Education of a University, should be given independent governing bodies. Although the administrative and financial control of teacher-training advocated by Robbins was not implemented, there nevertheless was a national move to revise the instruments and articles of colleges of education. The move was considerably accelerated by the publication of the Weaver Report[3] (1966) which made recommendations relating to college government, administrative and financial control, and the composition of a college's academic board. As an extension of the Robbins thinking Weaver, among other major recommendations for change, sought to secure for the academic staff of an institution of higher education the ultimate responsibility for the academic direction that institution might take. In addition the clerk to the governors was to be the senior administrative officer of the college and no longer, as in the case of L.E.A. colleges, the Chief Education Officer or his representative or, as in the case of the voluntary colleges, an elected governor.

The main repercussions on the governing body of King Alfred's College were the reduction of the main body from 30 to about twenty, the demise of the executive committee, and the appointment of Arnold Corkhill, the college's Senior Administrative Officer, as clerk to the governors. A standing committee without executive powers was established to scrutinise the estimates for the year ahead and the statement of accounts for the year just completed. For the first time the Principal instead of attending a governors' meeting by invitation was now an ex-officio governor himself. In addition the newly-formed Academic Board was allowed two representative members on the governing body. Apart from the nine Church places, six of which were required to be lay, representatives were also required from the L.E.A. and the University of Southampton. In this the Instrument of Government formalised what had long been practised.

The new Instrument was sealed in 1967, but significant amendments were soon to follow. The first elected members of the Academic Board were Guy Barnes, the Vice-Principal, and Harry Blamires. Had the Vice-Principal not been so elected he might have been placed in an invidious position in being called upon to act for the Principal without being fully conversant with the governors' deliberations. It was therefore agreed, and the Instrument so altered, that the Vice-Principal should become an ex-officio governor. The students, too, were anxious to secure representation, and on 12 February 1969 the Student Union president, Ned Foster, and Leslie Moores met the governors to put their case which the Principal had endorsed. The first stage was an invitation for two students to attend the meetings of governors. In 1970 the student president and vice-president, Alastair Snow and Rosemary Parsley, became the first student governors of the college. It was from this time that the constitution of the Student Union required the approval of the governing body, and it was also from this time that the Student Union *per capita* fee, which in 1970 was £3, was fixed by the governing body.

In 1968 Sir Desmond Lee's place as vice-chairman of governors was taken by the new headmaster of Winchester College, John Thorn. In 1971 Professor Pedley replaced Professor Wagner and Dr. Emmerson replaced Mr. Rushby as representatives of the University of Southampton. Jeffrey Aldam, the recently-appointed Chief Education Officer for Hampshire, replaced Robert Marsh. The Bishop of Winchester, Canon Wedderspoon, and Canon Manship were the clerics on the governing body. With other lay members, staff and students, the college was well poised at its highest administrative level to take the critical decisions that were to challenge it for the rest of the decade. With the post-Weaver governing body the old and significant roles of honorary treasurer and honorary secretary which had persisted since the foundation of the college in 1840 were no longer required. As an interim measure Arthur Edmonds, and after his retirement (1972), John Knight, continued to hold regular discussions with the administrative officers; but after Mr. Knight's resignation in 1973 the governors asked Robin Bishop to be the governor to take a particular interest in the college's financial concerns. Kenneth Kettle, who had acted as honorary secretary since 1953, relinquished the minute-keeping to the new clerk, but remained, as governor, the Principal's constant and valued counsellor. The clerk to the governing body, Arnold Corkhill, who had helped guide the prodigious development of the college since his appointment as Senior Administrative Officer in 1963, died suddenly in December 1972. In those crowded nine years his diligence, foresight, administrative skill and experience had been crucial factors in the college's development. His patience and kindliness in tutoring a raw Principal in the years following Mr. Stripe's death were deeply appreciated. In material terms Corkhill should perhaps be remembered most for his supervision of a major expansion within the college and as great an expansion off-site, with a bold sortie into the property market.

Student numbers for 1971-72 had reached 999, one short of that 1,000 for which overcrowding 'might be agreed'. For the two years 1966-68, while extensive building preparations were continuing on the main site, Wellington House was leased to the college. It is the very large house standing at the corner of Canon Street and Kingsgate Street, opposite the *Wykeham Arms*. Here for two years the Education Department had its headquarters and did its teaching. A special time-table was devised to allow students time to walk the distance from the main site and back, and each student in the college had to make many such regular journeys. 'Coffee breaks' were often taken at the *Wykeham Arms*. Both Vice-Principals had offices and taught in Wellington House. Miss Macintyre was then also in charge of the education programme.

Medecroft, the former preparatory section of St. Swithun's school, set in a 2½-acre site in Sparkford Road, was converted to become the art and design centre in 1966, and in 1967-68 a Vice-Principal's house, Beech Glade, was built in the grounds. Guy Barnes, appointed in 1968 on Miss Macintyre's retirement, was its first inhabitant. The *Carfax* hotel, now demolished, which stood near the station at the corner of Sussex Street and City Road, was leased as a hostel for 45 students in 1966. Lois Haynes was the warden responsible for this rather dilapidated residence, which after four years the students were loth to leave. A singular feature of the Carfax was a large windowless basement peculiarly fitted to the cellar-like entertainments in vogue with the young. Three other properties were leased for residence: 1 Christchurch Road, named Spicer Lodge—it was a city property and Stanley Spicer was then mayor of Winchester (1969); 6 St. James's Lane, also a city property, which became known as The Crescent; and St. Faith's, which had been the *St. Cross* hotel, at the corner of Barnes Close and St. Cross Road.

The most significant building development off-site was the purchase of Winchester property with D.E.S. approval and support. No. 4 Christchurch

Road (Macintyre Lodge) was bought and converted to a hostel in 1968. In fairly rapid succession the following properties were purchased and converted: 94 Christchurch Road (Allison Lodge); Gifford House; 14 Christchurch Road (Cotswold); 86 Christchurch Road (Edmonds Lodge); 78 Christchurch Road (Denstone). These were all large freehold properties, set in spacious grounds, providing shared accommodation for between 20 and 35 students. Wardens' accommodation was provided in each of these hostels. Former students, teaching locally, were among the early wardens of these hostels.

Development on the main site reflected the academic direction the college was taking. The provision of the Medecroft premises for the art and craft department, together with the addition of two purpose-built art studios, freed a whole floor in what later came to be called the Herbert Jarman Building for additional science laboratories. The Wessex Closed Circuit Television Consortium, serving originally four colleges of education, Salisbury, Southampton, Weymouth, and Winchester, had its headquarters in a specially designed single-storey building which contained the college's own television studio. In 1968 the new main teaching block was completed and used mainly for education and French. This was named the Tom Atkinson Building. There was no longer any need to renew the lease on Wellington House, and the daily trek of hundreds of students up and down St. James's Lane and Canon Street came to an end. At this time, too, the Student Union building was completed and the Principal and the president of the Students' Union celebrated with the first drinks pulled at the bar. The *John Stripe* theatre was officially opened by Sir Alec Clegg on 31 October 1969. Aristophanes' *Thesmophoriazusae* or *Ladies' Day,* presented by the staff—and about 35 were involved—and produced by the Principal, was one of the first plays to be performed in the new theatre. The John Stripe Memorial Fund had already assisted students in their foreign travel; now the theatre, another deep interest of the former Principal, was to offer the widest selection of plays and musicals by students and by visiting professional companies to the college and to the city.

In 1967 in response to a request from the Basingstoke teachers' associations the college looked into the possibility of setting up an outpost for mature students in Basingstoke. Hampshire L.E.A. was supportive and with the agreement of the Principal of Basingstoke Technical College, whose premises were at first used for the outpost, the enterprise got under way in September 1968. In 1969 the former Civil Defence headquarters were skilfully converted to form the Basingstoke Outpost of King Alfred's College. It was envisaged that the outpost would recruit about 25 students annually for the three-year certificate course. There were nine yearly intakes of about this number before the outpost closed. The average age of the first intake was 35 years. A few students in the last years of the outpost continued into a fourth year at Winchester to qualify for their B.Ed. The programme for the outpost had to be worked out entirely afresh from that obtaining at the main college. Hours of attendance were from 9.30 a.m. to 3.30 p.m. to take account of the students' school-aged children; one half-day a week throughout the training period was spent in a Basingstoke school; one day a week was spent at the parent college. Frank Carswell acted as tutor in charge and helped to make a great success of a thoroughly worthwhile venture.

In the early 1960s the college had been most generously supported in meeting its 25 per cent. of capital expenditure by contributions from the Central Board of Finance. When the expansion target moved from 400 to 800 students in 1963, Reggie Harvey had encouraged the college along this road without securing explicit commitment for financial support from the C.B.F. Expansion went ahead and one of the new Principal's tasks in 1967 was to find ways of paying the bills. Through Corkhill's accountancy skill, the increasing conference business, and the good offices of Canon James Robertson, the new general secretary of the Church of England Colleges of Education, a crisis was narrowly avoided. Canon Robertson secured from the C.B.F. sufficient financial support to tide the college over this difficult period. But a useful lesson had been learned. From this point the college had to look to its own resources.

At this time the college's physical resources made provision for something over 800 students. That the 'overcrowding' did not create greater difficulties for a college of just under a 1,000 was due to the founding of the outpost which catered for 75 students, and the inception of the Extra Entry Scheme in 1969 which was to cater for a further 125 students. The basis of this scheme was that once every three years in January an additional cohort of students should be admitted to a limited range of main subjects. These students would be taught in college, while the other groups of students were in schools on their teaching practice. When these students returned from teaching practice to be taught in college, the extra entry students went on school practice. The use of Guernsey and Jersey schools for practice purposes greatly facilitated the residential problems inherent in such a scheme. The scheme was sufficiently successful for it to recruit again in 1972, but under the title January Entry. The students were not endeared to being called 'Extra'. Their resilience, independence, and forthrightness brought an unexpected richness to college life.

In 1968 the college was among the first to offer within a three-year certificate or a four-year B.Ed. course a training for students who wished to teach educationally subnormal children. In 1971 15 teachers, so qualified, secured posts in either E.S.N.(M) or E.S.N.(S) schools. The staff under Peter Holden's leadership then went on to offer a one-year full-time diploma in special education, validated by the University of Southampton. The first group of serving teachers completed this course in 1972. The strengthening of staffing and the success of the college's work in this field, coupled with the growing number of initial and in-service K.A.C. trained students in special education, contributed to the later and extremely significant foundation of the Medecroft Opportunity Centre.

Other notable developments were the first offering of the one-year post-graduate certificate course in 1971, and the first in-service B.Ed. course in 1972. Both courses were validated by the University of Southampton. It had proved a struggle to secure validation and there had been what appeared to be unnecessary delay in mounting the B.Ed. for serving teachers, which comprised a part-time element followed by a year's full-time study. On the whole, however, relationships with the university were friendly and constructive. The B.Ed. for the initial teacher education course comprised education, main subject, and middle component. This last element was peculiar to the Southampton B.Ed. It required students from different main subject disciplines to form a group of about five, to choose a topic of current significance, and to contribute to the study of this topic both corporately and individually. This type of study brought serious problems of group dynamics and assessment, but the general response of students, staff, and examiners was enthusiastic. In 1969 11 college students were awarded the degree. In 1978 the last year a group of K.A.C. students entered, 122 received the degree, four securing 1st class awards. In all, between 1969 and 1978, about 540 students qualified for this four-year degree.

The college and the university had worked together closely and on the whole harmoniously in planning, together with the other colleges of this institute, the curriculum for the four-year B.Ed. course. The fourth year of the course contained no school experience, and a student completing the course and taking up a teaching post would have last been teaching children 18 months previously. This pattern of training raised doubts in college and in the teaching profession generally. The emphasis on degree work had led in the colleges generally to appointment of staff with high academic qualifications, but perhaps lacking any, or at least recent, experience of teaching in infant or primary schools, for which a large number of students were being trained. In 1967 the Plowden Report[4] had been critical of the insufficient experience of some college lecturers in the primary field, and had recommended a full-scale enquiry into teacher-training. This move gathered momentum as the employment prospects of the greatly increased number of newly-trained teachers began to wane. Local educational authorities and head-teachers were able to select with increasing discrimination and became critical of the training institutions in failing to turn out students who could teach the basic skills of reading and number in the classroom. Under pressure from the profession a Select Committee of the House of Commons was formed in 1969 to investigate the state of teacher-training. Members of the Committee visited the area, and the Principal was invited to give evidence. Members were keen to question the relationship between the colleges and the university and to probe university attitudes of tutelage or condescension. In February 1970 Edward Short, who was then Secretary of State for Education, initiated his A.T.O. Enquiry which called for an examination of the balance of elements within teacher-training courses, of the possibility of new patterns of training, of whether a common pattern was appropriate regardless of the age-range to be taught. Among other issues the enquiry, seemingly casting doubt on the theoretical underpinning of three-year certificate and four-year B.Ed. course, questioned the adequacy of the teacher-training course in relation to practical teaching patterns. Southampton A.T.O. called for a detailed response from its colleges. In its reply to the A.T.O. the college set its plans for teacher education against a broader development which included a two-fold programme of diversification: degree level work in the arts and technical studies; and courses for students preparing themselves for various types of social work. This reponse which had been prepared by the Academic Board in March 1971 and considered by the governors before it was sent to the university, contained the following: 'The College would expect to cater for a total of 2,000 students, half of whom would enter the teaching profession'.

Alan Chapman, the architect, had even drawn up preliminary plans to meet such proposed expansion. Two main factors had encouraged the Academic Board to plan in such an ambitious way. One was the A.T.C.D.E. (The Association of Teachers in Colleges and Departments of Education) 1970 publication known as *The Red Book, Higher Education and the Preparation for Teaching—A Policy for Colleges of Education*; and the other was the general direction given to the discussion about the Church colleges at the Board of Education of the General Synod, the Council of Principals, and in particular the Standing Conference of 1970.

The A.T.C.D.E. *Red Book,* which had been studied closely by both Academic Board and governing body, encouraged the college to look forward to the time when there was no longer any teacher shortage, when many more candidates with two 'A' level qualifications would be seeking higher education, and when diversified college courses, validated by the universities, might help meet such a growing demand. The academic development of the colleges into the field of general arts degrees and into courses leading to qualifications for the 'caring services' was in line with the Robbins proposals. The challenge of a rapidly expanding teacher-training programme had been successfully met. The challenge of the 1970s was seen as that of diversification. The A.T.C.D.E. had confidence that the universities were the proper bodies to validate the new college degrees. Edwin Peirson, Principal of Worcester College and a member of the working party which had prepared the *Red Book,* had reservations. His college was the first of the colleges of education to approach C.N.A.A. (The Council for National Academic Awards) for validation of one of its courses.

In 1970 King Alfred's was one of the largest Church of England colleges of education. At this stage there was no hint in Church House, Westminster, that closures might be on their way. Far from it, colleges were expected to continue planning for expansion but within a diversified field. Certainly, regional collaboration between colleges was recommended. Canon Robertson held talks on this matter with the Salisbury and Winchester Principals. But it was clear that the larger colleges with the greater spread of programmes and staff would be the better placed for a major expansion through a variety of new non-teacher training courses. The Standing Conference of Church of England Colleges in 1970 faced some of the religious, institutional and constitutional issues of a Church college of education becoming a Church college of higher education. The conference was feeling towards what James Robertson was later to call the 'Locus' of the colleges. In the Church colleges of education 'Evidence to the James Committee of Enquiry' in 1971, two alternatives were posed, A and B, as to the wisest 'Locus' of the colleges for the future.

A.   That the natural evolutionary point for most colleges would be the university to which they were affiliated as members of an Institute of Education, or a new university as yet without ATO/Institute status.

B.   That it would be possible to see a large number of colleges (voluntary or other) federated into a national, autonomous institution with degree awarding status and with a curriculum in higher education, rooted in teaching, but offering a breadth in higher education complementary to that which is at present distinctive of the university as we know it.

The alternative to university validation was seen not as the C.N.A.A., but as a new federation of mainly voluntary diversified institutions. The James Report did indeed propose as a validating body for the projected B.A.(Ed.), neither the universities nor C.N.A.A., but the National Council for Teacher Education and Training. But neither was to serve. The vision of B was, alas! to pass away because each of the Church colleges was too engrossed with its immediate and complex negotiations with its own university, concerning the next stage of development, to give to B the consideration it deserved.

The James Report[5] was published early in 1972. Its proposals were met with little enthusiasm. The pattern of training recommended was based on three cycles: a three-year degree course or a two-year course leading to a Diploma of Higher Education, followed by cycle two, a further year in a training institution including school experience and the subsequent year in a school, but not teaching full-time, as a licensed teacher. At the end of this period the student would qualify for a B.A.(Ed.). The third cycle concerned itself with in-service. In the Note of Extension to the Report, however, a four-year course of education and training for all was advocated. In its submission to James the A.T.C.D.E., sensing that a four-year course for all might have been beyond the government's means as well as not meeting the wishes of those students who required a shorter course, suggested a three-year pass B.Ed. for candidates entering with two 'A' level qualifications. When the government White Paper *Education: A Framework for Expansion* was issued in December 1972, it made the three-year B.Ed. the cornerstone of its teacher-training proposals. There was advocacy also for the Dip.H.E., for Nursery Education, which was already developing at Winchester, and for a sustained and more ambitious programme for induction and in-service. There had been growing resentment among teachers that with restricted employment prospects it was wiser to improve in-service opportunities rather than extend to four years the initial training programme.

The greatest impact of the White Paper, however, was not on curricula but on institutions. A major reduction of teacher-training was required by 1981. The falling birthrate and the recent national expansion of teacher education was leading to a substantial oversupply of teachers. It was the government's plan to locate teacher-training in large diversified institutions of higher education such as universities or polytechnics so that, according to national demand, the teacher-training courses might wax or wane without drastic consequences to the institutions themselves. The future of small colleges of education seemed very uncertain. To survive as a free-standing college with less than 1,000 students seemed doubtful. Even the largest colleges if they were situated in a city area near a polytechnic or university seemed almost destined to merge with one or the other. Within the White Paper, however, there were indications that mergers with polytechnics might be viewed with more favour than those proposed with universities. Possibilities were opened up for colleges of education to merge with each other or with colleges of further education. But there was not the slightest doubt that the institutional reorganisaion consequent upon the White Paper would lead to many colleges closing altogether. For King Alfred's College the rest of the decade was concentrated on ensuring that it would not be one of those closing colleges.

Taking the Strain (1972–1980)

The eight years that followed the publication of the 1972 government White Paper, *Education: A Framework for Expansion,* were filled with intensive planning. There were meetings about mergers with the University of Southampton, with the Winchester School of Art, with the College of Sarum St. Michael, Salisbury. Governors met, groups of governors met, Academic Boards met, students met. There were crucial matters of validation to be settled; there were the workings of Regional Advisory Councils to be understood and complied with. All at a time when the college was steadily expanding. In each phase of expansion the college received the full support of its H.M.Is, Mary Gordon Fraser, Peter Cadenhead, and John Hampson, and also its D.E.S. Territorial Officers, Peter Lane, Peter Clarke and Vernon Pines. Indeed much expansion occurred at Winchester when little was happening elsewhere. Ken Heyes, who succeeded Corkhill as bursar, controlled the most efficient team, administrative and financial, which dealt with the day-to-day running, the vacation letting business, and the general expansion of the college.

The sports hall was completed in 1974 and the new squash courts in 1976. Also in 1976 the Medecroft Opportunity Centre was opened. It was a nursery school for handicapped children and their normal siblings, containing special facilities for the mothers to meet each other and also the professional staff concerned with their children. Hampshire County Council maintained the school and contributed generously to its building cost, but considerable funds were found from voluntary sources, including the college, which also provided the site. The new library was completed in 1977 and the alteration to bring the audio-visual aids section as an extension of the schools section was completed in 1979. Additional residential accommodation, Christchurch Lodge (formerly Christchurch vicarage), was purchased with D.E.S. support in 1977 and opened as a most attractive and conveniently-placed hostel for 20 students in 1978. The architect had skilfully created an unusual but inviting common room in the cellarage. In 1980 the conversion of the stables afforded accommodation for a further eight resident students.

Alan Rannie's West Hayes field on the corner of Chilbolton Avenue and Romsey Road, which he had sold to the college in 1963, had been intended for residence, but the D.E.S. was not disposed to support the college in building new hostels after the completion of Alwyn Hall. Governors agreed that the architect should draw up a plan for the development of this 3½-acre site for self-catering accommodation for day students. The plan also contained a warden's house and some limited accommodation for married students. The first phase for 10 students, two married couples, and the warden and his wife was completed in 1978, and the second stage for a further 10 students and two married couples in 1980. This undertaking was without D.E.S. financial help.

The reasons why the college was able to respond to the demands of change so successfully are perhaps too complex to be amenable to full analysis. A significant contributing factor was the confidence shown by the governors in the academic and institutional judgements of the recently-formed Academic Board. There was a general air of confidence shared by governors, staff, and the students that the college would survive the harrowing times ahead. The college had reached a viable size; for 1,000 students 700 resident places were available; the social, medical, and general welfare services available to the students were excellent compared with other colleges; the staff were mainly accommodated in single studies; and wherever possible teaching was undertaken in small groups. A personal tutorial system, variable in its efficacy according to the personalities involved, staff and students, proved moderately successful. Since 1970 the college chaplain had been appointed by the bishop for a limited term. His duties were primarily pastoral not academic. During this period the chaplains were Paul Ayling, Robert Teare, and Norman Boakes. Their work greatly strengthened the community as a whole. Their concern was not just for the chapel congregation but for the whole college corpus, in sickness and in health. In 1973 Judith Ware, as dean of students, maintained excellent relations with the students at a time when they, too, were restless about their own careers, let alone the future of the college. Dennis Fancett, who for long had helped students to find their first appointments in schools, was later to become, as co-ordinator of students' services, the leader of a team which included the chaplain, Helen Gray as college counsellor, Pru Phipps as warden of students in lodgings, and John Matthews as an assistant in the careers guidance field.

In 1968, 23 new members of staff had been appointed. Five years later, when the college had to face reorganisation issues, most of these colleagues had been promoted; they were secure in their jobs and as in fellowship they had experienced a major college expansion together, so in 1973 they were the better able to overcome with the rest of their colleagues the problems of reorganisation. Of the senior members of staff four retired in 1974: Frank Blackburn (1946), Ralph White (1948), Wilfred Hodgkinson (1949), and Bill Minty (1959). In 1976 Harry Blamires (1948), Edmund Dobson (1948), Christopher Ludlow (1957), and Michael Bullivant (1962) retired. In 1978 Thomas Graty (1946) and Donald Venning (1959) retired. Within four years therefore 10 of the most senior and long-serving members of staff were to leave. But they did not leave before the issue of validation of courses had been decided. Their professional integrity and deep sense of loyalty were of incalculable importance in helping to steer the college through its most difficult period. Their posts were mostly filled by internal appointments, thus creating a number of vacancies, most of which were filled by new, younger members of staff to teach on the diversified courses. Some of the staff who left were declared redundant, but redundancy under the Crombie terms was seen by many as a welcome incentive to early retirement.

Guy Barnes, Vice-Principal since 1968, left in 1972 to take up his post as Principal of St. Paul's College, Cheltenham. His had been a key role in the developing college. At his going the governors made a special point of thanking him not only for his college work but for the excellent relationship he had built up with the Hampshire teachers and also for the contribution he had made as a lay preacher to the Winchester churches. His place was taken by R. W. Breach, head of the college's history department since 1968. Dr. Grace Jones was appointed in his place. At the University of Southampton two important new appointments had been made, Professor Lawrence Gower as Vice-Chancellor, and Professor Robin Pedley as Professor of Education. During the autumn of 1972 friendly and constructive talks were held at the university at the highest level discussing the possible reorganisational problems that would be attendant on the publication of the White Paper. The personal involvement of the Vice-Chancellor was particularly appreciated by the affiliated colleges. When the White Paper was published at the end of the year the Vice-Chancellor and Professor Pedley were well prepared for its contents, and in January 1973 the Vice-Chancellor's response was a closely argued paper which represented his personal view but which by 26 January 1973 had already been approved by the University Academic Planning Committee. It proposed that La Sainte Union College and King Alfred's College should be merged with the university and that the work of the University Department of Education should cease on the university site, but continue, in a modified form, in the colleges.

When the Vice-Chancellor's proposal was put to the governing body on 1 February 1973 the Academic Board had already given it their cautious approval. Professor Pedley and Dr. Emmerson clarified for the governors the Vice-Chancellor's plans for the disposition of the teaching and research responsibilities within an enlarged and unified school of education. The governors welcomed the proposals and agreed to exploratory discussions. Meanwhile at the university a number of members of staff of the Department of Education felt that not only was their centre of operations threatened by a take-over by the library or another faculty, but with the likely fall in the numbers of post-graduate students their livelihood, too, was at stake. The colleges, on the other hand, were basking in the Vice-Chancellor's generous reference to them as 'prestigious' and as having staff whose standards were as high as those of the University Department. Such anxieties and comparisons were, however, short-lived. The chairman of the University Grants Committee, Sir Kenneth Berrill, was quick to voice his disapproval of the Vice-Chancellor's plan. His stated objection for King Alfred's and the university merging was the 12 miles between them.

The White Paper's advocacy of a three-year B.Ed. at pass level, but which included a professional qualification, posed colleges with the choice of submitting new degree proposals to their university or turning for their validation to C.N.A.A. In 1972 and early 1973 King Alfred's had no thought of approaching C.N.A.A. In September 1972 Harry Blamires had been appointed Dean of Degrees. With his planning team he had prepared new degree proposals for the expected diversified area of the college's work. The new general degree was based on three elements—main (50 per cent.), complementary (30 per cent.), and related pursuits (20 per cent.). This last element owed a great deal to experience derived from the Middle Component Studies within the Southampton B.Ed. The main and complementary studies were related by thematic links. Within this first proposal were the seeds of the first B.A. degrees which eventually secured validation. In the conclusion to the document was written:

> We would submit these proposals to the University of Southampton in the first instance in the light of the Academic Board's prior wish to strengthen our links with that University.

At the university an Inter-Faculty Collegiate Board was formed to scrutinise the colleges' degree proposals. It became apparent that although progress was swift in consideration of a three-year B.Ed., the university itself was not interested in offering a Dip.H.E., nor was it likely to validate a three-year Honours B.A. or B.Sc. in any of its affiliated colleges. Furthermore, the degrees would be discrimininated from the normal university degree. For instance, a university arts student would secure a B.A. Southampton University; an affiliated college student a B.A. (Collegiate) Southampton University. The tradition of the college was to stay with the university, the good and friendly relationships of governors and staff argued for staying with the university, the apparent progress in planning the three-year B.Ed. greatly strengthened the case. There were, however, other serious considerations.

Between the lines of the White Paper might be read the government's preference for colleges seeking validation from C.N.A.A. rather than the universities. The same inferences had been drawn from some of the questions put by the Select Committee of the House of Commons, the A.T.O. Enquiry, and also from Hugh Harding's speech at the York Conference in 1970.[6] The inference was that a public body (C.N.A.A.) had been set up to validate courses run by colleges in the public sector. Why should a college, especially one maintained by an L.E.A., a public sector body, closely identified as employer with the teachers in its authority, continue to seek validation in the university sector? Had not the polytechnics, on the public side of the binary line, fared well under the C.N.A.A. aegis? Furthermore, had not the L.E.A.s been less than enthusiastic in taking up the places afforded them on Boards, Committees, Working Parties set up by the University Schools of Education? And would not independence of the universities strengthen colleges, in meeting additional resource requirements? Many colleges were pondering these matters when Circular 7/73 was issued by government requiring L.E.A.s to let the D.E.S. have by the end of November 1973 an account of the development of higher education in the non-university sector, including the voluntary colleges, within their authorities.

Suddenly, and for the first time, the fates of the voluntary colleges seemed placed more in the hands of the L.E.A.s than the D.E.S. Where L.E.A.s had both voluntary and maintained colleges of education within their authority it was entirely understandable that they should be especially concerned for the future of their own rather than the voluntary colleges. In 1973 in Hampshire King Alfred's was the only college of education within the Authority's boundaries. Moreover, in June 1973, Hampshire made it clear that it wished the Winchester School of Art to initiate talks with King Alfred's College with the prospect of the two colleges merging. The School of Art had 200 full-time students, of whom between 130 and 140 were taking the Diploma in Art and Design. The validation of this award, as a B.A., was shortly to be undertaken by C.N.A.A.

It was against this background that the college's Academic Planning Committee invited the Vice-Chancellor to meet them to discuss problems of securing validation. The meeting took place in the Principal's study on 5 December 1973. The Vice-Chancellor could offer every co-operation with the inception of the three-year B.Ed.; he was also hopeful of progress being made towards the validation of a Collegiate Arts degree in the traditional academic subjects in that field, but he had to stress that within the university's arts faculty there was little enthusiasm for validating arts degrees whose main components were associated with the performing arts: there was no scope for the development of art and design, music, drama, film, movement and dance. There was also little likelihood of the college's sciences or design and technology being validated as a Collegiate B.Sc. The Vice-Chancellor on the one hand wished very much to maintain the university link with the college, on the other hand he told the Academic Planning Committee frankly that for certain courses the college would have to seek validation of C.N.A.A. Furthermore, he made it clear that at a time of scarce financial resources many university staff were anxious about over-committing themselves to the validation and examination procedures involved in the launching of diversified courses. The following day the Academic Planning Committee weighed up the case, taking into account the significance of the U.G.C.'s categorical rejection of the Vice-Chancellor's earlier proposal for merger, and resolved to recommend to the Academic Board that the college should seek validation from C.N.A.A. The Academic Board accepted the committee's recommendation, and on 10 December the Principal wrote to the Vice-Chancellor notifying him of the decision. The following day the Vice-Chancellor replied with his customary warmth and understanding, accepting the decision (Appendix XI).

In June 1973, when the college still hoped for continuing university validation, the Academic Board had submitted a paper to the governing body setting out their view of the future of the college. It contained proposals for diversification into B.A. degrees, with a Dip.H.E. forming the first two years of such studies, and also a B.Sc.(Technical). Within the education department provision was made for additional induction and in-service courses as well as introducing within the initial teacher-training courses nursery and first school studies in September 1973. The optimum size of such a diversified college was seen as 1,500. This paper, approved by the governors, was passed on to the L.E.A. for inclusion within their response to the D.E.S. to Circular 7/73. It was at this time that the governors were informed of the L.E.A.'s wish that negotiations should be initiated by the Winchester School of Art with a view of a possible merger with the college. In the event the L.E.A.'s initial response to Circular 7/73 was made on 18 December, when such negotiations were in hand. As by then the Academic Board had decided to seek validation from C.N.A.A., such a proposal was less fraught by the complication of different validating authorities. The L.E.A.'s submission to the D.E.S. was in every respect as helpful as the college could wish. It supported the college's case for a further 500 places; it appended the Academic Board's paper on the future of the college; and it spoke of the discussions between the college and the School of Art in these terms, '. . . if the administrative problems associated with a combined College could be overcome there might well be advantages for both establishments'.

Negotiations with the School of Art did not prove fruitful. There were meetings of Principals, Academic Board representatives, and governing body representatives. In March 1974 the governing body and Academic Board of the college were invited to a delightful social evening at the School of Art. In the event although the college's Academic Board and governing body agreed in principle to a merger, the School of Art Academic Board decided not to. Negotiations were broken off in March 1975. One of the reasons given was that as negotiations had been initiated by the D.E.S. for a merger between the College of Sarum St. Michael, Salisbury, and King Alfred's, the School of Art should bide its time.

On 13 August 1974 two meetings were held at college concerning a possible merger between the two Anglican colleges of Winchester and Salisbury. Hugh

Harding attended both meetings. In the morning he met with the Bishop of Southampton, acting for the K.A.C. governors, the Dean of Salisbury, who was chairman of governors of the College of Sarum St. Michael, the two colleges' H.M.I.s, the two Principals, and David Bungey representing the Church of England Board of Education. In the afternoon Hampshire and Wiltshire L.E.A. representatives also attended. Mr. Harding pointed out that it would be difficult for the Salisbury College to continue alone and that there would not be more than 750 teacher-training places in the two colleges by 1981. He advocated a merged college of about 1,500 students with a rationalisation of courses on the two sites. He said that the Department envisaged one management with one Principal. College lawyers should look at the trust deeds and the new trust deeds would need to be submitted to the Charity Commissioners. He thought that Sarum St. Michael would need to make the most sacrifices, but if a merger were not possible that college's future might be even more difficult. It was agreed therefore that the initiative for the merger should come from the College of Sarum St. Michael.

This was the first of many joint meetings involving governors, Principals, members of both Academic Boards, and the colleges' solicitors. On 18 July 1975 at a meeting of the Joint Negotiating Committee of the governing bodies of the two colleges agreement seemed near with regard to the composition of the governing body of the merged college: the York-Ripon model met with general approval. Because the diocese of Salisbury leased to the college a substantial part of its property within the Close, there was concern that Salisbury, in the event of a merger, should be able to maintain separate custodian trustee rights. This the Charity Commission discouraged. However, the two sides seemed near enough in agreement to endorse a recommendation to merge to both governing bodies. The Principal and the Deputy Principal for the merged college were provisionally appointed pending an endorsement by the Salisbury governors at their next meeting on 23 September. It was also agreed that a letter of intent to merge, signed by the two chairmen of governors, be sent to the D.E.S. immediately. The proviso to be included was that at leat 900 teacher education places should be allowed the merged college in 1981. That letter was duly sent (Appendix XII). When the Salisbury governors met on 23 September, they decided unanimously not to proceed further with the merger. The result was that they received an instruction from the D.E.S. for a nil intake of students for 1976. This was virtually an instruction to close the college. The Salisbury College which had come into being in 1841 so closely associated with the Winchester College might have continued in even closer association. Anxieties about property, about complying with a different validation system, about being swallowed up by a larger institution, about not having equal representative rights when management and academic issues were under discussion, were all readily understandable reasons for the withdrawal. But yet the pity of it!

The crisis for the Church Colleges came to a head in 1975 at the York Conference over which the Archbishop of York presided. It was apparent that there would be a sharp reduction in the number of Church colleges and that it behoved the Church at the centre to develop a coherent policy in advising government on the distribution of teacher education places allotted to its colleges. Within the region Culham and Salisbury were the colleges most immediately affected. To the east Chichester was encountering difficulties in its negotiations with Bognor College of Education, and to the west St. Matthias, Bristol, and St. Peter's, Saltley, were closing, and St. Luke's, the most prestigious of the Church colleges, was to become part of Exeter University. From 1975–77 the Winchester Principal acted as chairman of the Council of Principals of the Church of England colleges. For the year 1977–78 he was chairman of the Colleges Committee of the National Association of Teachers in Further and Higher Education and also chairman of the Central Register and Clearing House Committee. From 1975–78 he was a member of the C.N.A.A. Committee of Education. A proliferation of sub-committee work stemmed from the main responsibilities relating to the Board of Education, N.A.T.F.H.E., and C.N.A.A. In such a critical and changing time it was helpful for the college to be kept informed of many of the most important pending developments within Church, professional association, and academic circles.

The college's application to C.N.A.A. for the validation of all its courses, commencing in September 1975, was made on 14 December 1973. Geoffrey Nokes, the C.N.A.A. Senior Assistant Registrar for Education, promptly accepted an invitation to meet the Academic Board on 14 January 1974. At this meeting plans were laid for the many stages leading to the college's submission of its various courses to C.N.A.A. A set of preliminary documents about the college's management structure, staffing, and academic intentions, were sent to C.N.A.A. and considered in Winchester on 13 May 1974 by a visiting party led by Sir Derman Christophersen, chairman of the C.N.A.A. Committee of Education. Keith Thompson, Principal of Madeley College of Education, was a member of the visiting party. He arrived the previous day and took the opportunity of seeing the premises before the rest of the visitors arrived. He was later to chair the C.N.A.A. team considering the B.Ed. sub-mission. The May visit passed off successfully. The college was encouraged to make a full submission of its main courses, and by July 1974 had delivered submissions for the three-year certificate, the three-year B.Ed., the four-year B.Ed. Honours, and the P.G.C.E. Dates for the first major C.N.A.A. visit were fixed for 21, 22, 23 October 1974. There were to be 38 visitors in all. Many stayed at Holm Lodge and St. James's. The governors were invited to meet the visitors over drinks on the evening of 22 October. Dr. Edwin Kerr, C.N.A.A.'s Chief Officer, was present, and he indicated to the governors that considerable confidence had been expressed by the visitors in the quality of the staff. However, at the end of the following day Keith Thompson, Geoffrey Nokes, and David Francis met with the Principal in his study and told him that validation could not be granted. There were many matters to put right, among which the most important were the coherence of the course and its control structure. The C.N.A.A. representatives were taken to catch their various trains and the Principal was left to enter a packed senior common room which went deathly quiet on his entry and stayed that way until he had given the main gist of what he had just been told, promising a full written report in the morning. It was a crushing moment for the college.

The academic staff of the college were acutely aware of the pressure of time to secure validation. They were reluctant to return to the university and ask for validation to be continued for a further year. Yet the C.N.A.A. visitors at their own final meeting were of the opinion that the college should make a further submission for a 1976 start. The C.N.A.A. core group, however, swung back in feeling that the college should at least be given the opportunity of considering a re-submission for 1975. If the college were to take up this challenge the C.N.A.A. would not rule out a 1975 start for a B.Ed. ordinary degree. In this case the college would have to respond to meet the C.N.A.A. recommendations by the end of the Michaelmas term as Stage 1. Stage 2 and the C.N.A.A. decision might come at the end of the Lent term 1975.

During the visit the postgraduade certificate submission had received only cursory attention. The staff knew that the Diploma in Special Education and a radically revised in-service B.Ed. from that validated by the university would have to stand longer in the queue awaiting C.N.A.A. scrutiny; and it was clear that C.N.A.A. would not be much concerned with the diversified awards until the main professional courses had received approval. Bulmershe and Didsbury Colleges had already started their three- and four-year B.Ed. courses, validated by C.N.A.A., in September 1974. In feeling the pressure of time there was a sense of inter-college competition and a sense of humiliation in returning to the university cap in hand for them to say 'I told you so'. But, much more important, was a sense that, nationally, time was running out for the former colleges of education. Many closures were already threatened, many more were imminent. Survival as a free-standing college depended on success in diversification, and Winchester's first B.A. seemed a long way off even from C.N.A.A. consideration. In addition, since 1 April 1974, with the L.E.A. boundary reorganisation, Hampshire had at last its first maintained college of education, at Portsmouth. In the final response to Circular 7/73, Hampshire was also to speak for Portsmouth as well as for La Sainte Union College, Southampton.

In those October days following the C.N.A.A. visit the college resolved to respond to C.N.A.A. by December 1974. There were major problems to overcome. Staffing changes were required; leadership roles were altered; above all, clarification had to be achieved in the relationship between the two main elements of the B.Ed. course, professional studies and special subjects. The new role of course director was to introduce a new concept into college: control of resources, human and material, across a wide range of subjects. With speed, vigour, and care the college put together a much revised submission. A small group of tutors led by the Principal met at the C.N.A.A. offices on

17 December 1974, and to their delight, relief and surprise, approval was given in principle for a 1975 start for the certificate, B.Ed., and B.Ed. honours courses. Re-submissions were required in certain subject areas, but these would be completed by mid-February for a meeting planned with C.N.A.A. in March. The certificate was offered in only three subjects, design and technology, physical education, and physical science. It was offered in physical science only in 1976 and 1977 and then withdrawn completely. Candidates for the degree courses were required to have two 'A' level passes on entry. The college's previous record in this respect gave little cause for anxiety. And so with validation achieved, with recruitment buoyant, a new wave of confidence swept through the college.

C.N.A.A. approval for the other professional courses followed in due time, but considerable difficulty was encountered in mounting the B.A. courses. In 1974 discussions were still taking place regarding mergers with the School of Art and the Salisbury College. The college was consequently unsure in making its submission to C.N.A.A. what its ultimate resource base would be. The government Circular 6/74 pointed the way to the former college of education securing general authority for offering advanced courses in a diversified field. One of the circular's underlying assumptions, shared by nearly all diversifying colleges, was that there would be common teaching for certain main subject studies within B.Ed., Dip.H.E., and B.A. courses. It was with this assumption that the college's first B.A. was submitted to C.N.A.A. It was entitled B.A. in Humane Studies and contained English and History as its main subject components. It soon became apparent that C.N.A.A. not only required distinct teaching groups and a clearly differentiated syllabus, but also a distinct teaching staff. The underlying argument was how can the college expect validation of a three-year Honours B.A. degree course, which by Charter is required to be no less rigorous than a university degree course, when the staff had been teaching on certificate of education courses and B.Ed. courses for so long? Would they not be lacking in experience of this new level of teaching, lacking in qualifications, and lacking in research and publications? In vain the college deployed its counter-arguments, but in the event distinct B.A. degrees were offered.

The reader will happily be spared a blow-by-blow account of the encounters with C.N.A.A. to secure validation of the diversified vourses, but it is a story in itself of immense human endeavour. In 4 February 1976 the C.N.A.A. approved the college as a centre for work leading to the Council's awards for the next five years. This was not merely course validation but institutional validation, and a landmark in the college's development. In September 1976 26 students were enrolled for the B.A. Honours History course with either Drama or English as associated subjects. In 1977 Archaeology was added as an associated subject. In 1977 49 students were enrolled for the B.A. honours English course with Drama or History as an associated subject. American Studies became an additional option in the range of associated subjects in 1980. In the same year the newly-validated three-year B.A. honours, Drama Theatre and Television studies was launched with 31 students. In 1977 a self-contained Dip.H.E. began with 22 students. Its field of studies was social and evironmental problems. Students completing the course successfully were offered one-year courses leading to the award of full Honours degrees at Plymouth or the City Polytechnic. In 1979 a five-year part-time B.A. honours History with English degree recruited with astonishing success. By 1980, therefore, the college had achieved not only validation of its diversified programme, but had also secured to it eminently satisfactory recruitment.

Within the teacher education programme although the induction and in-service plans as outlined in the 1972 White Paper had but stunted growth, new and fruitful patterns of in-service work were developed nationally, bringing together the schools and college of higher education into a new partnership. At Winchester with the severe restraint imposed by L.E.A.s on the full-time secondment of teachers, a great number of part-time long and short courses were set up following close collaboration between the L.E.A.s, the teachers, and the college staff. With the closing of the College of Sarum St. Michael the Wiltshire Authority welcomed the setting up of K.A.C. courses in the south-east part of the county. Furthermore, in both Wiltshire and Hampshire schools and teachers' centres, college staff were regularly employed on a wide range of teaching and in-service objectives. Economic contraints had precipitated the most beneficial professional collaboration that could have been wished. Wiltshire and Hampshire teachers gave regular support within college to the teaching of the professional courses. The work in special education particularly prospered. There were three different modes, one full-time and two part-time, of the Diploma in Special Education. Staff were engaged in the sixth form colleges and further education colleges running City and Guilds courses for F.E. teachers of handicapped young people; and plans for securing C.N.A.A. validation for an M.Ed. in Special Education for a 1981 start have met with success.

A new scheme of government was sealed for the new College of Higher Education on 24 November 1976. The custodian trustee remained 'the body corporate called the Winchester Diocesan Board of Finance', but the object of the college was no longer solely directed to the training of teachers. It was from now a 'College for higher and further education. The object of the charity shall be the provision, maintenance and development of a college . . . for the higher and further education of men and women including . . . the training of teachers'. Both the Universities of Reading and Southampton were to be represented on the governing body. Schemes of government for the college had changed many times in the 140 years of its history, but from the earliest time of Charles Sumner and George Moberly, to that of John Taylor and John Thorn, the Bishop of Winchester and the headmaster of Winchester College have continued to steer a steady course for the college on West Hill.

That steady course is held by the college itself. The association with C.N.A.A. has helped with the steadiness. In 1973 an anxiety expressed about the C.N.A.A. was that it was faceless, impersonal. It has not proved so. Through continuing contact with its officers, its Committee and Board members, and in particular external examiners, the validation exercise and subsequent running of courses have been as personalised as that experienced at the university. Indeed a number of staff serve on the C.N.A.A. Boards themselves. Dr. Brian Tippett, the Dean of the School of Arts and Sciences, is chairman of the English Studies Board.

The division of the college into two schools: the School of Education, of which Stephen Hewitt is Dean, and the School of Arts and Sciences, has not yet split the college into two separate camps because there are still a great number of colleagues who teach in both schools; and also within a senior common room of 115 full-time academic staff it is still possible for them to know each other fairly well, whichever school they may belong to. Moreover, the structure of courses in both schools depends on the interplay of the staff's academic expertise.

Staff research opportunities abound and staff publications are frequent. In 1977/78, 13 colleagues were granted further study leave. *Contexts and Connections*, issued first in 1978, has become the college's regular research publication. In recent years a number of students, too, have had their work published. Research and lecturing opportunities are now offered to staff, and study opportunities to students, through the American exchange which is now in its sixth year of operation. Staff and student exchanges have been made in America with the Universities of Southern Maine and Long Beach, California, and with the University of Calgary, Alberta, Canada. The extension of the college's work in the field of continuing education will be given new impetus by the Open University using college premises from 1980/81 as both a sub-office and a study centre.

For many years the Winton Club has been anxious about seeing at its reunions not only those who endured the harsher rigours of the college, the veterans of the 1930s and further back, but also the younger members who became students after 1960 when the college went mixed. In 1974 the Club celebrated its centenary in splendid style with a very large attendance. In the evening a 'Son et Lumière', organised by Derek Hill and the 1974 students, was given on the history of the college. Wintonians watched from the top of the present Student Union building. Sadly, however, there was not a great muster of post-1960 students. This, however, did happen in 1980, with some of those Wintonians brining their children. But perhaps no event could better have pleased Wintonians, living and dead, than the conferment of degrees to B.A. and B.Ed. graduates which took place in Winchester Cathedral on 4 November 1979. The Bishop of Winchester presided and conferred the degrees. The college after nearly 140 years was returning to its foundation. The cathedral clergy, the city representatives, the family and friends of the graduands, and that long line of spirits stretching back to the first Wintonian, George Monk, gave thanks for that long journey.

APPENDIX I

Winchester Diocesan Board of Education 1838

Permanent Members

President
The Lord Bishop of Winchester

The Lords Lieutenant of Hants and Surrey
The High Sheriffs of Hants and Surrey
The Dean and Chapter of Winchester
The Archdeacons of the Diocese
The Chancellor and the Commissary of the Diocese
The Wardens, Fellows, and Masters of Winchester College
The Chairmen of the Quarter Sessions of Hants and Surrey
The Mayor of Winchester
The Recorders of Winchester
All Noblemen and Privy Councillors; The Members of Parliament for the two
Counties and the Isle of Wight, and the Boroughs; the same being members of
the Church of England, and Subscribers to the Board
The Rural Deans
The Secretary of the Hampshire Society

Elected Members

Sir Thos. Baring Bart.	W. C. Yonge, Esq.
K. W. Blunt, Esq.	S. Wall, Esq.
Capt. Ducane, R.N.	Rev. J. Keble.
J. M. Elwes, Esq.	Rev. Edward M'All.
Geo. Eyre, Esq.	Rev. W. M. Nicholson
R. Littlehales, Esq.	Rev. J. E. Shadwell

Treasurer: Rev. Dr. Moberly, Head Master of Winchester College
Secretary: Rev. Philip Jacob, Canon of Winchester

APPENDIX II

The first regulations for the Winchester Diocesan Training School as they appear as Appendix, No. 4, of the 1840 Report of the Winchester Diocesan Board of Education.

APPENDIX, No. 4.

Winchester Diocesan Training School
(For Schoolmasters)

I.   The Training School is founded upon the Cathedral and College Chorister Schools. The College Choristers are under the domestic superintendence of the second master. The Cathedral Choristers are day boys.

II.   The training scholars board and lodge in the house of the principal, the Rev. D. I. Waugh, M.A. who superintends and directs the management of the whole school.

III.   The charge for every training scholar is £23 for his board, instruction, and lodging, including washing, to be paid on the quarter days in advance.

IV.   Ten exhibitions of £10 a year each have been founded in the training school, and are tenable for a term not exceeding three years.

V.   Every training scholar must produce, before he can be admitted into the establishment, his certificate of baptism, and of good character and conduct from his late schoolmaster, or the Clergyman of his parish.

VI.   In addition to the above certificate every candidate for an exhibition must produce—

1. A recommendation from some Local Board, or member of the Diocesan Board, certifying his fitness for training, the inability of his friends to undertake the whole expense without aid from the Board, and giving a guarantee for payment of the remaining £13.

2. A written statement, signed by the parent or guardian of the boy, the persons recommending him, and the boy himself, that (in the event of his obtaining an exhibition) it is intended that he shall pursue the profession of a schoolmaster within the diocese.

VII. No one will be eligible to an exhibition, unless he shall have attained the age of 15 years, and be able to read, write, and spell correctly; be versed in the first four rules of arithmetic, know the Church Catechism, and have a general knowledge of the contents of the Old and New Testaments.

VIII. The training scholar will be subject, in all matters of discipline and of a domestic nature, wholly to the control of the principal, except as regards the punishment of expulsion, which will not be resorted to without the sanction of the Training School Committee.

IX.   The training scholars attend the service at the Cathedral every morning at ten, and twice on Sundays.

X.   The holidays are, six weeks at Midsummer and four at Christmas. Wednesdays and Saturdays are half holidays.

XI.   Before a scholar leaves the Training School (on his appointment to any school), he will undergo an examination, and receive a testimonial according to his attainments, to be laid before the Bishop, in order that he may receive a licence to teach, according to the 77th Canon. No certificate will be given unless a person has resided in the house for six months at least.

XII.   Persons already engaged in tuition, or intending to be so, on their producing certificates of their baptism and of good conduct, will be permitted to attend portions of the course, without residing in the house, upon payment of £1 per quarter.

XIII. Boys of good and eligible character, on leaving the junior school, may be received at once, though under age, as boarders.

XIV. These arrangements are to be considered provisional, as it is hoped that the school may ultimately be made to support itself.

Names of the Scholars at the Winchester Diocesan Training School.

Names	Age	Admitted	Recommended by
Richard Pike	19	Sept. 10	Salisbury Diocesan Board
William Meaden	15	Aug. 15	ditto
William Lansdell	25	Nov. 10	Hon. and Rev. A. R. Percival, Rector of E. Horsley
Henry Potter	17	Aug. 15	Sir T. Baring, Bart.
Frederick Gatesman	16	Aug. 15	Ven. Archdeacon Hoare
William Stuart	15	Aug. 15	Rev. J. Keble, Vicar of Hursley
George Monk	15	Aug. 15	Rev. A. R. C. Dallas, Rector of Wonston

Exhibitioner in the Female Training School

Martha Gibson	17	—	Rev. R. C. Fell, Secretary of the Godstone Decanal Board.

APPENDIX III

Extracts from the report of the Inspector, Rev. Edward Feild, to the Bishop of Salisbury, after his inspection of schools in the Salisbury diocese. This extract forms part of Appendix No. 13 of the 1840 Report of the Winchester Diocese Board of Education.

How entirely the Rev. Inspector entered into the spirit of his instructions, the following extract from his report to the Bishop of Salisbury of his inspection of the schools of that diocese, will abundantly manifest. It would be well if this report, which is inserted in the report of the National Society for 1840, were studied by all the managers of our parochial schools.

'I entered upon the duties of my office (having spent some little time previously in preparing the questions to be addressed to the school-managers) on the 10th of May; and from that day till the 19th of August was constantly employed in examining schools, and in making reports to the diocesan secretary, with such interruptions only as were necessary for arranging and performing my journies from place to place. During that time I examined 143 schools, and made a full and particular report of all and each of them (except the

Sunday-schools), according to a previously prepared form. with the addition in every case of some general observations. These observations consisted, for the most part, of suggestions for the remedy of faults or the supply of deficiencies. In making such suggestions, I always wished it to be understood that I spoke under correction, being entirely aware that a single visit to a school, and only for a short time, could not qualify me to judge so fully and correctly of its actual state, and of the required or practicable improvements, as others might who enjoyed opportunities of more frequent attendance and closer investigation. I felt, indeed, much difficulty and much pain in many cases at being obliged (as I was in duty bound) to form and express an opinion on my own judgment and responsibility. As, how-ever, I did never presume to make suggestions or recommendations as with authority—I mean, as requiring or expecting they should presently be adopted without further inquiry or examination—a wrong judgment in any case can hardly prove the occasion of much inconvenience. If the school-managers are led thereby to a careful investigation of the points where defects or deficiences are supposed to lie, the purpose will be anwered, and benefit will ensue, though my opinion prove altogether a mistaken one. I am anxious to make these remarks in excuse to the school-mamagers for venturing to pass a sentence, and offer recommendations, where I felt, as entirely as they could do, that I required time, and other opportunities and advantages which I did not possess, to arrive at certain and satisfactory conclusions.

'In consequence of the desire expressed by other Diocesan Boards for the services of an Inspector, it was not considered expedient that I should examine every small school in the diocese which had been placed in union. Neither, of course, was I directed to any school not in union; neither, again, to any school in union where an objection existed to the visits of the Inspector. These remarks seem necessary to account for the small number of schools actually inspected. No doubt, when the objects of inspection are better understood, and more Inspectors have been appointed, they will be permitted and invited both to examine more schools, and to devote a longer time, as circumstances may require, to each; and their work will be more satisfactory to all parties concerned, both in its progress and results. Through the great kindness and hospitality of the clergy in entertaining and forwarding me on my journey, the expenses of my whole tour amounted only to a trifling sum.

'In obedience to the instructions I had received from the Secretary of the National Society, I endeavoured in every case to ascertain not only the general state and arrange-ments of the school, but also the attainments and proficiency of the scholars. With very few exceptions, I examined each and every child in every school. The examination must be supposed to have been cursory; but it was commonly sufficient to discover the progress making in each class, and in some degree the proficiency of each child. This statement will not appear so preposterous when it is remembered, that in the majority of schools the instruction is confined to reading, writing, and arithmetic, with the Church Catechism; and that, in writing and arithmetic, a few minutes would suffice to discover the attainments of each child in even a large class. A much longer time was, of course, required and given to the examinations in religious knowledge, as derived both from the Catechism and Bible.'

APPENDIX IV

Scheme of Instruction at the Winchester Training School, 1843

Scheme of Instruction at present followed in the Winchester Training School

Monday.—Before Breakfast—Prayers, Scripture Reading and Lecture. 2d Class, Latin Grammar.

Forenoon.—9 to 10, Writing and Arithmetic; 10 to 11, Church; 11 to 12, 1st Class, Caesar; 2d Class, Geography and Spelling.

Afternoon.—Writing from Dictation (for all); 2d Class, Euclid; English Grammar.

Tuesday.—Before Breakfast—Prayers, Scripture Reading and Lecture. 2d Class, Latin Grammar.

Forenoon.—Writing & Arithmetic; Church. 2nd Class, Algebra.

Afternoon.—1st Class, Latin Exercises; Lecture on Liturgy (for all); 2d Class, Delectus; 3rd ditto, Spelling, English Grammar, and Parsing.

Wednesday.—Before Breaktast—Prayers, &c. as above; 2d Class, Latin Syntax.

Forenoon.—9 to 10, Ecclesiastical History; Church; Music.

Afternoon.—Half Holiday.

Thursday.—Before Breakfast—Prayers, &c. Latin Gr.

Forenoon.—Writing & Arithmetic; Church; 1st Class, Caesar; 2d ditto, Geography and Spelling.

Afternoon.—2d Class, Delectus; 1st Class, Euclid; Writing from Dictation (for all).

Friday.—Before Breakfast—Prayers, &c. Latin Grammar.

Forenoon.—Writing and Arithmetic; Church; Natural Philosophy; Lecture.

Afternoon.—1st Class, Latin Exercises; 2d ditto, English History, English Grammar; Parsing & Spelling; 3d Class, Reading.

Saturday.—Before Breakfast—Prayers, &c. Latin Syntax.

Forenoon.—Lesson in Church Catechism; Church; Music.

Afternoon.—Half Holiday.

Scheme of Instruction at the Winchester Diocesan Training School, 1844

Scheme of Instruction at present followed in the Winchester Training School.

Monday.—Before Breakfast—six to eight o'clock, Washing, Clean Shoes. Preparation of Lessons, Prayers, Scripture Lecture. Forenoon.—nine to ten, Writing; ten to eleven, Church; eleven to twelve, Spelling, Latin, Grammar, English Grammar and Parsing—2d class. Afternoon—English History, Delectus—2d class; Caesar, Euclid—1st class.

Tuesday.—Before Breakfast—same as on Monday. Forenoon—nine to ten, Arithmetic; ten to eleven Church; eleven to twelve, Spelling, Latin Grammar, and Mensuration—2d class. Afternoon—Geography, English Parsing—1st class; delectus—2d class. Exercises, (Latin and English).

Wednesday.—Before Breakfast—Same. Forenoon—nine to ten, Ecclesiastical History, ten to eleven, Church, eleven to twelve, Prepare Music. Afternoon—Half Holiday.

Thursday.—Before Breakfast—Same. Forenoon—nine to ten, Writing; ten to eleven, Church; Eleven to twelve, Spelling, Chronology, and Latin Grammar—2d class. Afternoon—English History, Euclid, Caesar—1st class. Delectus and Dictation.

Friday.—Before Breakfast—Same. Forenoon—nine to ten, Arithmetic; ten to eleven, Church; eleven to twelve, English Grammar and Parsing, Latin Grammar—2nd class. Afternoon—Geography, Delectus, Caesar—1st class. Exercises, (Latin and English).

Saturday.—Before Breakfast—Same. Forenoon—nine to ten, Scripture, Catechism; ten to eleven, Church; eleven to twelve, Prepare Music. Afternoon—Half Holiday.

This is the table employed for the winter quarter of the present year:—

Dinner is served at one o'clock

The afternoon school hours are from two to four, or half-past four in winter; till five in summer. From five to six, voluntary study, or recreation. Six to half-past six, supper. Half-past six to eight, prepare lesson. Eight to quarter before nine, music (practice), or read in the books of the Library of the School. Quarter to nine, prayers and scripture lecture.

APPENDIX V
(1853)

DISTRIBUTION OF TIME.

The books and hours of study are essentially the same as those returned last year. The time appointed to each subject has been changed, and is nearly as follows, for the week :—

	Divis. 1.	Divis. 2.
Scripture and Liturgy . . .	8½	8½
Mathematics	13¾	14
History, Grammar, &c. Milton .	6	7¾
Geography	6½	6½
Music	6½	6½
Gardening	4	4
Family Worship and Cathedral .	5½	5½
Walking	10	10
Private Reading, or Leisure . .	8¾	8¾
Washing, Dressing, and Private Devotions	9½	9½
Latin and Physical Science . .	4	4 ·
Teaching with Criticism . . .	3½	3½
(This is exclusive of Training)		
Meals and Sleep	55½	55½

The times here given are exclusive of Sunday, on which day the Pupils have a Scripture Lecture from 7.30 to 8.0. Most of them attend Sunday Schools, and they often write notes of a Scripture Lesson for correction.

The Vacations are Six Weeks at Midsummer—Four Weeks at Christmas.

APPENDIX VI

TIME TABLE, for Michaelmas, 1851.

5¼ to 6.¼, Wash, Dress, and ¡Make Beds.

MONDAY.—6¼ to 7¼, Mathematics. Geography; 7¼—7¾, Bible Lecture; 7¾—8.25, Chapel Service; 8.25—9.0, Breakfast; 9.0—10.10, Garden Work; 10.10—10½, Prepare for Lessons; 10½—11½, Notes on Teaching and School Keeping, Mathematics; 11½—1.0, Mathematics, Notes on Teaching and School Keeping; 1.0—3.0, Dinner and Walking; 3.0—4.0, 4.0—5.0, Practising at St. Michael's School; 5.0—5.20, Intermission; 5.20—6¼, Mathematics, Prepare Music; 6¼—7.0, Supper; 7.0—8.0, Crit. of Lessons delivered at St. Michael's; 8.0—8¾, Practise Music; 8¾—9½, Learn Verses and Bible Lecture.

TUESDAY.—6¼ to 7¼, Geography, Mathematics; 7¼—7¾, Bible Lecture; 7¾—8.25, Chapel Service; 8.25—9.0, Breakfast; 9.0—10.10, Garden Work; 10.10—10½, Prepare for Lessons; 10½—11½, Mathematics, Grammar, &c.; 11½—1.0, Grammar, Mathematics; 1.0—3.0, Dinner and Walking; 3.0—4.0, Latin; 4.0—5.0, Mathematics, Prepare Music; 5.0—5.20, Intermission; 5.20—6¼, Mathematics, Prepare History; 6¼—7.0, Supper; 7.0—8.0, Dr. Wesley; 8.0—8¾, Practise Music; 8¾—9½ Learn Verses and Bible Lecture.

WEDNESDAY.—6¼ to 7¼, Prepare Liturgy and English Grammar; 7¼—7¾, Bible Lecture; 7¾—8.25, Chapel Service; 8.25—9.0, Breakfast; 9.0—10.10, Garden; 10.10—10½, Prepare for Lessons; 10½—11½, Mathematics; 11½—1.0, Chemistry; Half Holiday; 7.0—8.0, English Literature; 8.0—8¾, Practise Music; 8¾—9½, Learn Verses and Bible Lecture.

THURSDAY.—6¼ to 7¼, Mathematics, Geography; 7¼—7¾, Bible Lecture; 7¾—8.25, Chapel Service; 8.25—9.0, Breakfast; 9.0—10.10, Garden; 10.10—10½, Prepare for Lessons; 10½—11½, Notes on Teaching and School Keeping, Mathematics; 11½—1.0, Mathematics, Notes on Teaching and School Keeping; 1.0—3.0, Dinner and Walking; 3.0—4.0, Latin; 4.0—5.0, Prepare Music, Mathematics; 5.0—5.20, Intermission; 5.20—6¼, Mathematics, Prepare Music; 6¼—7.0, Supper; 7.0—8.0, Examination of Geography; 8.0—8¾, Practise Music; 8¾—9½, Learn Verses and Bible Lecture.

FRIDAY.—6¼ to 7¼, Geography, Mathematics; 7¼—7¾, Bible Lecture; 7¾—8.25, Family Prayer; 8.25—9.0, Breakfast; 8¾—9¾, Mathematics, Grammar; 9¾—11.0, Cathedral; 11.0—1.0, Grammar, Mathematics; 1.0—3.0, Dinner and Walking; 3.0—4.0, Latin; 4.0—5.0, Mathematics, Prepare Music; 5.0—5.20, Intermission; 5.20—6¼, Prepare Music, Mathematics; 6¼—7.0, Supper; 7.0—8.0, Dr. Wesley; 8.0—8¾, Practise Music; 8¾—9½, Learn Verses and Bible Lecture.

SATURDAY.—6¼ to 7¼, Geography of Colonies; 7¼—7¾, Bible Lecture; 7¾—8.25, Family Prayer; 8.25—9.0, Breakfast; 9.0—10.10, Garden; 10.10—10½—Prepare for Lessons; 10½—12, Examination of Mathematics; 12.0—1.0, Chemistry; Half Holiday and Cathedral.

10.0, Lights put out.

APPENDIX VII

TRAINING COLLEGES

Memorial to the Committee of Council on Education, addressed through her Majesty's Inspectors of Training Colleges (1863)

WE, the undersigned, being actively engaged in the management and support of Church-of-England Training Colleges under the inspection of the Committee of Council, respectfully desire to lay before your Lordships the following remarks on a draft Minute submitted to us through her Majesty's Inspectors.

We desire to preface these remarks by calling your Lordships' earnest attention to the following brief extracts from the Report of the Royal Commissioners on Popular Education:

'We do not propose any change in the relation of the Training Colleges to the State. We do not recommend any reduction in the amount of aid at present given to the Colleges in 'various forms.' It will be remembered that this amount is stated in the Commissioners' Report to be, in Church-of-England Training Colleges for masters, about 76 per cent of the total annual income. The Commissioners further say; 'no other Institutions stand so much in 'need of a permanent income.' And again: 'An Institution which produces good teachers 'may be the most efficient of all aids to education; but it appeals to no sympathy, it relieves 'no immediate distress, and it accordingly obtains subscriptions with difficulty.'

We have considered the principles laid down in the preamble to the draft Minute, and also the provision in the Minute itself, by which those principles are intended to be carried into effect.

We are of opinion that 25 per cent of the total expenditure of a Training College is a fair proportion to be raised by the Managers.

We believe, however, that the Training Colleges could not in general be maintained in a state of efficiency if the Managers be required to raise a larger proportion of the expenditure.

We have considered in detail the provision contained in the Minute itself, in order to ascertain how far we can rely on the receipt of 75 per cent of the total expenditure from the Parliamentary Grant.

The first point to be noticed is the great uncertainty resulting from the condition attached to the grant proposed to be contributed by the State.

Your Lordships are aware that those who undertake the financial responsiblility of Training Colleges do this as a labour of love, and not in the spirit of a commercial adventure. To place them in constant danger of incurring a serious pecuniary liability would compel many of them to discontinue their labour, and would deter others from undertaking it.

The following are some of the elements of the uncertainty to which we have referred.

The number of pupil-teachers under the operation of the Revised Code is in course of rapid diminution; and therefore the number of candidates for admission into Training Colleges will be diminished in proportion, as it can hardly be supposed that any considerable number of such candidates can be found except among pupil-teachers.

Your Lordships will perceive that the natural working of the draft Minute, in perhaps its most valuable provision is directly and injuriously affected by the operation of the Revised Code, inasmuch as under that Code inducements and temptations are held out to students to leave the Colleges after one year's training (Articles 72 and 90), whilst under the Minute no payment will be made to the Colleges for any pupils not remaining two years. Although we wholly deprecate any alteration in the Minute calculated to diminish the time of residence of the pupils, we cannot but draw your Lordships' attention to the additional uncertainty thus created as to the Colleges obtaining the necessary amount of assistance from the Parliamentary Grant.

A further element of uncertainty is, that no payment shall be made on account of any student who has not been in charge of the *same* elementary school for two years after leaving the Training College. Such provision would also obviously place the managers of the Training Colleges in a false position with respect to the managers of elementary schools; inasmuch as in many cases the interest of the elementary school would be to get rid of an unsuitable teacher, while it would be most important to the Training College that he should remain in the same employment two full years, or even longer, until certified.

In addition to this, to make every payment to a Training College depend on the residence of the students for two full years will have an injurious effect on the discipline of the Colleges. We believe that each second-year student will see that he or she respectively is worth 100*l*. or 82*l*. to the College, and also that, unless the College is to suffer loss, all the students, whatever may be their character or conduct, must be retained for the two full years, and be appointed to schools under inspection; so that in fact the authorities will, to some extent, be in the power of the students.

We observe that it is proposed by the draft Minute to withhold the Examination Grants for Christmas 1863. This we consider manifestly unjust; inasmuch as such grants are not only made in respect of the work of the past year, but were intended to assist in defraying the expenses of that year.

A plan for making the transition from the old to the new system has been suggested, as we understand, by Mr. Cowie. Many of us have not yet had an opportunity of considering it; but we trust that some satisfactory plan will be adopted, which, combined with payment of the Examination Grants for Christmas 1863, will prevent the Managers of the Training Colleges from being unduly involved in pecuniary responsibilities.

Having thus pointed out various objections in the draft Minute as at present constructed, we respectfully request that your Lordships will so far modify the proposed plan as to hold out to the Managers of Training Colleges a reasonable prospect of their obtaining 75 per cent of their expenditure from the Parliamentary Grant.

In concluding this representation, we wish to express our desire to continue to co-operate cordially with your Lordships in measures for rendering the system of training teachers as efficient and as economical as possible; and we will do our best to carry into effect any plan which seems likely to secure this most important object.

Chas. Cowie

Principal of the
Winchester Training College

APPENDIX VIII

STUDENTS' REGISTER

Jan: 31. 1863

*We do hereby sincerely declare that it is our intention
& our desire, if admitted into the Winchester Diocesan Training
School, to continue our period of training in that Institution
to the end of the second year, & thereafter mindful of the advantages conferred upon us in our training to follow the profession
of a School master at least until we have
obtained our Certificate.*

Signed

John Atkins.   George Howell.   James Watson
John Belchare   John A. Jones.   Henry Hackwood
Raymund Bryer   Thomas Lupman   James Newhook.
Henry Brummell   John Maslen.   Alfred Fabian
Charles Challew   William Paddock   Charles Haynes
Edward Cane   Thomas Painter.   Henry Woodman.
John Cotier   Henry Taylor.   George Paddock.
Thomas Day   Charles H. West.   Alfred Henry Poultney.
Charles Carle   John G. Whenman
Thomas Edwards   Richmond G White
Edwin Everett   George Leith Veal
Henry Found   James Blake
Farren Frederick   Geo. Fran: Jones
John Hammond
Samuel Harris
William Jillins

The last page of the Students' Register which began with the entry of the first students in 1840.

In 1863 the students on entry were required to sign a declaration of intent that they would remain at College for two years and subsequently stay in the profession for at least a further two years. On such conditions the college received government grant.

APPENDIX IX

Extract from the *Hampshire Chronicle*, 29 August 1874

WINCHESTER TRAINING COLLEGE.—It has long been the wish of the National school-masters and others who have been trained at this College to form some society, or club, in order that they might meet together occasionally, and thus, by mutual intercourse, preserve old friendships and show a more real appreciation of their place of education. This year a committee of old students (schoolmasters) was formed, and a successful attempt to set on foot such a society has been the result. A large party of schoolmasters, formerly trained at the Winchester Training College, met yesterday at that institution, and, after divine service and a meeting of the committee, sat down to an excellent cold collation provided by Mr. Grant (of the *Old Market* inn), under the presidency of the Principal. Excellent addresses were made by Archdeacon Jacob, the Rev. J. Smith, former Principal, and the Rev. N. Midwinter. After the ordinary loyal toasts, proposed by the Chairman and heartily responded to, the following were given:—'The Board of the College', by Mr. Atkins, of the Central Schools, Winchester; 'the former Principal', by Archdeacon Jacob; 'the present Principal', by Mr. Bush, of Botley School; 'the Masters of the College', by Mr. Brummell, of Woking; 'Success to the Winchester Training College', by Mr. Sandford, of Alverstoke; 'Success to the New Club', by Mr. Archard, of the Training College. Glees were sung by the members present, assisted by the students. We congratulate the indefatigable secretary and the members of the committee on their success. The club has now got a fair start, and we are quite sure that next year, by which time it is hoped that the addresses of the old students will be better known to the committee, there will be a larger, and, if possible, a more enthusiastic meeting.

APPENDIX X

(1158) 20th June

WINCHESTER DIOCESAN TRAINING SCHOOL

Dated June 16, 1860   6A 225. 23

Copy of

CONVEYANCE OF SITE

for

Training School at Winchester

Dean and Chapter of Winchester
to   Conveyance of Site for
The Lord Bishop of Winchester   Training School at Winchester

---

Enrolled in Her Majesty's High Court of Chancery the twentieth day of June, in the year of our Lord 1860 (being first duly stamped), according to the tenor of the Statutes made for that purpose.

672   *(Signed)*   E. GRABB

WE, the Right Worshipful Thomas Garnier, Clerk, D.C.L. Dean of the Cathedral Church of the Holy Trinity of Winchester, in the county of Southampton, and the Chapter of the same Church, under the authority of an Act passed in the Session of Parliament, and of the other Acts made to amend and explain the said Act, do hereby freely and voluntarily, and without any valuable consideration, grant and convey to the Right Reverend Father in God, Charles Richard, by divine permission Lord Bishop of Winchester, and his successors, all that piece of Land, containing by estimation five acres, more or less, situated in the Parish of St. Faith, within the borough of Winchester, which piece of Land is more particularly described, with its boundaries, in the plan annexed to these presents, and therein edged with a green colour, and all our right, title, and interest to and in the same and every part thereof, to hold under the said Lord Bishop of Winchester and his successors for the purposes of the said Acts, and to be appropriated and used as a site for a School for educating, and instructing, and of boarding during the time of such education and instruction, persons intended to be masters of elementary schools, in connection with the Church of England, for poor persons and for the residence of the principal and other master or masters, and other officers of such institution, and for no other purpose; and it is hereby agreed and declared that the said institution shall be called the Winchester Diocesan Training School.

That the said School shall always be conducted upon the principles and in furtherance of the ends and designs of the Incorporated National Society for promoting the education of the poor in the principles of the Established Church.

That the said School shall be at all times open to the inspection of the inspector or inspectors for the time being, appointed or to be appointed in conformity with the order of Her Majesty in Council, bearing date the 10th date of August, 1840, and also of any inspector or inspectors who may from time to time be appointed by the said Lord Bishop of Winchester and his successors for the time being.

APPENDIX XI

10th December, 1973

L. C. B. Gower, Esq., LL.M., F.B.A.,
Vice-Chancellor,
The University of Southampton,
Southampton, SO9 5NH.

Dear Vice-Chancellor,

At this morning's meeting of the College's Academic Board the following
resolutions were passed:

1. "That the College seek validation of its awards from C.N.A.A.
   for courses which will be planned to begin in September 1975."

2. "The College is asking the University to continue to validate
   all established courses beginning in 1974. In the event of the
   College not securing validation of its awards through C.N.A.A.
   the College would ask the University to extend its validation
   procedures for a further year."

These resolutions will be forwarded to the Governing Body and, if confirmed,
be followed by a submission of courses for validation to C.N.A.A.

It is to be hoped that this decision by the Academic Board will not lead to the
lessening of the good relationships this College has enjoyed with the University,
academically, personally, and institutionally, over very many years. In
particular we are conscious of your own and Professor Pedley's friendly concern
for the Colleges and of your vigorous endeavour to retain the traditional
associations. You will readily appreciate that the Academic Board did not make
its decision lightly nor without recalling the very considerable benefits derived
by our close association with the University, nor ignorant of the hazards that
lie ahead.

Yours sincerely,

M. Rose.

THE UNIVERSITY SOUTHAMPTON SO9 5NH

FROM THE VICE-CHANCELLOR PROFESSOR L. C. B. GOWER, LL.M., F.B.A.

TELEPHONE 559122
TELEX 47661   11th December, 1973

Dear Principal

        Thank you for your letter of 10th December.   I was
sorry to hear this news but your Academic Board's decisions
are entirely understandable and there will certainly be no
hard feelings on our part.   Inevitably the decisions will
lead to a loosening of the ties between our respective
institutions, but I sincerely hope that they will not lead to
any lessening of friendly relationships.

            With warmest good wishes,

                        Yours
                        Jim

Martial Rose, Esq., M.A.,
King Alfred's College,
Winchester.

APPENDIX XII

21st July, 1975

Secretary of State for Education and Science,
Department of Education and Science,
Elizabeth House,
York Road,
London, SE1 7PH.

Dear Sir,

We the undersigned, on behalf of our respective Governing Bodies, agree to the merger of King Alfred's College, Winchester and the College of Sarum St. Michael, Salisbury with effect from the 1st August, 1976. From the 1st August, 1976, there will be one Governing Body, one Academic Board, one Principal and one Administration of the new College.

This agreement is made on the understanding that there should be within the merged College by 1981 no less than 900 places allotted to teacher education.

Yours faithfully,

Chairman of Governors,
King Alfred's College.

Chairman of Governors,
College of Sarum St. Michael.

APPENDIX XIII

PRINCIPALS OF THE COLLEGE

Rev. David Waugh	1840–1846
Rev. John Smith	1846–1858
Rev. Canon Charles Collier	1859–1878
Rev. Canon Henry Martin	1878–1912
Rev. Canon Ernest Wainwright	1912–1933
Rev. Richard Clement White	1933–1945
William Parker Dickinson	1946–1958
John Arthur Stripe	1959–1967
Martial Rose	1967–

NOTES

KEY

C.C.E.	The Committee of Council on Education, Reports and Minutes.
H.C.	*The Hampshire Chronicle.*
W.D.B.E.	The Winchester Diocesan Board of Education, Reports and Minutes.
W.Q.R.	The Winchester Quarterly Record.

Chapter One

1. Curtis, S. J., *History of Education in Great Britain* (London, 1950), p. 231.
2. H.C., 17 February 1840.
3. Schools founded by the National Society for the Education of the Poor in the Principles of the Church of England.

Chapter Two

1. Newsome, D., *The Parting of Friends* (London, 1966), p. 220.
2. *Ibid.*, p. 211.
3. Hooper, P., *William Whiting* (Southampton, 1978), p. 84.
4. W.D.B.E., *First Report.* 1840, p. 6.
5. *Ibid.*, p. 7.
6. *Ibid.*, pp. 7–8.
7. *Ibid.*, p. 21.
8. *Ibid.*, p. 9.
9. *Ibid.*, p. 9.
10. *Ibid.*, p. 13.
11. *Ibid.*, p. 13.
12. *Ibid.*, p. 10.
13. H.C., 27 April 1840.
14. H.C., 11 June 1840.
15. Society for the Nurturing and Education of the Infant Poor within the County of Hampshire (hereafter called the Hampshire Society) *Minutes,* 19 November 1811.
16. Hampshire Society, *Minutes,* 17 December 1811.
17. Rich, R. W., *The Training of Teachers in England and Wales During The Nineteenth Century.* (Cambridge, 1933), p. 18.
18. Hampshire Society, *Minutes.* 5 November 1812.
19. *Ibid.,* 1 July 1813.
20. *Ibid.,* 17 October 1816.
21. W.D.B.E., 1840, p. 18.
22. *Ibid.,* p. 19.
23. Hampshire Society, *Annual Report,* 1830.
24. Hampshire Society, *Minutes,* 1829.
25. C.C.E., *Minutes,* 1844, p. 87.
26. *Ibid.,* p. 88.
27. C.C.E., *Minutes,* 1845, pp..87–88.
28. *Ibid.,* pp. 89–90.
29. W.D.B.E., 1840, p. 43.
30. C.C.E., *Minutes,* 1845, p. 45.
31. *Ibid.,* p. 90.
32. *Ibid.,* p. 57.
33. *Ibid.,* p. 94.
34. *Ibid.,* p. 105.
35. W.D.B.E., 1840, p. 32.
36. W.D.B.E., 1846, p. 3.
37. Hooper, *op. cit.,* p. 66.
38. Students' Register, 1840–1872.

39.   Bradbury, J. L., *Chester College* (Chester, 1975), p. 59.
40.   W.D.B.E., 1844, p. 4.
41.   W.D.B.E., 1842, p. 10.
42.   W.D.B.E., 1843, p. 6.
43.   W.D.B.E., 1840, p. 34.
44.   W.D.B.E., 1841, p. 31.
45.   W.D.B.E., 1843, p. 8.
46.   H.C., 28 December 1840.
47.   W.D.B.E., *Reports*, 1840–1846.
48.   C.C.E., *Minutes*, 1840–1841, p. 46.
49.   *Ibid.*, p. 45.
50.   W.D.B.E., 1846, p. 3.
51.   W.D.B.E., 1845, p. 3.
52.   W.D.B.E., 1844, p. 4.
53.   W.D.B.E., 1846, p. 3.
54.   W.D.B.E., 1847, p. 4.
55.   *Ibid.*

Chapter Three

1.   Macky, John, *A Journey Through England* (London, 1722), Vol. II, p. 21.
2.   Bussby, F., *Winchester Cathedral, 1079–1979* (Southampton, 1979), p. 215.
3.   Burgess, H. J., *Enterprise in Education.* (London, 1958), p. 121.
4.   W.D.B.E., *Minutes*, 1847, p. 8.
5.   *Ibid.*, p. 4.
6.   *Ibid.*
7.   Edward Sheppard entered the Winchester Training School in January 1847, at the age of twenty-two. Much of his time was spent 'instructing the daily pupils'. In January 1848 he was sent to Battersea College for 12 months at the expense of the Winchester Board to qualify him for the office of third master at the Winchester College, to which he returned in January 1849.
8.   W.D.B.E., 1847, p. 5.
9.   Burgess, *op. cit.*, p. 65.
10.   W.Q.R., November, 1850.
11.   W.Q.R., April 1855.
12.   Rich, *op. cit.*, p. 4.
13.   *Ibid.*, p. 33.
14.   Dent, H. C., *The Training of Teachers in England and Wales, 1800–1975* (London, 1975), p. 14.
15.   Drewett, W., *The Wintonian*, 1924.
16.   W.D.B.E., 1857–58.
17.   C.C.E., 1860, p. 312.
18.   W.D.B.E., 1851, p. 3.
19.   *Ibid.*, p. 4.
20.   The Dean of Hereford in 1851 was Richard Dawes, formerly vicar of King's Somborne, Hants.
21.   Drewett, *op. cit.*
22.   C.C.E., 1857–58, p. 729.
23.   W.D.B.E., 1851, p. 3.
24.   H.C., 17 December 1853.
25.   How, F. D., *Six Great Schoolmasters* (London, 1904), p. 51.
26.   C.C.E., 1852, p. 244.
27.   W.D.B.E., 1853.
28.   H.C., 13 December 1849.
29.   H.C., 13 June 1857.
30.   H.C., 2 June 1852.

31. H.C., 14 June 1849.
32. H.C., 30 November 1848.
33. C.C.E., 1852–53, p. 282.
34. W.D.B.E., 1847, p. 4.
35. Students' Register, 1847–62.
36. *Ibid.*
37. W.D.B.E., 1859, p. 3.
38. H.C., 10 January 1859.
39. H.C., 29 January 1859.
40. H.C., 6 April 1861.

Chapter Four
1. Maclure, J. S., *Educational Documents* (London, 1965), p. 70.
2. *Ibid.*
3. Lawson, J., and Silver, H., *A Social History of Education in England* (London, 1973),
       p. 290.
4. Burgess, H. J., *Enterprise in Education* (London, 1958), p. 175.
5. National Society Library, Correspondence with Winchester Diocesan Training School.
6. *Ibid.*
7. *Ibid.*
8. *Ibid.*
9. C.C.E., 1862–63, p. xiii.
10. Rich, *op. cit.*, p. 188.
11. H.C., 2 May 1863.
12. H.C., 30 April 1864.
13. H.C., 28 April 1866.
14. H.C., 28 April 1866.
15. H.C., 7 February 1863.
16. C.C.E. *Report*, 1863–64, p. 310.
17. H.C., 26 January 1867.
18. C.C.E. *Report*, 1864–65, p. 352.
19. Maclure, *op. cit.*, p. 98.
20. National Society Library.
21. Lawson and Silver, *op. cit.*, p. 321.
22. C.C.E. *Reports*, 1866–67, p. 438.
23. H.C., 27 February 1864.
24. H.C., 15 October 1864.
25. H.C., 26 February 1870.
26. H.C., 2 June 1866.
27. W.Q.R., 21 October 1854.
28. H.C., 8 April 1854.
29. H.C., 29 August 1874.
30. H.C., 29 June 1878.
31. H.C., 10 May 1890.
32. *Ibid.*
33. H.C., 21 December 1878.
34. H.C., 20 December 1879.
35. H.C., 17 April 1880.
36. *Ibid.*
37. H.C., 5 February 1881.

Chapter Five
1. Thomas, R. A., *The History of the Volunteer Company* (Winchester, 1910.)
2. C.C.E., 1886–87, p. 431.

3.   C.C.E., 1886–87, p. 408.
4.   C.C.E., 1887–88, p. 481.
5.   H.C., 27 July 1906.
6.   College archives.
7.   Minutes of the Committee of the Winchester Diocesan Training College, 28 January 1913.
8.   Dent, *op. cit.*, pp. 75–80.
9.   *Ibid.*
10.   C.C.E., 1889–90, p. 471.
11.   C.C.E., 1890–91, p. 419.

Chapter Six

1.   College archives.
2.   Dent, *op. cit.*, p. 131.
3.   Dent, *cp. cit.*, p. 100.
4.   Wing, R. G., *The Wintonian*, Easter term, 1924.
5.   Dent, *op. cit.*, p. 104.
6.   *The Wintonian*, Christmas term, 1923.
7.   Breach, R. W., 'Wintonians and the General Strike, 4th–12th May, 1926', College archives.
8.   *Ibid.*
9.   Wing, R. G., *College Year Book*, 1949.
10.   *The Wintonian*, Christmas term, 1924.
11.   *The Wintonian*, Christmas term, 1923.

Chapter Seven

1.   *The Wintonian*, Summer, 1955, pp. 21, 22.
2.   For this information I am indebted to Thomas Graty.
3.   *Ibid.*
4.   *The Wintonian*, Summer, 1949.

Chapter Eight

1.   Report of the Committee on Higher Education. (H.M.S.O., 1963.)
2.   Report of the Minister of Education's Central Advisory Council entitled 'Half Our Future' (H.M.S.O., 1963.)
3.   Report of the Study Group on the Government of Colleges (H.M.S.O., 1966.)
4.   *Children and their Primary Schools*, Vol. I (H.M.S.O., 1967.)
5.   *Teacher Education and Training*—a Report of a Committee of Inquiry under the Chairmanship of Lord James of Rusholme (H.M.S.O., 1972.)
6.   H. A. Harding, Under-Secretary, D.E.S., address to the A.T.C.D.E. Conference of Principals (York, 1970.)

BIBLIOGRAPHY

(A) BOOKS

Allen, A. O., *John Allen and his Friends* (London, 1922).

Ashwell, A. R., *Life of Bishop Wilberforce* (London, 1880).

Biddle, M., ed., *Winchester in the Early Middle Ages, Winchester Studies I* (Oxford, 1977).

Bradbury, J. L., *Chester College* (Chester, 1975).

Bronte, C., *Jane Eyre* (Oxford, 1975).

Browne, J., *Teachers of Teachers, A History of the Association of Teachers in Colleges and Departments of Education* (London, 1979).

Burgess, H. J., *Enterprise in Education* (London, 1958).

Bussby, F., *Winchester Cathedral* (Southampton, 1979).

Curtis, S. J., *History of Education in Great Britain* (London, 1950).

Dent, H. C., *The Training of Teachers in England and Wales, 1800-1975* (London, 1977).

Dickens, C., *Nicholas Nickleby* (London, 1960).

Grier, R. M., *John Allen, Vicar of Prees, Archdeacon of Salop* (London, 1889).

Hardy, T., *Jude the Obscure* (London, 1975).

Hooper, P., *William Whiting* (Southampton, 1978).

How, F. D., *Six Great Schoolmasters* (London, 1904).

Laski, M., *Jane Austen and her World* (London, 1969).

Lawson, J., and Silver, H., *A Social History of Education in England* (London, 1973).

Long, W. H., *A Dictionary of the Isle of Wight Dialect* (London, 1888).

Maclure, J. S., *Educational Documents* (London, 1965).

Merson, E., *The Village School* (Southampton, 1979).

Naylor, L., *Culham, Church of England Training College for Schoolmasters, 1853-1953* (Abingdon, 1953).

Newsome, D., *Godliness and Good Learning* (London, 1961).

Newsome, D., *The Parting of Friends* (London, 1966).

Priestley, J., *St. Luke's College, 1839-1978* (Exeter, 1978).

Rich, R. W., *The Training of Teachers in England and Wales during the Nineteenth Century* (Cambridge, 1933).

Seaborne, M., *Education* (Visual History of Modern Britain) (London, 1966).

Trench, R. C., *English, Past and Present* (London, 1868).

Trench, R. C., *The Study of Words* (London, 1859).

Trevelyan, G. M., *British History in the Nineteenth Century and After (1782-1919)* (London, 1947).

Trollope, A., *The Warden* (London, 1932).

Wood, A., *Nineteenth Century Britain* (London, 1977).

(B) EDUCATION REPORTS AND OFFICIAL PUBLICATIONS

Great Britain, Privy Council Committee on Education, Minutes and Reports of the Committee of Council on Education (London, 1839-1899).

British and Foreign School Society. Thirty-eighth Report (London, 1843).

Newcastle Commission (Elementary Education) (H.M.S.O., 1861).

Clarendon Commission (Public Schools) (H.M.S.O., 1864).

Cross Commission (Elementary Education) (H.M.S.O., 1888).

Training College Returns, The Royal Commission Appointed to Inquire into the Working of the Elementary Education Acts (England and Wales) (London, 1888).

Bryce Commission (Secondary Education) (H.M.S.O., 1895).

McNair Report (Training of Teachers and Youth Leaders) (H.M.S.O., 1944).

Robbins Report, Report of the Committee on Higher Education (H.M.S.O., 1963).

Newsom Report, Report of the Minister of Education's Central Advisory Council entitled 'Half Our Future' (H.M.S.O., 1963).

Weaver Report, Report of the Study Group on the Government of Colleges (H.M.S.O., 1966).

Plowden Report, Children and Their Primary Schools (H.M.S.O., 1967).

James Report, Teacher Education and Training (H.M.S.O., 1972).

Government White Paper, Education: A Framework for expansion (H.M.S.O., 1972).

(C) LOCAL AND MANUSCRIPT SOURCES

Breach, R. W. *Wintonians and the General Strike, 4th-12th May, 1926* (College Archives).

Colson, A. M., *Revolt of the Hampshire Agricultural Labourers, 1812-1831, and its causes* (M.A. Thesis, 1937, University of Southampton).

Davey, C. R., ed., *Education in Hampshire and the Isle of Wight* (Hampshire Archivists Group Publication, No. 3, 1977).

Dickinson, W. P., Notebooks (College Archives).

Hampshire Chronicle, 1839-1980.

Thomas, R. A., *History of the Volunteer Company, Winchester* (1910).

Winchester

Diocesan Board of Education, Reports, 1840-1861 (Winchester).

Diocesan Training College Report, 1914 (Winchester).

Diocesan Training College, Minutes of the Meetings of the Committee of Governors, 1909-1927.

King Alfred's College, Minutes of the Meetings of the Governing Body, 1928-1980.

King Alfred's College, Minutes of the Meetings of the Sub Committee of the Governing Body, 1926-1945.

King Alfred's College, Minutes of the Meetings of the Executive Committee of the Governing Body, 1946-1965.

The Wintonian, 1893-1970 (College Archives).

Diocesan Training School, Correspondence with the National Society (National Society Library, London).

Training College Club, Report and Balance Sheet, 1915 and 1916, Supplementary Year Book and Special War Issue, July 1916 (Winchester).

Training College Club, College Year Book, 1949 (Portsmouth).

Quarterly Record, 1848-1866 (Winchester).

Reports for the Diocese of Winchester, 1818-1853 (National Society Library, London).

INDEX